D1520337

Ronald Dworkin's Theory of Equality

Also By Alexander Brown

PERSONAL RESPONSIBILITY: Why It Matters

Ronald Dworkin's Theory of Equality

Domestic and Global Perspectives

Alexander Brown
University College London

First published 2009 by
PALGRAVE MACMILLAN

Palgrave Macmillan in the UK is an imprint of Macmillan Publishers Limited,
registered in England, company number 785998, of Houndmills, Basingstoke,
Hampshire RG21 6XS.

Palgrave Macmillan in the US is a division of St Martin's Press LLC,
175 Fifth Avenue, New York, NY 10010.

Palgrave Macmillan is the global academic imprint of the above companies
and has companies and representatives throughout the world.

Palgrave® and Macmillan® are registered trademarks in the United States,
the United Kingdom, Europe and other countries.

ISBN-13: 978–0–230–21015–8 hardback

This book is printed on paper suitable for recycling and made from fully
managed and sustained forest sources. Logging, pulping and manufacturing
processes are expected to conform to the environmental regulations of the
country of origin.

A catalogue record for this book is available from the British Library.

A catalog record for this book is available from the Library of Congress.

10   9   8   7   6   5   4   3   2   1
18 17 16 15 14 13 12 11 10 09

Printed and bound in Great Britain by
CPI Antony Rowe, Chippenham and Eastbourne

for *June*

Contents

Part II

Preface

The genesis of this book bears a resemblance to the Ship of Theseus. During my graduate studies in the Department of Philosophy at University College London (UCL) I became interested in the 'Equality of what?' debate within contemporary political philosophy. Dworkin's two seminal articles, 'Equality of Welfare' and 'Equality of Resources' were my obsession for a while, but I found that I did not have enough space to do justice to the full complexity of his system of ideas. I was fascinated not merely by his rejection of equality of welfare and defence of equality of resources but also by his nuanced interpretation of the choice/luck distinction and by what he said about the abstract right to equal concern and respect, the relationship between equality and liberty, the nature of a true political community, the method of constructive interpretation, and much more besides. Over time I stripped away a number of Dworkinian planks from my dissertation and found a new home for them in a folder marked 'Dworkin'. In 2005 I joined the School of Public Policy as a lecturer in political theory and it occurred to me to salvage the old planks and to revisit my reflections on Dworkin.

During this time I was regularly attending the Colloquium in Legal and Social Philosophy held within the Faculty of Laws at UCL and chaired by Professor Dworkin. His performances at the Colloquium were a *tour de force* in sustained analytical thought. I also had the good luck of being seated next to Ronald during one of the equally invigorating post-Colloquium suppers. I found his conversation open, inquisitive and profoundly interesting. But it was working in the School of Public Policy itself which had the greater influence on my thinking. The School has a strong record of teaching and research in the fields of international relations, human rights and global justice. Reading the work of John Rawls, Charles Beitz and Thomas Pogge it became clear to me that I was dissatisfied with the version of liberal equality that was being (or not being) globalised. I wondered if something like Dworkin's equality of resources might work better. The main stumbling block, however, was that Dworkin himself had, to use his own words to me after one Colloquium, 'ducked the issue'. On top of that, nearly all of what he has written about the scope of equal concern suggests that it is a bounded value and not to be globalised. I believed then, I still do now, that if I could make headway in challenging this assumption I would have achieved something of value. It is up to the reader to decide how successful I have been, of course. But what I can say with absolute certainty is that this project has been every bit as stimulating as I hoped it would be.

Acknowledgements

When I first started to think seriously about Dworkin's theory of equality I benefited greatly by attending a reading seminar on *Sovereign Virtue* held within the Department of Philosophy at UCL in 2001 under the thoughtful stewardship of Jo Wolff, Michael Otsuka and Veronique Munoz Darde.

Previous incarnations of Chapters 4, 5, 6 and 7 were presented at the ALSP Annual Conference, University College Dublin, June 2006, the Department of Philosophy Seminar, University of Essex, February 2007, as the Royal Institute of Philosophy Lecture, Roehampton University, March 2007, the GSA Annual Conference, University of Birmingham, September 2007, the ECPR Annual Conference, Pisa, September 2007, the School of Public Policy Seminar Series, UCL, December 2007, the ALSP Annual Conference, University of Nottingham, March 2008, and the Former Research Students Conference, UCL, June 2008. For their useful questions and observations I would like to thank Robin Attfield, Clara Brandi, Clare Chambers, Chiara Cordelli, John Exdell, Brian Feltham, Donald Franklin, Stephen Gardiner, Béatrice Han-Pile, Mark Hannam, David Hudson, Carl Knight, Sune Laegaard, Bruce Landesman, Seth Lazar, Graham Long, Colin MacLeod, Christian Schemmel, Margaret Moore, Michael Otsuka, Adina Preda, Miriam Ronzoni, Raj Segal, Fabian Schuppert, Daniel Schwartz, Shlomi Segall, Jonathan Seglow, Neomal Silva, Joel Smith, Mario Solis, Kok-Chor Tan, Lorella Terzi, Jo Wolff and Lea Ypi.

I am also very grateful to Chris Armstrong, Basak Cali, Liz Cripps, David Karp, Saladin Meckled-Garcia, David Miller, Julio Montero, Andrea Sangiovanni, Agir Savoir, Laura Valentini and Gabriel Wollner who each provided invaluable critical comments on earlier drafts of the book (or parts thereof).

Credit must also go to the two anonymous referees from Palgrave Macmillan whose recommendations greatly improved the project in its fledgling stages. I am equally indebted to Priyanka Pathak for her generous encouragement and support throughout.

Finally, I thank *Res Publica* and *Human Rights Review* for permitting me to use revised material from 'An Egalitarian Plateau? Challenging the Importance of Ronald Dworkin's Abstract Egalitarian Rights', *Res Publica*, 13 (2007), 255–291 and 'Are There Any Global Egalitarian Rights?' *Human Rights Review*, 9 (2008), 435–464.

Part I

1
Introduction

For nearly three decades Ronald Dworkin's work on equality has helped to shape the debate on distributive justice. His own theory of equality, which draws on the idea of an abstract right to equal concern and respect and is realised through his account of equality of resources, has been by turns hugely influential and hugely controversial.

This book has two main ambitions. The first is to provide a sympathetic, though not uncritical, assessment of Dworkin's theory of equality in the domestic sphere. This theory has attracted numerous objections, of course. Some challenge his case against equality of welfare. Others demur at the desert island auction and hypothetical insurance markets. One or two suggest that by focusing on the choice/luck distinction he has fundamentally misunderstood the point of equality. Dworkin has responded to most of these criticisms. But what, if any, conclusions can we draw from these exchanges? I shall argue that although some aspects stand in need of further clarification and defence, Dworkin's detractors are mistaken if they believe that their objections demolish the foundations of the view. Nevertheless, I will argue that further weaknesses come to the fore when we ask 'Equality among whom?' as opposed to 'Equality of what?' I also try to explain a subtle shift in Dworkin's interest from questions of justice to questions of legitimacy. While his two original articles (Dworkin, 1981a; 1981b) focused on the best, most accurate account of justice as equal concern, *Sovereign Virtue* also develops the slightly different idea that if a government fails to act on a minimally adequate conception of equal concern it is not merely unjust but a tyranny (2000, p. 1). This idea is taken to its logical conclusion in *Is Democracy Possible Here?* in which he claims to be interested in what it would mean to achieve a 'minimum standard' of equal concern, where this is intended as an account of legitimacy as opposed to the 'gold standard' of justice (2006, ch. 4). How should we understand Dworkin's theory of equality in the light of this new preoccupation? My answer will be as follows. Justice and legitimacy are often assumed to have distinct normative foundations. Justice has to do with achieving a fair distribution of benefits and burdens, while legitimacy is a matter of gaining the consent of the governed. According to Dworkin, however, questions of justice and legitimacy are two sides of the same coin. Whereas justice asks what a government is required to do in order to live up to the best possible account of what it means to treat citizens with equal concern and respect, legitimacy asks what a government is required to do in order to show that it has made a good faith attempt to treat its citizens with equal concern and respect according to a minimally adequate interpretation of what that means.

My second ambition is to consider what, if anything, a Dworkinian approach might bring to current work in the field of global distributive justice. Dworkin evidently accepts certain basic precepts of international justice but resists the idea that agents owe equal concern to members of other political communities, where this implies a duty to reduce global inequality (Dworkin, 1986, ch. 6; 2006, ch. 2). I query this assumption and argue instead that there are good reasons for applying some aspects of his thinking to questions of global distributive justice despite Dworkin himself. One is that his methodology allows an interpreter to focus his or her imagination on the purpose and value of a practice as something we would all have reason to care about. It also encourages the interpreter to adopt a more critical attitude towards his or her subject, to say what it really is or ought to be and not merely what it is widely supposed to be. A second, related reason has to do with identifying possible sites of global distributive justice. The temptation may be to focus exclusively on trade tariffs, dispute settlement procedures and structural adjustment policies as things to which principles of justice apply. It seems to me right, however, to widen the interpretive net to capture additional things such as the distribution of natural resources and the giving or withholding of foreign aid. A third reason involves Dworkin's desert island thought experiment. That every human being is entitled, *ex ante*, to an equal share of the planet's natural resources is an intuition shared by many cosmopolitan theorists. Spelling out what, more precisely, global equality of resources would mean is quite another matter. I think that a suitably modified version of Dworkin's auction has the potential to explain much. A final reason is that Dworkin's analysis of the genesis of inequality may provide some useful conceptual tools for making normative sense of global inequality. Given the Byzantine interplay between international, local and natural causes of inequality, individual and collective, I argue that an amended version of the hypothetical insurance approach may provide a way of converting brute luck into option luck around the world and thereby of understanding the concrete demands of global equality of resources.

Dworkin in the context of contemporary political philosophy

As one of the leading figures in legal and political philosophy over the past 40 years or so, the size of Dworkin's literary corpus is matched only by the depth and range of the philosophical curiosity which stands behind it. Unlike some of his contemporaries, he has confidently taken his place as a public intellectual and is a regular contributor to *The New York Review of Books*, *The Times Literary Supplement* and *The Guardian*. Among the numerous important questions to have benefited from his careful attention are those relating to the nature of law and legality, the limits of state authority, the rights of citizens, the need for a free press, the basis of a tolerant society, the justification of political obligation, the distinction between different forms of democracy, what it means to be a good citizen, the decisions of the US Supreme Court, the rights and wrongs of abortion and euthanasia, and the relationship between politics, law and morality.

The aim of this book, however, is not to provide a comprehensive introduction to, or overview of, every component of Dworkin's extensive body of work. Instead, I focus on his theory of equality as it relates to matters of distributive justice. Of course, his account of the abstract right to equal concern and respect is itself closely connected with his interpretation of a range of other political values, most notably liberty, democracy, integrity and community (cf. Dworkin, 2004a, p. 377). So questions relating to the connection between distributive justice and these other important political values will also figure prominently. Even so, the following six propositions make up the nucleus of Dworkin's theory of equality as I shall understand it here. Firstly, that virtually every normative theory of social arrangement from Kant onwards can be presented as providing a competing interpretation of the same abstract egalitarian principle: that every citizen has a right to be treated with equal concern and respect by his or her own government (1977, p. 180; 1983, pp. 24–5; 1986, pp. 296–7; 1987a, pp. 7–8; 2000, p. 2). Secondly, that equality of welfare is a defective conception of this abstract egalitarian right in the genre of distributive justice because it cannot be specified without drawing on a prior conception of fair shares (the radical criticism) and is counter-intuitive (the objection from expensive tastes) (1981a; 1981b; 2000, ch. 7; 2004a). Thirdly, that equality of resources is the correct realisation of the right to equal concern and respect in matters of distributive justice, where this includes both 'personal' and 'impersonal' resources (1981b; 2000, pp. 322–3). Fourthly, that equality of resources encompasses two abstract requirements – to make the distribution of income and wealth at any given time sensitive to choice but not sensitive to brute luck – but that in order to fully understand what these requirements mean it is instructive to appeal to the artificial devices of persons shipwrecked on a desert island, an auction for natural resources and various hypothetical insurance markets (1981b; 2000; 2006, ch. 4). Fifthly, that the model of conflicting values defended by Isaiah Berlin (and others) is erroneous,[1] since it is possible to reconcile equality and liberty once we understand the true nature of each (1987a). Finally, that governments owe equal concern and respect to their own citizens and members of political communities owe equal concern and respect to each other, but they do not owe this to non-members (1986, ch. 6). This is not to deny that we owe non-members a degree of concern, especially with respect to human rights, but there is no obvious justification for extending egalitarian justice to global distribution (2006, ch. 2).

Taken together these propositions set Dworkin's theory apart from other leading approaches in the field of contemporary political philosophy. John Rawls, for example, locates questions of distributive justice within a broader question about which principles of justice should govern the basic institutions of 'a well-ordered democratic society' viewed as 'a cooperative venture for mutual advantage' (Rawls, 1971, p. 4). Rawls' two principles of justice describe the fair background conditions for cooperation within that society, including the way its basic institutions assign rights and liberties and regulate the distribution of primary goods. At the heart of Rawls' vision is the idea that the principles of justice must be those which can be the subject of agreement in the original position (1971) and which can provide a basis for overlapping consensus and public justification among citizens viewed as free and equal (1996). Dworkin's account of justice also fits into a broader picture of political society, but he is less interested in society as a cooperative venture for mutual advantage and more interested in what he calls *a true political community*. For Dworkin, something is a true political community only if its government demonstrates the virtues of legitimacy, democracy and integrity, and when members of the community conduct their public lives in ways that can be interpreted under an ideal of fraternity (Dworkin, 1986, ch. 6). According to Rawls, a well-ordered democratic society is *not* a community, 'if we mean by a community a society governed by a shared comprehensive, religious, philosophical, or moral doctrine' (Rawls, 1996, p. 42). To insist on community in this sense, argues Rawls, is to fly in the face of diversity and is likely to require the use of coercive force to impose a single comprehensive doctrine (p. 146, n. 13). Dworkin, for his part, acknowledges the fact of diversity, but does not accept the further assumption that we must therefore abandon the idea of political community altogether. In contrast to Rawls' narrow understanding of community, Dworkin's conception allows individuals to pursue their diverse conceptions of the good under the umbrella of equal concern and respect.

It is important, however, not to confuse Dworkin's doctrine of true political community with that of the communitarian school of political thought. Communitarians argue that the nature and value of community is not adequately reflected in Rawls' account of justice as fairness since according to this account agents must select principles of justice on the basis of a 'thin theory of the good'. This is flawed either because it is impossible to leave one's communal identity behind when selecting principles of justice or because the rights of the community ought to be given more prominence in the principles of justice (see Sandel, 1982; Taylor, 1989; 1992). Unlike Rawls, Dworkin puts the idea of community at the centre of his theory of equality, but his theory is not communitarian in the above sense, and for two good reasons. The first is that members of true political communities accept that they owe obligations to each other rather than to the group as a collective entity (Dworkin, 1986, p. 199). A true political community is not an agent or living thing with an ontological status and life of its own over and above the activities of its members (1989, p. 494). The second reason is that in order to show equal concern and respect to its citizens a government must, according to Dworkin's equality of resources, distribute resources among individuals. If a group of persons wish to club together to build a temple of worship, then justice will be served provided that each individual has an equal share of resources with which to engage in this collective project as opposed to saying that justice will be served provided that each *group* has an equal share of resources for its temples. In this way equal concern is an individualistic virtue. Even so, Dworkin does not wish to imply that 'the success of a person's life can be achieved or even conceived independently of the success of some community or tradition to which he belongs'. His theory of equality would not provide a common ground for all the members of diverse political communities if it were individualistic in that 'different and more substantive sense' (2006, p. 10). On the contrary, each individual is entitled to devote his or her fair share of resources to the particular religious, moral or cultural tradition he or she belongs to or has come to identify with. Dworkin can accept these sorts of associative obligations provided that they operate within the shared communal principle of equal concern and respect. Indeed, individual citizens are encouraged to integrate their life, interests and basic values with the life, interests and basic values of the political community by making use of their fair share of resources and by taking an interest in the various practices and activities that make up the health and vitality of that political community (1989, p. 500).

Returning to the comparison between Dworkin and Rawls, further differences come to the fore when we reflect on the relationship between liberty and equality. Rawls argues that basic rights and liberties can conflict with the demands of socio-economic equality but should be considered lexically prior in the sense that liberty may only be sacrificed for the sake of liberty and not for equality (Rawls, 1971, ch. 4). Dworkin, however, believes that the right to equal concern and respect provides a single value from which to interpret the content of liberty and equality. In the case of liberty, he maintains that citizens do not have a general right to liberty as such, but they do have a right to certain liberties, where the answer to the question 'Which liberties?' depends on our best conception of equal concern and respect (Dworkin, 1977, p. 272). With regards to equality, the claim is that 'if we accept equality of resources as the best conception of distributional equality, liberty becomes an aspect of equality rather than, as it often thought to be, an independent political ideal potentially in conflict with it' (1987a, pp. 1–2). Consequently, 'anyone who thinks that liberty and equality really do conflict on some occasion must think that protecting liberty means acting in some way that does not show equal concern for all citizens.' Dworkin doubts whether this could ever be justified (p. 8).[2]

Another difference emerges when we reflect on the right way to respond to the distribution of natural advantages. Both Dworkin and Rawls affirm that the distribution of natural talents can be a source of unfairness depending on how institutions deal with these facts. But whereas Rawls advocates the difference principle as the right way to deal with unequal talents, Dworkin asks us to imagine what income people would have if, contrary to fact, they had been given ample opportunity to purchase insurance against lack of natural talent. He argues that on average people prefer a 'bet' under which the percentage of income they pay in premiums would rise as their income rises (Dworkin, 1981b, p. 325). 'If we modelled our tax structure on the hypothetical insurance story,' explains Dworkin, 'we would insist on a fairly steep progressive tax-rate system so that those with more income would pay at a higher rate' (2006, p. 117). Rawls argues that the demands of distributive justice (as in, the difference principle) might be better served by a consumption tax rather than an income tax. He suggests that a consumption tax is preferable to an income tax 'at the level of common sense precepts of justice', 'since it imposes a levy according to how much a person takes out of the common store of goods and not according to how much he contributes (assuming here that income is fairly earned)' (Rawls, 1971, p. 278). According to Rawls, income tax should be reserved for circumstances in which it is required to safeguard the first principle of justice and fair equality of opportunity; that is, when it is necessary to forestall the accumulation of wealth and power which threatens to undermine the exercise of equal political rights and fair access to positions (p. 279).

Dworkin also bears contrast with Robert Nozick. Nozick is less concerned with offering an account of the nature of fair terms of social cooperation or true political community as with understanding how even a 'minimal state' can be justified. The main task is to explain how individuals can come to have 'just entitlements' to private property and income. For Nozick, it is through original acquisition and voluntary transfers of land, natural resources and labour power that just entitlements are created. This is not a matter of social cooperation for reciprocal benefit in Rawls' sense. Nor is it living in a true political community in Dworkin's sense. Rather, it is simply a matter of the exercise of individual rights (Nozick, 1974, p. ix). Dworkin, however, rejects the entitlement theory on two main grounds. The first is that it is a 'starting-gate' theory of justice which upholds the rights of first-grabbers irrespective of inequalities in their size, strength and temporal advantage. The second is that Nozick wrongly treats natural talents as a legitimate source of economic inequality. The promise of Dworkin's equality of resources is that it can marry together traditional right-wing support for the free market with traditional left-wing concerns about the plight of people who start off with nothing or whose talents the market does not value (see Dworkin, 1981b, pp. 308–11; 2000, p. 7; 2006, pp. 103–4).

A key component of equality of resources is the hypothetical insurance device. Dworkin has applied this device to a wide variety of disadvantages ranging from physical disability and lack of talent through to ill-health and on to redundancy and being born to poor parents (Dworkin, 1981b; 2000, chs. 8, 9; 2006, ch. 4). Although he is by no means the only liberal egalitarian philosopher to employ a thought experiment to flesh out the principles of justice — Rawls, of course, asks us to imagine ourselves behind a veil of ignorance — Dworkin's contribution has been to underscore the potential usefulness of insurance as a device for turning the theory of equality into practice.[3] While political philosophers have been good at specifying ideal conditions, they have been far less diligent at saying how exactly their principles are to be applied to the real world where there is complex interplay between different causes of inequality. Dworkin wishes to be an exception to this. He places Rawls in the social contract tradition of political thought, but places himself in a tradition of 'practical politics' which includes 'the Fabian movement in Britain, Franklin Roosevelt's New Deal in America, and the social democratic parties of post-war Europe'. All of these movements, argues Dworkin, 'proposed that the redistributive programs they sponsored, like social security, workmen's compensation, and poverty relief programs, be understood as vast insurance schemes against accident, sickness, unemployment and other forms of bad luck' (2006, p. 112). That being said, Dworkin also exploits the artificial device of hypothetical insurance to remedy some of the more problematic iniquities exhibited by actual insurance schemes.

Returning to the comparison with Rawls, another key difference is the work they have each undertaken (or not undertaken) in developing a set of principles of international justice. Rawls' *A Theory of Justice* contains a version of the original position in which the representatives of different peoples come together to choose principles of international justice *inter alia* the right of non-intervention, the right of self-defence and the duty to honour treaties (Rawls, 1971, pp. 378–9). *The Law of Peoples* supplements this list with a duty to assist what he calls 'burdened peoples' and a qualification to the duty of non-intervention in the case of 'outlaw states and grave violations of human rights' (1999, p. 37). Dworkin's work in the field of political theory is striking for the absence of a full-length treatment of international justice. That is not to say he never touches on these sorts of questions. It is fairly clear from *Law's Empire* that he believes countries do not have a right to engage in wars of self-interest against other sovereign countries (Dworkin, 1986, p. 206). Furthermore, in *Is Democracy Possible Here?* he addresses the US government's treatment of foreign detainees at Guantánamo Bay and Abu Ghraib, and briefly considers the question of economic sanctions against countries with a track record of human rights violations. In both cases he argues that an appropriate deeper test of the rightness of such activities is whether or not they can be interpreted as respecting human dignity (2006, ch. 2). Nevertheless, Dworkin has yet to write a book similar in ambition to *The Law of Peoples*.

Like Rawls, Dworkin believes that socio-economic inequalities only raise questions of justice within a domestic political setting and not across state borders. The pressing question is *why* Dworkin eschews the idea of global distributive justice in this way. Rawls provides a relatively long explanation as to why there can be no identikit version of justice as fairness in the global context: the main reason being the need to show 'due toleration' for the political cultures of other societies. Because liberal peoples must show due toleration for decent yet non-liberal peoples there is no reason to regard as unjust material inequalities between societies which reflect differences in political culture (Rawls, 1999, pp. 115–19). At first glance, Dworkin's thinking seems to be more influenced by the question of dominion. He writes that equal concern and respect is 'the special and indispensable virtue of sovereigns' (Dworkin, 2000, p. 6). If there is no global sovereign, individuals of the world cannot reasonably expect global equality of resources. But then this raises a question about other possible sites of global egalitarian justice; that is, institutions, rules, practices and activities to which principles of egalitarian justice could apply even in the absence of a global state. It also raises a question about the role of true political community and why there can be true political community in the domestic but not the global context.

Dworkin's methodology

Whilst keeping these questions at the back of our minds, let us now turn to Dworkin's methodology. This has two elements, the first of which is *constructivism*. In contrast to intuitionism, constructivism 'treats intuitions of justice not as clues to the existence of independent principles, but rather as stipulated features of a general theory to be constructed, as if a sculptor set himself to carve the animal that best fits a pile of bones he happened to find together'. It does not, in other words, assume 'that principles of justice have some fixed, objective existence, so that descriptions of these principles must be true or false in some standard way. It does not assume that the animal it matches to the bones actually exists.' Instead, it 'makes the different, and in some ways more complex, assumption that men and women have a responsibility to fit the particular judgments on which they act into a coherent program of action' (Dworkin, 1977, p. 160).

The second part is *interpretivism*. To continue with Dworkin's metaphor, we might say that the interpreter seeks to carve out an attractive-looking animal from the pile of bones. Naturally the interpretation of political practices and concepts will involve disputes, where different interpretations must compete for the honour of being the 'best' interpretation. So

what makes something a good interpretation? This is also open to interpretation, but two requirements seem especially important in Dworkin's
eyes. The first is that it must provide a good 'fit' with the data. In the case
of concepts, linguistic use will set some limits on possible interpretations.
Although political philosophers 'cannot develop semantic theories that
provide rules for "justice" like the rules we contemplated for "book"', they
can 'try to capture the plateau from which arguments about justice largely
proceed, and try to describe this in some abstract proposition taken to
define the "concept" of justice for their community, so that arguments
over justice can be understood as arguments about the best conception of
that concept' (Dworkin, 1986, p. 74). Dworkin also suggests that a good
interpretation of the concept of justice must be 'continuous' with our
conventional personal ethics. We have every reason to be sceptical of an
interpretation of justice in public life that depends on normative ideas
which cut against the grain of our conventional personal ethics (as in,
people's ordinary ethical experience) (2000, p. 294). As for practices, these
too will constrain feasible interpretations as to purpose or value. For
instance, some people find libertarianism to be an unattractive theory of
the practice of justice. Even so, we at least all agree that it is such a theory.
'But the thesis that abstract art is unjust is not even unattractive; it is
incomprehensible as a theory about justice because no competent preinterpretive account of the practice of justice embraces the criticism and
evaluation of art' (1986, p. 75).

The second requirement is that an interpretation must tell an attractive story about its subject. That is to say, we should 'aim to make the
object of interpretation the best it can be'. 'It means making the best of
it, given what we believe to be the right view of the point of the enterprise in question' (Dworkin, 1994, p. 474). It can also involve interpreting the practice as though it were attempting to exemplify a value or
ideal that any of us would have reason to care about – an ideal such as
integrity (1986, pp. 49–55). Like practices, showing a concept in its
best possible light may involve both identifying the particular functions it serves in our lives and presenting it in terms of deeper values
that many people share, so that the best interpretation of the concept
is the one that best encapsulates those deeper values. Philosophical
analysis must be able to tell us what values such as justice, equality and
liberty really are. But knowing what these things really are is not the
same as learning what gold really is by dint of chemical analysis. 'We
believe that gold is what it is quite independently of human concerns,
ambitions, or needs. But that is not even remotely plausible about a
political virtue like equality or liberty.' 'They are what they are because

we are what we are: we believe that a government that respects liberty and equality in some way improves the lives of those whom it governs' (2001, p. 255).

Some of the things which are likely to make for successful interpretation across various different genres of interpretation are that an interpretation is complete, systematic, simple, elegant and true to the point of interpretation in the given genre. According to Dworkin, one of the key features of political interpretation − as distinct from literary interpretation − is that interpretation should not be conservative in the sense of merely reporting and thereby endorsing the intentions of those involved in creating or maintaining its subject matter. Practices are constituted out of human activity and naturally as the authors of their own practices it is only natural that people should take a view about what it is they are doing. But this subjective interpretation lacks the critical edge of *constructive interpretation*. This, as Dworkin puts it, 'is a matter of imposing purpose on an object or practice in order to make of it the best possible example of the form or genre to which it is taken to belong' (Dworkin, 1986, p. 52). This critical aspect is significant because once the interpretive attitude takes hold people will 'try to impose meaning on the institution − to see it in its best light − and then to restructure it in the light of that meaning' (p. 47). Interpretation, in other words, 'folds back into the practice, altering its shape' (p. 48). Thus constructive interpretations of the concepts of justice, equality, liberty, integrity, democracy, community and so on are not supposed to be neutral. They 'are as substantive, normative and engaged as any of the contending opinions in the political battles that rage about those ideas' (2004b, p. 3).

Putting these elements together, we might say that constructive interpretation involves making the best of a given practice or concept and where necessary transforming that practice or concept to bring it closer to its ideal. According to Dworkin, this method consists in three stages (Dworkin, 1986, p. 66). First, an interpreter must identify the preinterpretive data from which his or her theory is to be constructed. In the case of a social practice, this will include all the rules, standards and modes of behaviour that might be associated with the practice. With respect to a concept, this is the customary ways in which the concept is used as well as common intuitions about its correct usage. Second, an interpreter must identify the main or core elements of the practice or concept and spell out his or her reasons or justification for thinking that these are the core elements. This justification might simply be an account of what is purposeful or valuable about the particular practice or concept, but it might also draw on deeper values that could be common to various practices or concepts and shared by a great many people. Third, an interpreter must revisit the preinterpretive data in the light of the second stage and in some instances discard elements which are not really part of the practice or concept. For example, an interpreter might take the view that a key purpose of the concept of justice is to guide the actions of agents and to impose strong duties of compliance upon them. As a result, he or she might disregard certain intuitions about justice on the grounds that they fall outside of these core purposes.

In his book *Spheres of Justice,* Michael Walzer famously defends a form of constructivism according to which the cultural meanings of goods such as health care determine the principles of distributive justice according to which they are rightly distributed. What is more, 'every substantive account of distributive justice is a local account', that is, relative to its own social meanings, so there can be 'no external or universal principles' of justice with which to judge a society (Walzer, 1983, p. 314). This may or may not be a promising slant on what it means to resolve questions of justice, but it is not one that Dworkin accepts. His criticism of Walzer is unequivocal: 'Walzer's relativism is faithless to the single most important social practice we have: the practice of worrying about what justice really is' (Dworkin, 1985, p. 219). So Dworkin wishes to stress the fact that when a constructive interpreter says that something 'really is' part of a particular practice or concept this signifies something about his utterance. The language signals the fact that he wishes to make an argument about how things ought to be and this is something we understand when he speaks (1986, pp. 103–4). In other words, the interpreter wishes to make it clear that he is not merely reporting a taste – he thinks that his interpretation is best for everyone and not merely for himself. According to Dworkin, however, we do not automatically assume that by using this sort of language an interpreter must be affirming the existence of a metaphysical realm of moral facts to which he somehow has special access (p. 81). On the contrary, the 'practices of interpretation and morality give these claims all the meaning they need or could have' (p. 83).[4]

In the next section I shall say more about Dworkin's use of constructive interpretation in the case of justice and equality, but before doing so I want to reflect for a moment on the similarities and differences between this methodology and Rawls' reflective equilibrium. I shall also try to explain why I think that constructive interpretation is a superior method and respond to some possible objections.

Rawls describes reflective equilibrium as the search to find a 'match' between ordinary beliefs about the nature of society, pre-reflective intuitions about the right and the good and considered moral judgements in particular cases. Reflection gives rise to a set of proposed principles of justice for society and the reasoner goes back and forth between beliefs, intuitions, judgements and proposed principles, making revisions where necessary, until he has achieved equilibrium in the shape of one particular conception (Rawls, 1971, pp. 48–51). All of this may sound reasonable enough, but Rawls begins with some not uncontroversial descriptions of society. He characterises domestic political society as 'a cooperative scheme for reciprocal advantage' or 'a fair system of cooperation over time'. He also claims that 'mutual recognition' is an essential part of a society of peoples. According to Rawls, these ideas are 'implicit in the public political culture of a democratic society' – including its 'political institutions', the practices of the judiciary and 'historical texts and documents that are common knowledge' (1996, pp. 13–14) – and in the political cultural of the society of peoples (1999, pp. 103, 122).

These characterisations have led some commentators to wonder whether Rawls really is constructing a theory from widely held beliefs about society or actually interpreting those beliefs in particular ways. Aaron James, for example, suggests that the 'original position reasoning is partly grounded in what has come to be called "constructive interpretation" of existing practices' (James, 2005, pp. 284–5, 300–1). Dworkin also characterises Rawls' reflective equilibrium as an 'interpretive enterprise' (cf. Dworkin, 2004c: 1391–2). Even if Rawls' characterisations are interpretations, however, it is not clear to me whether this kind of interpretation is exactly on a par with Dworkin's brand of interpretation. After all, Rawls' characterisations are supposed to explain or articulate ideas of society and a society of peoples that are present within the relevant political culture and within the institutions they have created and the founding documents. The aim is to render more explicit these existing ideas whilst at the same time being faithful to the intentions of the creators of these institutions. The ambition of constructive interpretation, by contrast, is to make its subject the best it can be and where necessary to impose an interpretation of its point or value. So what makes the interpretation successful is not that it explains what is already widely supposed to be the case, but that it shows its subject in its best light. In this way the constructive interpreter is explicit about what *he* regards as the real point or value of his subject and this, I think, opens up the possibility for a more critical brand of interpretation. In other words, Dworkin's method underscores the fact that there are many possible fits or matches with the data, that is, many possible explanations of the point or value of the institutions or practices at hand, and therefore no reason to be slavish to the intentions of those responsible for creating or maintaining them.

This in itself, however, raises a number of worries. If constructive interpretation is a matter of foisting an interpreter's beliefs and values on others, what is the justification for doing so? With what authority does the interpreter disregard what it is that the persons who actually created the practice and help to sustain it think they are doing? I assume that Dworkin's answer to this question is that whatever justification there is must derive from the point or value of political interpretation itself. Consider the alternative, he might say. If all reasoning about justice begins and ends with retrieving the beliefs and values that are alive and well in the public political culture of the society in question, then inevitably there will be a bias towards viewing current practices as just. That is, the reasoning will not tell us what kinds of social practices we ought to have and whether or not major revisions to current practices are justified. The point or value of political interpretation is that we can step beyond the status quo. That being said, for Dworkin political interpretation is likely to be most successful when the interpreter makes an appeal to deeper ground that everyone can share. In other words, a process of justification allows us to discriminate between competing interpretations that satisfy the requirement of fit, but in the case of politics the most powerful justification is likely to be one of human dignity.

A second set of worries concerns the issue of who the constructive interpreters are supposed to be. If any rational thinker is entitled to turn a critical eye to political practices or concepts and thereby to become a constructive interpreter, how do we adjudicate between competing interpretations? How can any single interpreter claim to be offering the most authoritative account? Would something like a poll of interpretations have more authority than a single interpretation? Are people who live outside of a society automatically better placed for critical interpretation than those inside it? I suspect that Dworkin's response to these worries would be twofold. First, he would point out that some interpreters are better than others. We must be on the lookout for interpreters who are apt to bias or prejudice, for example. In his philosophy of law Dworkin appeals to the idea of a perfect judge, Hercules, who is blessed with 'superhuman intellectual power and patience'. He is the personification of law as integrity, which is to say that he exploits his gifts of being fully informed, scrupulously impartial, calm, unpartisan and perfectly fair-minded to settle hard cases in the law (Dworkin, 1977, p. 105; 1986, p. 239). Ordinary people cannot expect to achieve these high standards, of course, but they are nonetheless some of the standards to which we should aspire in the interpretation of law. Perhaps if Hercules turned his attention to questions of political morality, he would also come to one right answer. In actual political life we know that interpreters are not always impartial. However, from the mere fact that someone offers an interpretation from inside a practice it does not automatically follow that it is tainted. When Dworkin asks whether or not his own government treats its citizens with equal concern and respect it is not necessary to disregard his critique merely because he is himself an American citizen: for we know that he intends to consider in good faith whether the kind of justice meted out by his government is as just as it could be. The second response would be to say that whatever authority attaches to a particular interpretation does so in ways that are quite familiar to ordinary political argument. After all, to interpret a political practice or concept is itself to take a stand in a political argument. It is to nail one's colours to the mast in the face of opponents who offer conflicting interpretations. So we ask: does an interpreter impose on his subject matter a coherent and attractive account of its purpose or value? Does he provide a satisfactory elaboration of that purpose or value? Is the interpretation adequately coherent and tolerably complete?

Interpreting the idea of equal concern and respect

Although Dworkin has applied the interpretive method to a number of important concepts, in this book I shall concentrate on the concept of distributive justice. It is to be expected, says Dworkin, for people to have deep theoretical disagreements about the nature of distributive justice. This is surely right. People who use the concept will disagree about the scope of distributive justice (what kinds of things can be treated justly or unjustly?), the sites of distributive justice (what sorts of things are appropriately governed by principles of justice − rules, institutions, collective practices, individual actions?), the point of distributive justice (is the point of justice to resolve disputes, to allow more advanced forms of cooperation or to make certain other kinds of community possible?), and the content of distributive justice (what are the principles of justice − equality, sufficiency or something else entirely?). According to Dworkin, that there exists this sort of deep disagreement is part and parcel of this and many other concepts; which is itself, of course, an interpretation (Dworkin, 1986, p. 49).

Dworkin's own interpretation of distributive justice appeals to the notion of an abstract right to equal concern and respect. He asks: which principles of distributive justice provide the best interpretation of this abstract right? But consider now those people who would disclaim the existence of this right, who would say that justice is not necessarily about treating people as equals. How do we justify the existence of this right to them? Dworkin sets out to motivate the abstract egalitarian right without recourse to either utilitarianism or the assumption of natural rights. His suggestion is that we seek a deeper common ground that people can share: 'we must not look to principles that are distinctly political or even moral but rather to principles that identify more abstract value in the human situation' (Dworkin, 2006, p. 9). To this end, he proposes what he calls two principles of 'ethical individualism' or 'human dignity'. The first is 'the principle of equal importance' or 'intrinsic value'. This is the 'vague but powerful idea' that every human life is something of intrinsic value and objectively so. That is to say, it matters how well or badly people's lives go and it matters not just to them but to everyone (1977, pp. 198–9; 2000, p. 5; 2006, p. 9). The second is 'the principle of special responsibility' or 'personal responsibility'. It adds to the principle that every human life has intrinsic value the idea that every individual has a special responsibility for identifying and realising that value (2000, p. 6; 2006, p. 10). Dworkin declares at the start of *Sovereign Virtue* that together these two principles 'shape and support the account of equality defended in this book' (2000, p. 5).

At first glance, there are some intuitive connections between the two principles of ethical individualism and the abstract political right to equal concern and respect that citizens can claim against their own governments. We might think that the right to equal concern piggybacks on the idea of equal moral worth, while the right to equal respect seems to flow quite naturally from the notion that each individual has a special responsibility for the success or failure of his or her own life. Dworkin makes it clear, however, that the relationship between the two principles of ethical individualism and the abstract political right to equal concern and respect is one of constructive interpretation or abduction rather than logical entailment or deduction. Hence, he does not suppose that the principle of equal importance always translates into a right to equal concern. Rather, it only does so 'in certain circumstances' (2000, p. 6). So when he claims that equal concern is the sovereign virtue of political community what he means is that there is something special about a true political community which makes such an interpretation appropriate (2000, p. 1; 2006, p. 95). People's private lives are a different matter. Here 'we owe all other human beings a *measure* of concern, but we do not owe them concern equal to that we have for ourselves, our families, and others close to us' (p. 94). For example, 'most of us do not suppose that we must, as individuals, treat our neighbours children with the same concern as our own, or treat everyone we meet with the same respect' (1978, p. 125). Indeed, according to Dworkin, '[w]e believe that someone who showed equal concern for all members of his political community, in his private life, would be defective' (1989, p. 503). The sphere of international affairs is also different from the sphere of domestic politics. Once again we owe members of other political communities a measure of concern, as expressed by the recognition of baseline human rights, but not equal concern as such and certainly not in matters of economic distribution (2006, ch. 2).

My project

My project has two main parts. The first part is to scrutinise Dworkin's theory of equality as articulated in the following body of work. Dworkin's abstract egalitarian principle first appeared in his *Taking Rights Seriously* (1977). Here he draws a distinction between the right to equal treatment and the right to treatment as an equal. This distinction is further explored in 'What is Equality? Part 1: Equality of Welfare' (1981a) and 'Part 2: Equality of Resources' (1981b) which specify different ways of treating people as equals in matters of distribution. He followed up these articles with a reply to Jan Narveson in *Social Philosophy and Policy* (1983) and a chapter in his book *A Matter of Principle* entitled 'Why Liberals Should Care about Equality' (1985). This material looks at how one might go about trying to justify the abstract egalitarian principle. Following on from there, chapter 6 of *Law's Empire* (1986) fleshes out the concept of a true political community, while 'What is Equality? Part 3: The Place of Liberty' (1987a) examines the alleged tension between equality and liberty. For the purposes of this book the next major landmark in the development of Dworkin's theory of equality came in the shape of *Sovereign Virtue* (2000). It not only reprints a number of the earlier articles but also includes a response to objections (ch. 7) and an attempt to apply the hypothetical insurance device to new areas of distributive justice such as health care (ch. 8). The book's central thesis is deceptively simple: 'Equal concern is the sovereign virtue of political community' (Dworkin, 2000, p. 1). Dworkin has also replied to his critics in *Ethics* (2002), *Philosophy and Public Affairs* (2003) and Justine Burley's edited collection *Dworkin and His Critics* (2004a). More recently, chapter 4 of *Is Democracy Possible Here?* (2006) revisits many of the earlier themes and explores in detail the question of taxation and legitimacy in the context of US politics. Studying this work seldom requires the reader to reflect on incomplete suggestions about what a complete theory might look like. Few of his commentators are more detailed or systematic than Dworkin himself. This does not mean, however, that there is no work to be done in terms of clarifying his main arguments so that we might better understand their nature and force as well as how they fit together over time; exposing to critical assessment why the right to equal concern and respect matters; explaining the nature of his interest in justice and legitimacy respectively; scrutinising equality of resources; and evaluating the success or failure of his replies to critics.

The second part of my project, by contrast, is to try to develop a Dworkinian approach to questions of global justice. Chapter 6 of *Law's Empire* will again be important, since it is here that Dworkin anchors the right to equal concern to political communities, and this gives pause for thought about the possibility of a global political community. I shall also look at chapter 2 of *Is Democracy Possible Here?* in which he considers a number of political questions that have international significance and makes an appeal to human dignity in answering them. In addition to this, I intend to revisit 'Equality of Resources' to see what light, if any, it might shed on questions of global distribution. I take seriously the possibility of extending equality of resources globally and try to spell out what such a theory might look like, what problems it could face and why it would be worth defending. Part of this project will be to measure the proposal against approaches taken by other political theorists in this area, most notably Charles Beitz's *Political Theory and International Relations* (1979), John Rawls' *The Law of Peoples* (1999), Thomas Pogge's *World Poverty and Human Rights* (2002a), Kok-Chor Tan's *Justice without Borders* (2004) and David Miller's *National Responsibility and Global Justice* (2007).

Nevertheless, two fallacies threaten this project right from the start. The first is a fallacy of doctrine. Why should we think that it is possible to construct a Dworkinian theory of global distributive justice when the man himself is at best silent on the issue and at worse hints at the absurdity of such an idea? Wouldn't such an enterprise be mere pretence? Wouldn't it produce only a bogus reincarnation of the Dworkinian spirit? The second is a fallacy of scope. Why should we think that it is appropriate to extend a theory of domestic distributive justice into the global sphere given numerous possible disanalogies between the two? Why should we assume that the best account of global justice has anything in common with Dworkin's equality of resources? I fully acknowledge these pitfalls at the outset and so proceed with a healthy degree of caution. But I do not think that they should discourage the project entirely. Of course, Dworkin believes that in the case of domestic justice '[w]e share a preinterpretive sense of the rough boundaries of the practice on which our imagination must be trained.' Furthermore, '[w]e use this to distinguish conceptions of justice we reject, even deplore, from positions we would not count as conceptions of justice at all even if they were presented under that title' (Dworkin, 1986, p. 75). The task of interpreting the concept of global justice is even more difficult – allegedly – because there is as much disagreement about the kinds of things to which it applies as there is about the contents of justice. But from the mere fact that thinking about global justice may be more difficult than thinking about domestic justice it does not automatically follow that doing so is impossible.

In fact, I shall try to show that Dworkin's method of constructive interpretation lends itself rather well to this other field of study. As suggested above, there are three stages of interpretation to be undertaken. The first is to identify the preinterpretive data, which in this case might include the many institutions, rules, practices and activities in which individuals, states and non-state actors are involved at the international or global level. The second stage is to reflect on the point, purpose or value of these various things. Evidently this reflection will lead some interpreters to say that abstract egalitarian rights do *not* apply within this domain. But this is not necessarily the case. Others may develop an interpretation according to which these rights *do* apply. They might even appeal to deeper values of the human situation in order to lend support to this interpretation. That is, they will ask not 'What is the conventional point of these things?' but 'What is the real point of these things given the deeper common ground that we all share?' If it is appropriate to speak of such rights, the third stage involves an interpretation of the content of these rights in the light of the data. At this stage an interpreter will revisit his preinterpretive reflections on the subject, sometimes discarding elements which are not really part of the subject, sometimes adding elements which are relevant after all.

The constructive interpreter cannot be oblivious to what might distinguish different domains of human life. But neither can he or she afford to ignore potentially important similarities between domains. For this reason, I leave open the possibility that the best interpretations of institutions, rules, practices and even individual actions within both the domestic and global domains could draw upon roughly the same two principles of human dignity, that these principles could imply roughly the same abstract rights to equal concern and respect and, finally, that these rights could have a somewhat similar content with regards to more substantive principles of justice. Nevertheless, prior to embarking on a detailed interpretation of domestic and global politics and of the various possible principles of justice which might be suitable to each, we should no more assume in advance the truth of dogmatic universalism, the view that the same principles of justice should be applied across different domains of human life, than we should assume in advance the truth of dogmatic contextualism, the view that there must be major variation of principles across different domains of human life (cf. Miller, 2002a, pp. 7–14; Pogge, 2002c, pp. 37–9). It is, of course, a further issue how egalitarian rights are best realised or implemented in the different domains, and here it is quite possible that larger differences will arise.

One of the problems for my project going forward, however, is that Dworkin has remained more or less silent on the sorts of preinterpretive data that he thinks might be suitable for thinking about principles of global justice. Asking the following questions suggests a bewildering array of possible data. To what extent can we blame poor people for their own predicament? Have they taken gambles which simply didn't pay off or were they never in a situation of taking chances on a level playing field? What about their governments? Have they pursued policies that actually harmed successful development? What about the role of economic globalisation in all of this? In an economy incorporating virtually every region of the world, to what extent does the trade protectionism practised by rich countries unfairly hinder the economic prospects of poorer countries? Indeed, don't international bodies such as the IMF and World Bank prescribe certain structural adjustment policies as conditions for much needed loans and don't such conditions actually hold poorer countries back in some respects? Aren't poorer countries required to open their economies to compete with each other and with more powerful and established industrialised nations and doesn't this worsen inequality? Don't international investors demand that poorer countries enter into a crippling competition to provide lower taxes, reduced wages and cheaper resources all of which blights the lives of local people? Besides, aren't the residents of many of the world's most impoverished countries still paying the price for their colonial past? Furthermore, what about inequalities in access to natural resources in different parts of the world? Even when countries are blessed with reserves of valuable minerals, gas and oil deposits, what if they lack the development skills and technological required for exploiting their resources? What if they are blighted by tyrants, civil wars and weak property rights? Don't foreign companies sometimes exploit or trade in oil, coltan, diamonds and other precious materials that have been taken without the permission of local people? What level of official development assistance is given to poor countries and what is its real purpose? And what of the numerous natural disasters that strike different parts of our planet ruining the lives of some people and not others? How do national governments and international aid organisations deal with these disasters and what kind of impact does this have on local people? Indeed, what role do local people play in making good or bad use of foreign aid?

Although a number of writers have tried to answer some or all of these questions, I look at them afresh using the method of constructive interpretation. In order to construct the best possible interpretation of these various institutions, rules, practices and individual actions I try to provide a clearer account of their point and purpose, of the concepts we use to judge them and of the deeper principles of human value that show them in their best light. At a high level of abstraction, I appeal to the idea of an abstract right to global equal concern and respect supported by Dworkin's two principles of human dignity. At the more concrete level I defend a compound approach to global distributive justice which comprises not only principles of justice for the regulation of trade rules, dispute settlements and international fiscal arrangements but also principles governing international exploitation of, and trade in, natural resources and foreign aid. More specifically, I defend a version of global equality of resources inspired by the familiar Dworkinian devices of an imaginary auction for natural resources, hypothetical insurance and the distinctions between choice and luck, option luck and brute luck, ambition and endowment. In each case, however, I attempt to remodel and amend these original ideas in ways better suited to the global sphere.

Few books and articles written on the subject of global distributive justice begin without listing at least some brute facts about global inequality. Pogge's *World Poverty and Human Rights* is no exception. Page two offers the striking statistic that '2,800 million people together have about 1.2 percent of aggregate global income, while the 903 million people of the "high income economies" together have 79.7 percent' (Pogge, 2002a, p. 2). This raises the following difficult question, why does global inequality matter? Pogge includes this statistic in order to make the point that shifting 1 per cent of aggregate global income from the first group to the second group could eradicate severe poverty worldwide. In his work with Sanjay Reddy, for example, Pogge develops an account of absolute poverty based on the local cost of a basket of basic necessities (Pogge and Reddy, 2002). In his 'Why Inequality Matters', however, Pogge offers the further reason that relative poverty matters because it translates into and sustains power imbalances, meaning that the poorest people in the world typically have the least influence over the global institutional order (Pogge, 2007). I do not disagree with this reason, but I intend to argue that there is perhaps another reason why relative deprivation matters. That it is based on factors that are arbitrary from a moral point of view and leaves people unequally placed with respect to meeting the challenge of life, including the challenge of risk and uncertainty. Hence I construct a thought experiment in which all individuals around the world face the same antecedent risks and have an equal share of resources with which to purchase insurance.

In short, my intention is to spell out and defend global equality of resources as a principle of political morality. When I say 'political' morality I mean not only the background rules and practices of the global realm but also the individual choices that are made in the shadow of that institutional backdrop, including the choices of individuals and collectives. By 'principle' I mean a tenet of public morality whose job it is to govern rules, practices and individual actions. A principle is the embodiment of a sense of the requirements and obligations of right conduct in a domain. One thing that makes something a principle as opposed to a rigid rule is that it points in favour of a course of action but may not necessitate a particular decision. The point of using principles rather than rules is that principles have a dynamic nature: they allow us to construct all plausible versions of the principle under its underlying theme or spirit in different contexts and changing circumstances. But note that a principle will itself depend on particular interpretations of the things which it is supposed to govern, which is to say that what makes something an appropriate principle to govern X will depend on the nature and function of X, which is itself open to interpretation. Take the examples of official development assistance and humanitarian aid. Hitherto political theorists working on the question of global distributive justice have tended to interpret foreign aid (which includes rules, practices and individual actions) in terms of duties of compassion or philanthropy, whereas scholars of international relations have depicted it as largely a matter of self-interest. My own view is that a single thing can be interpreted as having more than one kind of purpose or value. Thus I intend to interpret foreign aid as being appropriately governed by principles of justice as global equal concern and respect by pointing out features that are best interpreted in this light.

The structure of the book

This book is divided into two parts, consisting of four chapters each. The remainder of Part I looks at Dworkin's theory of equality as it applies domestically.

Chapter 2 considers Dworkin's two most powerful arguments against equality of welfare: the radical criticism and the objection from expensive tastes. I shall argue that the radical criticism is difficult to defeat, since it is not clear whether any theory of equality of welfare can gain a foothold without an independent theory of fair shares. The objection from expensive tastes, by contrast, is widely regarded as being much less convincing. I shall argue, however, that most critics fail to grasp the true significance of the objection. They tend to assume that Dworkin wishes to make the crude point that some people deliberately cultivate expensive tastes. If that were the point of the objection, then it would indeed have had little force against equality of opportunity for welfare. In fact, Dworkin's argument is different. Since we typically identify with our personal tastes and preferences, it would strike us as 'bizarre' for persons to expect compensation for their expensive tastes, even if they are not deliberately cultivated. Other disputants do understand this argument, but insist that it *does* make sense for people to ask for assistance from the rest of society for their expensive tastes on account of the arbitrary expense of these things. I try to show, however, that this reply overlooks what Dworkin calls *the challenge model of ethical life*.

Chapter 3 examines Dworkin's conception of equality of resources including the distinction between personal and impersonal resources, the twin requirements that the distribution of income and wealth should be at any given time ambition-sensitive but not endowment-sensitive, and the technical devices of the desert island auction and hypothetical insurance markets. I try to explain how these different components fit together and I address a number of objections targeted at equality of resources: the objection that the auction is not integral to knowing what an equal distribution of resources would be like; the argument that ample opportunity to purchase insurance is not a sufficient condition for imposing consequential responsibility as Dworkin suggests; the objection that the hypothetical insurance scheme ignores the separateness of persons; the capabilities objection; and the objection that equality of resources misunderstands the point of equality. I then assess Dworkin's replies to these objections and ask what implications these replies have for the kind of theory he wishes to defend. More generally, I consider what it means for a theory of just distribution to be 'egalitarian' or even 'luck egalitarian' and whether Dworkin's own theory qualifies as either.

Chapter 4 addresses Dworkin's claim that the abstract egalitarian principle represents a kind of plateau in contemporary political thought. The chapter considers a number of reasons for supposing that this plateau matters in political debates and concludes that these reasons are less powerful than we might reasonably expect them to be. However, I shall argue that there is another, more fundamental question we can ask about abstract equality, the answer to which might ultimately help to explain the deep nature and importance of the right to equal concern and respect. Asking the question 'Equality among whom?' has the potential to shed light on a range of pressing political issues concerning a government's treatment of citizens and non-citizens.

Part II seeks to extend Dworkin's theory of equality – or an amended version of that theory – to questions of global distributive justice.

Chapter 5 critically examines Dworkin's assumption that equal concern and respect is idiosyncratic to true political communities, first, by asking whether or not the community of nations could be interpreted as a form of true political community and, second, by challenging the view that in the absence of such a community the right to equal concern and respect stops at state borders. I shall argue that Dworkin's limited conception of community makes it almost impossible to talk of a true global political community, but that nevertheless there can be other sites of global justice in its absence. Many sites have been ably identified in the literature, but in this chapter I choose to concentrate on foreign aid, which at first glance looks to be an unlikely site of justice. Not surprisingly foreign aid can be interpreted in more than one way. Nevertheless, I attempt to impose meaning and value by concentrating on the ideal of justice as global equal concern rather than on the ideal of humanitarian compassion or the ideal of national self-interest.

Chapter 6 defends a compound approach to global justice which recognises not only forms of injustice associated with colonialism, slavery, genocide, exploitation, trade protectionism, borrowing and resource privileges but also the injustice of failing to mitigate *brute luck*. Focusing on the last of these components, I distinguish between three different conceptions of global luck egalitarianism, and then compare and contrast the third conception, which I call *interpretive global luck egalitarianism*, with the theories of international justice defended by Beitz and Rawls. Finally, I defend interpretive global luck egalitarianism against two objections commonly made against cosmopolitan theories of justice. The agency objection claims that this sort of theory is unable to specify duty bearers in the right way, whereas the nationalism objection claims that contrary to cosmopolitan political theory we actually owe more to members of our nation than to strangers. I argue that the first objection can be met by keeping in mind the individualistic dimension of global luck egalitarianism, while the second can be avoided by endorsing a weak as opposed to a strong version of the view.

Chapter 7 completes the interpretation of global equal concern and respect by developing a theory of global equality of resources. Here I recast Dworkin's desert island thought experiment by supposing that the people of Earth are forced to flee the planet after an unprovoked alien onslaught only to become space-shipwrecked on a planet called Mini-Earth. I first explore how the auction procedure might operate on Mini-Earth and then turn to consider how, if at all, Dworkin's distinctions between ambition and endowment, option and brute luck might apply to emerging inequalities. As with domestic inequality, the complex interplay between these factors can make it hard to determine which proportion of inequality is due to which factor. In order to resolve this problem I suppose that the survivors are faced with an equal antecedent risk of suffering the resource curse and various kinds of natural disasters and must make choices about what level and type of insurance to purchase. I also address the objection that significant cultural differences in the world today can render it problematic to articulate, apply and implement global equality of resources without favouring some cultural beliefs and attitudes over others. I try to show that despite this pluralism it is possible to develop versions of the auction and hypothetical insurance devices which can operate at the global level without such favouritism. Finally, I explain how global equality of resources is an appropriate principle or set of principles to govern exploitation of, and trade in, natural resources and foreign aid. I shall argue that agents involved in these things do the right thing when they transfer resources in a way that mimics an equal distribution of the world's natural resources as well as the insurance that individuals from around the world would be likely to purchase against a range of risks under conditions of *ex ante* equality.

Chapter 8 recapitulates the various argumentative steps taken in the book, and tries to spell out what it is I hope to have demonstrated along the way.

2
Equality of Welfare

Any thoughtful person coming to the 'Equality of what?' debate for the first time might be forgiven for thinking that it puts the cart before the horse. Surely the more crucial question is 'Why equality?' I shall return to that question in Chapter 4, to which I shall add a further question, 'Equality among whom?' But it is worth emphasising here that in his two famous articles of 1981, Dworkin does not ask the question, 'Equality of what?' Rather, he asks the subtly different question, 'What is equality?' Whereas Amartya Sen and G. A. Cohen start with the assumption that there is something substantive which justice requires people to have equal amounts of (Sen, 1980; Cohen, 1989), Dworkin begins with the different fundamental assumption that every citizen has a highly abstract right to be treated with equal concern. His task is to work out what it means to be treated with equal concern in matters of distribution. Hence, 'What is equality?'

The first article, 'Equality of Welfare', begins with the simple but extremely powerful observation that making people equal in one respect of their situation can make them unequal in other respects of their situation (Dworkin, 1981a, p. 185). This being the case, we must determine whether or not a government that achieves equality in *any* particular respect is one that treats its citizens with equal concern. That is, which of the possible distributive schemes treats people as equals (p. 186; see also 2000, pp. 1–2)? His lengthy analysis begins with a distinction between two kinds of theories.

The first (which I shall call equality of welfare) holds that a distributional scheme treats people as equals when it distributes or transfers resources among them until no further transfer would leave them more equal in welfare. The second (equality of resources) holds that it treats them as equals when it distributes or transfers resources among them until no further transfer would leave their shares of the total resources more equal.

(1981a, p. 186)

The aim of this chapter is to try to make sense of Dworkin's initial arguments against equality of welfare in the light of his later clarifications and to address what I believe is widespread confusion among his critics. I argue that his rejection of equality of welfare remains sound not only because of the underlying purpose of the expensive tastes objection, which I believe has been widely misinterpreted, but also because of the strength of his radical criticism, which is too often overlooked.

The radical criticism

Dworkin's 'radical criticism' − as he puts it − of equality of welfare is that as it stands it is too ambiguous to serve as a theory of distributive justice but once it is fully specified it loses any appeal it might otherwise have had because no conception of welfare can figure in such a theory without recourse to a prior conception of fair distribution. The criticism begins with the disarmingly plain observation that personal tastes, preferences, desires and ambitions are not given, meaning that people develop or form these things in the light of their deeper beliefs and convictions and in the light of their circumstances including their expected shares of resources. Dworkin's further claim is that the ethical standing of tastes and preferences must therefore depend, to a large extent, on the fairness or otherwise of the prior division of resources. The upshot is that in order to develop a true picture of someone's welfare it is necessary to call on an independent theory of what an appropriate division of resources would be. But to do this is to settle the problem that equality of welfare was supposed to solve: how to distribute resources fairly. Thus any conception of equality of welfare must ultimately provide a 'self-defeating' principle of equality in distribution (Dworkin, 1981a, p. 227; 2000, p. 285; 2004a, p. 340).[1]

Dworkin deploys the radical criticism against a number of different conceptions of welfare. One version targets 'relative success' theories of welfare. Relative success is defined by how successful an individual has been in fulfilling his or her preferences, goals and ambitions. Dworkin claims that individuals 'make their choices, about what sort of life to lead, against a background of assumptions about the rough type and quantity of resources they will have available with which to lead differ-ent sorts of life' (Dworkin, 1981a, p. 205). Given this fact, the problem is to explain how equality of relative success can be measured without drawing on a prior conception of fair shares. How would we know what resources to transfer to each person such that everybody has equal suc-cess and therefore equality of welfare if the contents of relative success depend on background assumptions about the very resources that we want to know how to distribute? There is, as Dworkin puts it, 'danger of a fatal circle here' (ibid.).

Another version of the criticism targets theories of welfare based on people's judgements of their 'overall success'. Such judgements are not only a measure of the value persons place on their relative success but reflects a larger ambition to find value in life, where this is based on what 'are best described as philosophical convictions about what can give meaning to any particular human life' (Dworkin, 1981a, p. 207). To see why this conception is flawed, we are asked to consider Jack and Jill. Despite having the same share of resources and roughly the same level of relative success and life enjoyment, Jack and Jill have different views about the overall value of their lives. 'If each is asked to assess the over-all value of his or her own life, Jack would rate his high and Jill hers low' (p. 213). However, these different evaluations are based on 'specu-lative fantasies' about how good or bad their lives would be under alter-native arrangements, that is, about whether or not a larger share of resources could give greater value to their lives. Dworkin argues that we cannot fairly compare their lives without asking whether or not one or other has 'reasonable regrets' about his or her life (p. 216). Yet any perti-nent test of what someone could reasonably regret about his or her life 'must rely on assumptions about what resources an individual is enti-tled to have at his disposal in leading any life at all' (pp. 225–6).

Richard Arneson, however, takes issue with Dworkin on whether the radical criticism applies to *all* relevant theories of welfare. He argues that

> if our standard of individual welfare is objective, then whether an individual is well off or badly off will not vary arbitrarily with her opinions and attitudes, but will be fixed by the degree to which over the course of her life she obtains what is truly valuable and worthwhile. With a list of objective goods and a weighting of their relative significance, one does not need to suppose that what is good for a person depends on her circumstances [...] There is no temptation whatsoever to suppose that a welfarist ideal with this

> yardstick of individual welfare needs anything like the fatal 'reasonable regret' idea that Dworkin proposes in order to carry out interpersonal comparisons. Welfarist justice is not a non-starter as Dworkin alleges.
>
> (Arneson, 2000a, p. 512)

Even if a welfare-based theory can be coherently expressed without the idea of reasonable regret, however, the key issue is whether or not a welfare-based theory can be coherently expressed without *some* account of fair background circumstances including a fair distribution of resources. Suppose we say that a person enjoys equality of welfare if and only if his life embodies less objective value or meaning than the life of other people. Would it be possible to describe the essential ingredients of such a life without referring to the share of resources that would accompany it?

Arneson cites a life of artistic achievement as something that could be objectively good for a person independently of a prior account of fair shares (Arneson, 2000a, p. 512). But citing one example will not do. For what is at stake here is whether or not it is possible to work out something like a complete list of objective goods that are involved in giving overall meaning to a range of human lives. Arneson argues that the articulation of such a list is not especially difficult. We might assume for the sake of argument that a good life includes such things as useful labour, friendship, love, enjoyment, knowledge and so on. Dworkin insists that it is part and parcel of having a good life to have a fair share of resources. But Arneson replies that having a fair share of resources *is* to have a share that is compatible with everyone being able to achieve an objectively good life. So, if giving resources x to person A, resources y to person B and resources z to person C means that A, B and C are able to achieve useful labour, friendship, love, enjoyment, knowledge and so on, then they can regard themselves as having fair shares and an objectively good life. So far so good for the welfarist: for he appears to have defined fair shares in terms of an objective conception of welfare without appealing to some prior conception of equality of resources. If this is true, then in Arneson's words, 'Dworkin's master argument fails' (2002, p. 369).

Dworkin's likely response to this line of argument, I suggest, is to retreat to the challenge model of ethical life. In *Sovereign Virtue* he maintains that most ordinary people have the conviction − or can be interpreted as having the conviction − that 'the value of a good life consists in its product, that is, in its consequences for the rest of the word'. Rather, 'the goodness of a good life lies in its inherent value as a performance', that is, meeting the challenge of life (Dworkin, 2000, p. 251). The challenge model of ethical life has two features which are relevant to the present discussion. First, the challenge model regards shares of resources as the 'parameters' against which people are to shape a good life. That is, we determine what a good life is by first assessing what share of resources rightfully belong to ourselves as opposed to trying to determine what share of resources rightfully belong to us by first assessing what a good life is (1990, p. 259; 2000, p. 277). Perhaps this model would be profoundly wrong as applied to a world of limitless resources, where all people can have all things at all times. But the real world is not like this, and meeting the challenge of the real world is a model by which most ordinary people try to live.

Secondly, it is an essential feature of life's performance that persons define for themselves what gives value to life. Therefore, it is contrary to this performance for officials to decide an objective list of elements of a good life and distribute resources accordingly: for this means that officials would 'usurp' the role of each person in deciding for himself what a good life is (Dworkin, 2000, p. 276). Part of the intuitive pull of welfare is that it is supposed to make people well off in what really matters. However, according to Dworkin, if we assume as a minimum adequacy constraint for any theory of distributive justice that it must not propose as a fixed goal of distribution anything that any individual could not endorse either as her highest-order interest or as a derivative goal of her highest-order interest, then we see that welfare cannot be adequate. If a government picks an objective conception, there is no guarantee that it will be something that all individuals can endorse. Alternatively, suppose a government employs equality of relative success as a fixed goal of distribution for everybody. The problem is that people disagree markedly over how much enjoyment, satisfaction and achievement of goals respectively make up a good life. So, whichever conception government selects inevitably some people will be made equal in respects that they scarcely value at all (1981a, p. 208; 2000, p. 277; 2004a, p. 340). Or suppose instead a government adopts equality of overall success as a fixed goal of distribution tailored to each individual, where this is based on each person's beliefs about the best life at that particular time. The problem is that people's beliefs about an overall successful life will change over time. So they cannot in good faith endorse that fixed goal in perpetuity (1983, p. 30).

On one level, Dworkin's challenge model of ethical life relies on an agent-dependent conception of what it means to live well. That is, living well must be understood from the perspective of the person whose life it is, where this includes his or her own sense of how best to rise to the challenge of certain parameters. But even if this is a superior interpretation of what it means to live well, why must the parameters encompass the distribution of resources including as it does facts of supply and demand? Why cannot someone rise to the challenge of identifying a good life independently of knowing what share of resources he or she has with which to live that life? I think that this knowledge is necessary, and to see why consider two aspects of most people's definition of living well: doing good deeds and physical activity. It seems to me that in order to define a good life in a way that will guide my activities, I must specify how, more precisely, doing good deeds and physical exercise are to figure in my life and how they are going to manifest themselves. If doing good deeds includes being charitable with *my* money, then I will need to know what money I can reasonably expect to have at my disposal with which to be charitable. Likewise, if physical exercise relies on a set of working body parts, I need to know which body parts in particular and to what degree of functioning. This means that I require some prior account of fair shares of resources in order to define what a good life is. Otherwise my definition will be empty or incomplete.

So Dworkin's radical criticism is that equality of welfare is able to gain support by remaining incomplete and as soon as one begins the task of trying to render it complete one finds that it depends on a prior account of fair shares.[2] Of course, that is not to say that equality of resources is itself complete to begin with. This conception also requires further specification both in terms of what we mean by 'resources' and how many resources each person is entitled to. Nevertheless, Dworkin's claim, to which I shall return in the next chapter, is that equality of resources can be made complete without recourse to a prior conception of fair shares (Dworkin, 2000, pp. 285–6). Now some commentators read Dworkin as attempting yet failing to 'derive' an argument for equality of resources from the radical criticism (Guest, 1991, p. 263). That is, they interpret Dworkin's radical criticism as operating both as an argument *against* equality of welfare and as an argument *for* equality of resources. I have a different reading. It is that the radical criticism is only intended to clear the ground for the defence of equality of resources. This reading is based on the fact that Dworkin is careful to say that conceptions of equality of welfare depend on '*an* independent theory of fair shares of social resources' rather than making the stronger claim that they depend on one particular theory of fair shares. He asserts that 'this might, for example, be the theory that everyone is entitled to an equal share of resources'. Even so, this is offered merely as an illustration and leaves open the possibility of other theories (Dworkin, 1981a, p. 217). Hence,

I think it is wrong to criticise Dworkin for failing to derive equality of resources from the radical criticism, since the radical criticism does not seek to show that equality of welfare can *only* be made intelligible with the help of equality of resources.

The objection from expensive tastes

However, Dworkin is not done yet. He argues that even before the radical criticism enters the story equality of welfare falls to counter-examples (Dworkin, 1981a, p. 228). Perhaps Dworkin's best-known counter-example is that of Louis and his expensive tastes. He asks us to imagine that 'someone (Louis) sets out deliberately to cultivate some taste or ambition he does not now have, but which will be expensive in the sense that once it has been cultivated he will not have as much welfare on the chosen conception as he had before unless he acquires more wealth.' If, on the one hand, Louis is denied extra wealth, taken from those who acquire or already have less expensive tastes, this would contradict equality of welfare. If, on the other hand, he is given additional wealth, this result seems intuitively unfair (p. 229).

Few examples in the 'Equality of what?' literature are as commonly misunderstood as that of Louis. It is widely assumed that Dworkin's principal argument against equality of welfare is that it implies giving additional resources to people, like Louis, who deliberately set out to cultivate expensive tastes (see Cohen, 1989, p. 923; Rakowski, 1991, p. 41; Macleod, 1998, p. 25; Ripstein, 2007, p. 87). Thus according to most commentators the lesson we are supposed to glean from the Louis example is that taxpayers should not be forced to subsidise Louis' expensive tastes because they were deliberately cultivated. Colin Macleod, for example, writes that '[t]he particular aetiology of Louis's tastes – i.e., they are deliberately cultivated – disqualifies his claim to extra resources' (Macleod, 1998, p. 25). Not surprisingly, then, the standard response to this example has been to point out that it defeats equality of welfare but nonetheless fails to defeat equality of opportunity for welfare (see Arneson, 1989; 1993; Cohen, 1989; 1993). Thus Cohen writes that '[t]he revised welfare principle, unlike equality of welfare, permits and indeed enjoins departures from welfare equality when they reflect choices of relevant agents, as opposed to deficient *opportunity* for welfare' (Cohen, 1989, p. 916).

Although I think that Dworkin has not done quite enough to make clear the real purpose of the example – certainly there are passages where Dworkin foregrounds the fact that Louis is acting deliberately

(Dworkin, 1981a, p. 230) – what his critics fail to understand is that the example does not hinge on whether or not Louis deliberately set out to develop expensive tastes. There are two pieces of textual evidence that tell against the common reading of the Louis example. The first is that, having introduced the case, Dworkin immediately plays down the significance of the fact that Louis deliberately set out to cultivate his expensive tastes. He begins by explaining *why* Louis did what he did:

> if someone like Louis wishes to lead the life of people in *New York* magazine ads, this must be because he supposes that a life in which rare and costly goods are savored is a life better because it knows a greater variety of pleasures, or more sophisticated pleasures, or, indeed, simply pleasures that others do not know, in spite of containing less pleasure overall.
>
> (pp. 231–2)

For Dworkin, then, what is significant about Louis' new tastes is that they reflect his new beliefs about what kind of life is better overall. He continues,

> This explanation of Louis' behavior challenges the importance of the distinction we have thus far been assuming between expensive tastes that are deliberately cultivated and other aspects of personality or person, such as native desires or socially imposed tastes, that affect people's welfare. For the explanation suggests that such tastes are often cultivated in response to beliefs-beliefs about what sort of life is overall more successful-and such beliefs are not themselves cultivated or chosen. Not, that is, in any sense that provides a reason for ignoring differences in welfare caused by these beliefs in a community otherwise committed to evening out differences in welfare. I do not mean that beliefs are afflictions, like blindness, that people find that they have and are stuck with. People reason about their theories of what gives value to life in something of the same way in which they reason about other sorts of beliefs. But they do not choose that a life of service to others, for example, or a life of creative art or scholarship, or a life of exquisite flavors, be the most valuable sort of life for them to lead, and therefore do not choose that they shall believe that it is. We may still distinguish between the voluntary

decision someone makes to become a person with certain tastes, or to lead the sort of life likely to have that consequence, and his discovery of tastes and ambitions that he just has. But the distinction is less important than is sometimes thought, because that decision is rarely if ever voluntary all the way down.

(p. 232)

If there is a point to the Louis example, this passage clearly shows that it must be subtler than the distinction between deliberately and non-deliberately cultivated tastes or even between voluntary and involuntary decisions to cultivate expensive tastes.

The second piece of evidence comes from the fact that Dworkin's explicitly rebuts the idea that involuntary tastes raise a case for compensation or subsidy. His discussion of Cohen's example of Paul and Fred is highly instructive. Compare Paul who loves photography and Fred who loves fishing. Paul's problem is that whilst he cannot afford to pursue his love of photography, because it is so expensive, he also hates fishing, a much cheaper pastime. The effect is that he has less welfare than Fred. Cohen argues that in so far as Paul has a 'genuinely involuntary expensive taste' a commitment to equality of opportunity for welfare implies that we should subsidise his photography. If, on the other hand, he voluntarily cultivated his expensive taste, then egalitarians have good reason not to pay a subsidy (Cohen, 1989, p. 923).[3] Dworkin, however, rejects the idea that compensation is owed to people in so far as their tastes are genuinely involuntary (Dworkin, 2000, p. 298). What is more, he reasons that if it is morally fitting to hang the right to subsidy on the peg of involuntary tastes, then Cohen's view 'collapses back into the simple equality of welfare he wants to abandon', since it is likely that none of our tastes are genuinely voluntary all the way down (p. 289).

Thus a more careful reading of what Dworkin actually says about the Louis case suggests that the point is not about voluntary versus involuntary tastes. If the argument had been of that simple character, then of course it would have invited the standard retreat to equality of opportunity for welfare. Nor do I think the example turns on an argument from human agency, namely, that because most people are capable of adjusting their tastes and preferences over time it is inappropriate to hold them responsible for expensive tastes (cf. Rakowski, 1991, pp. 43, 108). Such an argument would also have been susceptible to the claim that if some people are not capable, then they at least are entitled to equality of welfare.[4] So what *is* the point of the Louis example?

One possible way of reading the example is to pursue an analogy with Thomas Scanlon's case of someone who acquires onerous or guilt-inducing religious beliefs. Scanlon claims that it would be odd to compensate such a person not least because 'it might destroy the point of religious burdens to have them lightened by social compensation' (Scanlon, 1986, pp. 116–17). Likewise, we might say that if Louis develops a taste for plovers' eggs and pre-phylloxera clarets because these things are expensive and he wants to ape the lifestyles of the rich and famous, then arguably it would destroy the point of having these particular tastes if free coupons for plovers' eggs and pre-phylloxera claret were readily available to average people. If virtually everyone had free access to these items, they would no longer be 'champagne tastes' and the aping would fail. That free coupons would destroy the point of Louis' way of life is surely a reason that he and everybody else can share.[5]

Obviously much more could be said both for and against the proposed analogy between religious guilt and expensive tastes.[6] Nevertheless, it seems to me that Dworkin wishes to make a more general point about the relationship between Louis' expensive tastes and his other beliefs and convictions, and it is to this point that I now turn.

Dworkin's ethical argument against compensating expensive tastes

With careful scrutiny I think that it is possible to reconstruct from 'Equality of Welfare' and chapter 7 of *Sovereign Virtue* what I shall call Dworkin's ethical argument against compensating people with expensive tastes:

(1) It is part of our ordinary first-personal ethical experience to identify with various features of our personality (as in, our tastes, preferences, desires, goals and ambitions) but not necessarily with a range of elements that make up our circumstances (as in, our talents, physical capacities, opportunities, income and wealth) (Dworkin, 1981b, p. 303; 2000, pp. 289–90, 293).

(2) Because of (1) it is part of our ordinary ethical practice to take consequential responsibility for, and to expect to be held consequentially responsible for, features of our personality but not features of our circumstances (pp. 290, 294).

(3) There should be continuity between public principles of distributive justice and ordinary ethical distinctions and practices (pp. 294–6, 323–4).

(4) Expensive tastes are ordinarily regarded as features of our personality rather than our circumstances (pp. 297–9). Therefore,

(5) Government agencies should, as a matter of distributive justice, hold individuals responsible for their expensive tastes (p. 298).

The conclusion of this argument, (5), is further supported by two hypothetical arguments to be discussed in Chapter 3. The first is that shipwreck survivors faced with the task of dividing the available resources on a desert island are unlikely to agree to divide resources in a way that makes special accommodations for people's expensive tastes (Dworkin, 1981b, pp. 287–8). The second is that faced with questions about what kinds of insurance they would purchase against a range of misfortunes, the shipwreck survivors are unlikely to want to purchase insurance against having unsatisfied tastes and preferences; unless, that is, these things constitute obsessions or cravings 'so severe and disabling as to fall under the category of mental disease' (p. 303).[7] But I shall put these two hypothetical arguments aside for the moment and concentrate on the ethical argument as it stands. One immediate response to the argument might be to question the validity of its conclusion. Perhaps we think that government agencies should take other aspects of justice into consideration which are not connected to ordinary ethical distinctions and practices. In which case, it may not follow that government agencies should hold individuals responsible for their expensive tastes. Nevertheless, I do not intend to challenge the validity of this argument in that way. I do, however, wish to examine each of the premises in more detail to determine whether or not the argument is sound.

Premise (1)

What does it mean to say that it is part of our ordinary ethical experience to identify with our personality but not with our circumstances? Dworkin's contention is that we tend to look upon our tastes, preferences, ambitions, desires and character traits as defining our ends, whereas we tend to regard our natural talents, physical abilities, opportunities, income and wealth as defining the means we have at our disposal for achieving our ends (Dworkin, 1981b, p. 303; 2000, p. 293). How is this separation manifest? He suggests that we typically identify with our tastes and preferences in the sense that we do not regret having them and do not believe we would be better off without them, but will typically regard our circumstances as potential limitations, in the sense that we often wish our circumstances could be different so that we might pursue our ends more easily (1981b, pp. 302–3).

Of course, it can be pointed out that we do not always identify with the contents of our personality. Think about people with obsessions and cravings. Surely they do not regard these things as defining what they really want out of life.[8] Dworkin accepts this point and argues that while people identify with their ordinary tastes and preferences, they tend to regard obsessions and cravings, if they have them, as impediments to a successful life. An obsession or craving is something that people do not see as an aspect of their personality but as a difficulty they would be better off without (Dworkin, 1981b, pp. 302–3). This distinction is certainly interesting but not difficult to find fault with. One problem is that preference-repudiating attitudes may be less helpful in identifying cravings than Dworkin seems to think. Cohen, for example, points out that someone in the grip of a genuine obsession or craving is often too unreflective to form the kind of second-order attitudes which Dworkin thinks is necessary to generate a claim to remedy or mitigation (Cohen, 1989, p. 926). Nevertheless, I think that much depends on what kind of repudiation is necessary. The inability to engage in detailed or sustained critical self-reflection about a particular feature of one's personality may be characteristic of an obsession or craving. But this does not automatically mean that the victim is rendered utterly senseless with respect to his own state of mind. Moments of lucidity may punctuate the haze of desire, and all that may be required in those moments is a sense that it might be better if things were different than they are, even if the person cannot bring himself to formulate any concrete ideas.

Another important clue to the meaning and purpose of premise (1) can be sought in Dworkin's discussion of the free will problem. Arneson and Cohen both maintain that the idea of choice and responsibility is incompatible with the philosophical theory of hard determinism. This means that if hard determinism is true, then no individual should be held responsible for expensive tastes and all differential welfare is unjust (see Arneson, 1989, p. 86; Cohen, 1993, p. 28). As Cohen ironically puts it:

> We may indeed be up to our necks in the free will problem, but that is just 'tough luck'. It is not a reason for not following the argument where it goes.
>
> (Cohen, 1989, p. 934)

Dworkin, however, rejects the suggestion that whether or not people are owed compensation depends on the existence of free will. He argues instead that people commonly accept responsibility for outcomes that reflect aspects of their personality, and they do so without the assumption that they have in some deep metaphysical sense chosen their personality (Dworkin, 2000, pp. 6, 294, 323; 2002, pp. 107, 118–19). Indeed:

> The distinction between choice and circumstances is not only familiar in first-person ethics but is essential to it. We might think ourselves persuaded, intellectually, of the philosophical thesis that people have no free will, and that we are no more causally responsible for our fate when it is the upshot of our choices than when it flows only from a handicap or from society's distribution of wealth. But we cannot lead a life out of that philosophical conviction. We cannot plan or judge our lives except by distinguishing what we must take responsibility for, because we chose it, and what we cannot take responsibility for because it was beyond our control.
>
> (2000, p. 323)

Dworkin tries to add weight to this argument by suggesting that almost everything that we are willing to count as *our* tastes, preferences, desires, goals and ambitions are suffused with deeply held beliefs and judgements of value. Louis, for example, develops a taste for plovers' eggs and pre-phylloxera clarets because he believes that having these tastes will make his life better overall. According to Dworkin, this is something that differentiates normal human beings from 'buzz' or 'tick addicts' who identify with their tastes and ambitions only in an impersonal way. For the addict, the fundamental goal in life is to get as many cheap thrills or satisfy as many preferences as he can irrespective of the quality of the particular experience and the content of the particular preference. Most normal people, by contrast, are more intimately connected with the objects of their desire (Dworkin, 2000, p. 293). For this reason,

> It would strike us as bizarre for someone to say that he should be pitied, or compensated by his fellow citizens, because he had the bad luck to have decided that he should help his friend in need, or that Mozart is more intriguing than hip-hop, or that a life well lived includes foreign travel.
>
> (p. 290)

However, would it always strike us as 'bizarre' for someone to ask for additional resources for the satisfaction of expensive tastes which he or she actually identifies with? It is not difficult to think of possible counter-examples. Would it be so strange for a person with a passion for live opera (say) to ask the government to subsidise the high cost of his musical experience on the grounds that it is entirely beyond his control that opera is a relatively expensive interest to pursue? Surely not. It might be argued that such a person would be willing to ask for public funds not in spite of his strong identification with his taste but because of the importance he places on it and his frustration at how costly it is. Cohen queries Dworkin on similar grounds:

> the person regards the relevant taste as bad luck *only* in the light of its price. And people can certainly without any self-misrepresentation or incoherence ask for compensation for (what might be, in every relevant sense) the *circumstance* that their taste is expensive. Whether or not it is weird to regret one's preference for reading certain kinds of books (that *happen* to be expensive), there is nothing weird or self-alienating in regretting precisely this: that the kinds one wants to read are expensive.
>
> (Cohen, 2004, p. 11)

Nevertheless, Dworkin's reply to this line of criticism has been to shift the onus of proof back onto the welfarist: it is Cohen who must provide a plausible theory of welfare to capture the relevant disadvantage. Even if we can understand in a fairly ambiguous way the idea that someone suffers bad luck if the kinds of books he wants to read are expensive, that is not the same as offering a complete conception of equality of welfare or even equality of opportunity for welfare. In order to show that someone with expensive tastes suffers from *bad luck*, the welfarist must be able to demonstrate that he is worse off *on some particular conception of welfare*. The problem is that such a person already thinks that his life is better overall than the person with more modest tastes: that is why he has the tastes he does. So, according to what other plausible conception of welfare is he worse off (Dworkin, 2004, pp. 345–6)? It may be tempting at this stage to petition an objective list conception of welfare. Thus one might conjecture that the reading of some types of books has more objective value than the reading of other, cheaper books. But Dworkin's response to this, I suspect, would be to reiterate that part of the challenge model of life is to decide for oneself what kinds of books have particular value in the light of the parameters set by the choices of other people concerning what kinds of books they find valuable. The consequence is that Cohen is unable to provide an adequately complete account of the sense in which the expensive book lover is worse off.

Premise (2)

According to Dworkin: 'Ordinary people, in their ordinary lives, take consequential responsibility for their own personalities' (Dworkin, 2000, p. 290). But what does this mean? Perhaps the idea is that most ordinary people develop and adjust their personal ends to make themselves happy without hope or expectation that others will compensate them for having expensive tastes. That is, the vast majority of people work hard to pay for the items they desire or else they try to change tastes, preferences and ambitions they cannot achieve or simply come to terms with their unhappy lot. Only in philosophy articles do people expect other taxpayers to subsidise their expensive tastes.

But could one imagine a world in which ordinary people have the propensity *not* to take responsibility for their tastes and preferences even though they identify with these features of their personality? It is certainly true that the terms 'welfare state' and 'welfare worker' are traditionally associated with the essentials of life such as food, clothing, housing, health care and so on. But one can certainly envisage a possible world in which there are many more strands to public spending besides these staples. After all, some mainstream politicians are now saying that personal happiness should be a political goal.[9] Hence, the mere fact that few people currently make redistributive claims against the rest of society for their expensive tastes does not prove that it would be wrong for them to do so in the future if that became an option. That is, one cannot proceed from a factual statement about the claims that people currently make to a moral conclusion about how state authorities should treat possible claims in the future. So long as the claims that people currently make (or do not make) reflect their expectations about what government agencies will accept or decline, those agencies are not justified in denying alternative claims simply on the basis that people do not presently make them.

However, I think that for Dworkin it is not enough to show that we can *imagine* other possible worlds in which people would be willing to make redistributive claims based on something like equality of opportunity for welfare. Given the constructivist project in which he is engaged, what we require is a theory of justice tailored to the kinds of societies in which we actually live. That is, the aim is to construct a fully developed description of equality that will provide an adequate standard for judging distributive institutions given our ordinary ethical experiences. On Dworkin's view, Cohen's proposals are discontinuous since they require active widespread support for the idea of compensating for involuntary expensive tastes, support which relies on a radically different set of ethical attitudes and practices to those we currently subscribe to both in our public and private lives. We might be able to imagine a world in which our state of mind is such that we identify with our tastes but do not feel ourselves to be responsible for them. But this is not *our* world. So the onus of proof is on the welfarist to explain why such a world would be valuable.

Premise (3)

One of the central themes of *Sovereign Virtue* is that there ought to be continuity between the political principles of justice and ordinary ethical distinctions and practices (Dworkin, 2000, pp. 294–5, 323–4). Consider once again the exchange between Cohen and Dworkin. Although Cohen recognises Dworkin's 'considerable service' to contemporary political philosophy (in utilising the idea of choice and responsibility), he urges that 'a proper insistence on the centrality of choice leads to a different development of the insight from Dworkin's own' (Cohen, 1989, p. 933). For his part, Dworkin claims that his own way of drawing the distinction between choice and luck is continuous with people's ordinary ethical experience in a way that Cohen's is not (Dworkin, 2000, pp. 289–90). The task of evaluating this claim, however, is made more difficult by the fact that he offers scant analysis of the term 'continuity' and little evidence for supposing that continuity is always to be cherished. Even so, Dworkin does offer two illustrations.

This first concerns the buzz and tick addicts described above, people who identify with their tastes and ambitions in an impersonal way. Dworkin argues that welfare egalitarians, vis-à-vis Cohen, adopt dis-continuous theories because they 'propose that we should all pretend, in politics, that we are addicts – that we should all act collectively in ways that we would find demeaning individually'. He adds, 'There may be a reason for such collective self-degradation, but I do not know what it is' (Dworkin, 2000, p. 295). The basic thought appears to be this. Few people in their private lives − addicts aside − live *only* for brute enjoyment or preference satisfaction. Most ordinary people develop, cling on to or revise their tastes and preferences on the basis of judgements of value: 'these judgements include both ethical convictions about the shape of an overall successful life and moral judgements about the reasonableness, fairness, and justice of any particular assignment of resources' (ibid.). Suppose someone has a passion for live opera because he believes it is a beautiful art form. He will also have an understanding of whether or not the fulfilment of this passion is expensive, whether he can afford to see live opera, and the reasonableness, justice and fairness of imposing on other people the cost of his taste. Consequently, to say that he *simply* wants the buzz that opera brings him would be to demean him individually. And since we recognise that he knowingly develops or clings on to his taste in the light of this information, to offer compensation would be collective self-degradation.

Dworkin's second illustration has to do with unemployment, and this time it is utilitarianism under the microscope. He claims that a utilitarian society would support a policy of redistributing income and wealth from the rich to the poor if and only if this would maximise aggregate welfare. This means that if welfare can be maximised by redistributing wealth without regard to whether or not people are responsible for the situations in which they find themselves, then we should do so. Consequently, a utilitarian theory of justice 'is discontinuous because it makes no room, at the ultimate level of assessment, for any distinction between choice and circumstance' (Dworkin, 2000, p. 324). For the sake of balance, however, it is important to bear in mind that a utilitarian theory of justice need not be discontinuous at the level of practical assessment. After all, a more sophisticated utilitarian analysis of the question of economic redistribution might take into consideration certain utility-enhancing consequences of imposing a regime of choice and responsibility. Moreover, some utilitarians may include living a life of personal responsibility as a feature of welfare, and so responsibility enters into the utility function at the ultimate level.

Even if these illustrations are granted, however, can we really say that continuity between public principles and personal ethics is always a good thing? At first glance, counter-examples seem easy to call to mind. In our personal lives we may be only too willing to call upon our friends for emotional succour when our pursuit of the good life causes us nothing but misery and heartbreak. In the context of friendship, the virtue of compassion or loving kindness may be more important to us than the virtue of personal responsibility. We feel responsible for our troubles but we ask for help nevertheless. This may not be fitting for public life, by contrast, where the government is accountable for taxpayers' money. Rather than seeing such a policy as harsh and unforgiving it might be viewed as achieving a fair balance between the interests of people with expensive tastes and the interests of more responsible taxpayers.[10] On closer reflection, however, the gap between public and private morality may not be so great after all. Although we may be ready to seek comfort from friends if we are unable to satisfy our expensive tastes, this does not mean that we are willing to beg, steal and borrow from them just to make ourselves happy. Friendship may involve emotional support, but it does not mean that we expect other people to fund our expensive tastes or hopeless dreams. Personal responsibility may be less important in this context but it is still important enough to make most people feel extremely uncomfortable at the prospect of asking their friends to bear the financial costs of their personalities.

It is also worth making clear that saying public principles of distributive justice should be continuous with ordinary ethical distinctions and practices is not the same as saying there should be continuity with *all* ethical distinctions and practices. After all, there may be more buzz and tick addicts in our midst than Dworkin realises, but this is not to say that *their* distinctions and practices should radically reshape the principles of justice for the majority. Rather, the pursuit of continuity must be understood within the broader enterprise of constructive interpretation. This means that as well as interpreting justice in its best light we must also try to interpret ordinary ethical distinctions and practices in their best light. Only when we are armed with the best interpretations of both can we say with conviction that there should be continuity. Accordingly, Dworkin wants to say that principles of just distribution should reflect the ethical distinctions and assignments of responsibility we make in leading our lives from the inside whilst at the same time discounting some ethical experiences and practices if they are not central to our best ethical distinctions and assignments of responsibility.

Premise (4)

Why should we place expensive tastes on the side of uncompensable personality rather than on the side of compensable circumstances or bad luck? Dworkin provides an answer to this question in the shape of the following distinction:

> [There are] two forms of bad luck that people might claim because their tastes are expensive: bad *preference* luck, which is their bad luck in having the preferences they do because these preferences are expensive, and bad *price luck*, which is bad luck in the high cost of the preferences they have. The difference appears when we ask whether the claimant would rid himself of the preference if he could; whether he would take a costless pill with no side effects to do that.
>
> (Dworkin, 2004a, p. 344)

According to Dworkin's analysis, if the claimant would take the pill that would rid him of the preference, then he has bad preference luck. But if he would not take the pill, then he suffers bad price luck. However, he goes on to argue that neither form of bad luck may ground claims for assistance in respect of unequal welfare. On the one hand, bad price luck is not something that merits compensation. Far from being a source of injustice, the tastes and preferences of other people constitute part of the background conditions or 'parameters' of justice (2000, pp. 298–9). That is, we must decide what sorts of lives to pursue against a background of information about the social value of the resources we need in order to plan and conduct different kinds of lives. So, if someone would not take the pill to rid himself of a preference for opera − because his preference is suffused with beliefs about how wonderful opera is − he does not suffer a form of compensable bad luck. If, on the other hand, he would take the pill, then Dworkin accepts that he does have a claim to assistance. Yet the claim for assistance is not in respect of his lack of preference satisfaction as such − that is, he has no claim to be brought up to the same level of welfare as others − but for the psychological handicap (2004, p. 350).[11]

One of the consequences of the pill test is that it establishes a clear link between preference-repudiation *as a state of mind* and preference-repudiation *as an activity*. After all, it may be difficult to give credence to someone who claims to genuinely regret having his tastes yet at the same time refuses to take a harmless pill that will rid him of those tastes forever. In the above description of preference-luck, bad luck is signalled very clearly by the willingness to perform a simple *act* of repudiation, taking the pill. However, could not someone in the grip of a genuine obsession or craving find himself unable even to take a costless pill? I think that this question identifies a reasonable concern but one that does little genuine damage. The thought experiment is not designed to replace proper medical diagnoses of psychological flaws. The appropriate medical test for deciding whether or not someone is the victim of a problem which merits medical assistance will be determined by appropriate experts. Rather, it is merely intended to illustrate a distinction between two kinds of luck.

Having now analysed the four main premises of Dworkin's ethical argument against compensating expensive tastes, I think that the pressing question is why bad price luck should be regarded as part of the background conditions of just distribution rather than as something which might be compensable. That is, why should people accept bad price luck as part of the normal way of things? I propose that part of the answer lies in the value of the practice of personal responsibility.

On the value of personal responsibility

What exactly does Dworkin mean when he asserts that 'It would strike *us* as bizarre' for someone to request compensation from his fellow citizens for his expensive tastes? No doubt there will be cases when the request will seem bizarre considered from the person's own perspective. The request may destroy the point of the taste. But suppose it could make sense. Suppose someone draws a distinction in his own mind between what he likes, for which he accepts responsibility, and the arbitrary expense of what he likes, for which he does not accept responsibility. What then? I suggest that Dworkin's underlying argument is that such a distinction sits uncomfortably with the task of showing the idea of responsibility in its best light. The 'us' in this case is the constructive interpreter. If as constructive interpreters we sit down and reflect on most ordinary people's ethical distinctions and practices and on the institutions of the free market and the welfare state and many other aspects of human life, we see that these practices and institutions are at their best when they hold people responsible for the tastes they form against the background of other people's tastes.

As an aside, I also think that focusing on Dworkin's commitment to the method of constructive interpretation helps to explain why he somewhat provokingly accuses Cohen of not being interested in continuity (Dworkin, 2000, pp. 294–5). Dworkin is not suggesting that Cohen is disinterested in intuitions about justice. After all, Cohen regards intuitions as perhaps the best clues we have. Rather, he is highlighting Cohen's conviction that discovering the truth about justice stands free from a process of constructive interpretation: that it is fitting to divorce the process of understanding what justice is from facts about (or an interpretation of) the kinds of social practices it is to govern (cf. Cohen, 2003).

Even if we accept the method of constructive interpretation, however, it is still open to other interpreters besides Dworkin to construct something different out of the pile of bones. So why prefer Dworkin's interpretation? What is the value of interpreting personal ethics and public morality in a way that does not regard bad price luck as compensable bad luck and that holds individuals responsible for their own welfare?

Consider four possible reasons. The first draws on the familiar idea of moral hazard. If people are not expected to pay the costs of satisfying their tastes or realising their ambitions, then (so the argument goes) they will tend to develop evermore extravagant tastes and ambitions. Given the likelihood that it would be impossible to satisfy everyone's tastes and ambitions, the result will be a world in which a great many people are miserable and disappointed. It is hard to see how anyone who believes in the intrinsic value of human life could seriously believe that this would be a desirable state of affairs.

A second reason touches on a point I made earlier in relation to the case of Louis. Living in a world where I must pay for the satisfaction of my own tastes and for the realisation of my own ambitions has the potential for providing me with a powerful mechanism for self-expression. If I decide to cultivate a taste for the most expensive things in life or to develop a difficult and perhaps unattainable ambition, then I can thereby send out a clear signal to everyone else about the kind of person I am and what I value most. To be given whatever I desire merely because I desire it could render the choice of what to desire less meaningful in that sense (cf. Scanlon, 1998, p. 253).

A third reason is that a government fails to treat citizens with equal concern and respect when it views the success of some people's lives as more important than that of others, or regards some people's definitions of living well as superior to those of others. Louis believes that his life is more successful overall with expensive tastes even if it now contains less enjoyment than it would otherwise have with cheaper tastes. Other people take a different view. Given a world of diverse conceptions of living well, it seems right that Louis should not be able to lead a life that is more expensive with no sacrifice of enjoyment to himself. To do otherwise would be to treat his life or his conception of the good as somehow more important than, or superior to, the life or conception of other people (see Dworkin, 1977, pp. 272–3; 1981a, pp. 237–8; 1990, p. 255).

A fourth reason is that being required to bear the consequences of our expensive tastes is essential to the normal exercise of our personal responsibility. This reflects the second of the two principles of human dignity – which 'holds that each person has a special responsibility for realizing the success of his own life, a responsibility that includes exercising his judgment about what kind of life would be successful for him' (Dworkin, 2006, p. 10). We might say that economic institutions are at their best when they give people the space to specify or judge what it means for them to lead a good life against the parameters set by other people's judgements.

In these four ways it is possible to identify meaning and value in the practice of holding persons responsible for their personal ends, meaning and value that we all have reason to care about, even Louis. Of course, it might be argued that a regime of equality of opportunity (which *does* regard bad price luck as compensable) could also be interpreted as expressing the aforementioned values. There are weaker and stronger responses to this proposal. The weaker response is that the extent to which and the particular ways in which equality of opportunity for welfare could be interpreted as embodying these values is not as attractive as the extent to which and the particular ways in which equality of resources can be so interpreted. The stronger response is that equality of oppurtunity for welfare collapses back into equality of welfare once we realise that nobody is responsible either for their personality or their price luck. At any rate, all of this highlights the crucial importance, for Dworkin, in finding a viable alternative to equality of welfare: for he believes that without it, we will not be able to give proper expression to what it means to treat people as equals in matters of distribution. So the question is, what is the alternative?

3
Equality of Resources

According to Dworkin's initial characterisation, equality of resources is the view that a distributional scheme treats people as equals when it 'distributes or transfers resources among them until no further transfer would leave their shares of the total resources more equal' (Dworkin, 1981a, p. 186). He later clarifies that equal shares are best interpreted in terms of what he regards as two widely held intuitions about justice. The first is that the distribution of income and wealth is not fair when it reflects inequalities in the distribution of physical endowments and other features of brute luck. The second is that a fair distribution is dynamic in the sense that it allows the distribution at any given time to be sensitive to people's ambitions, that is, choices about occupation, investment and consumption. So to treat people as equals is to try to make sure that the distribution of income and wealth at any given moment is ambition-sensitive but not endowment-sensitive (1981b, p. 311; 1985, p. 207). This abstract picture of equality of resources is complicated, however, by the interplay between endowment and ambition. This interplay means that it is nigh-on impossible to know what proportion of people's income and wealth is due to each causal determinant *ex post*. In response to this 'strategic problem', Dworkin offers the hypothetical insurance scheme, where the aim is to realise equality of resources *ex ante*. The purpose of this chapter is to examine in more detail the key features of this view and to critically assess whether or not it provides the best or even an adequate interpretation of equal concern. I will also investigate what it means for a theory of distributive justice to be 'egalitarian' and try to develop a Dworkinian response to standard objections levelled against the luck egalitarian family of views.

Resources

We can quickly move to the core of equality of resources by focusing on what Dworkin means by the word 'resources'. His opening gambit is to ask the reader to: 'Suppose a number of shipwreck survivors are washed up on a desert island which has abundant resources and no native population, and any likely rescue is many years away' (Dworkin, 1981b, p. 285). The survivors choose to divide the resources, and let us suppose this includes raw materials, arable land, food, plants and so on, equally between them. Furthermore, the survivors have the chance to purchase insurance against lacking certain other kinds of resources such as healthy limbs and talents. In this way equality of resources ranges over very different kinds of resources. The rationale for doing so is to give expression to what Dworkin regards as a commonly held intuition that it is unfair for a person born with a physical disability or lack of talent or mental ability to have less income and wealth simply by virtue of this brute luck.

I shall return to the thought experiment in a moment, but for now I wish to focus on the concept of resources. One problem is that Dworkin fails to disambiguate the meaning of 'a desert island which has abundant resources'. If he has in mind such things as coal, oil, gas, timber, arable land, metals, edible plants, fruits, bush meat, farm animals and drinking water, then, as Tim Hayward quite rightly points out, strictly speaking these are not naturally occurring phenomena but things that human beings must create through extracting, purifying, chopping, collecting, gathering, ploughing, harnessing, growing, cooking, rearing and so on. In other words, turning them into human resources – things valuable for human ends and purposes – requires doing something to or with them (Hayward, 2006). This has obvious implications for the auction: for people will be less inclined to bid for items which they lack the requisite skills and knowledge to exploit (Miller, 1999b, p. 193). I shall have more to say about this problem in Chapter 7. In order to concentrate on the distribution of the island's resources, however, Dworkin starts with the simplifying assumption that 'all the immigrants are in fact sufficiently equal in talent at the few modes of production that the resources allow so that each could produce roughly the same goods from the same set of resources' (Dworkin, 1981b, p. 304).

In *Sovereign Virtue* Dworkin clarifies that equality of resources covers a person's 'personal resources' (i.e., 'his physical and mental health and ability – his general fitness and capacities, including his wealth-talent, that is, his innate capacity to produce goods or services that other will pay to have') as well as his 'impersonal resources' (i.e., 'those resources that can be reassigned from one person to another – his wealth and the other property he commands, and the opportunities provided him, under the reigning legal system, to use that property') (Dworkin, 2000, pp. 322–3). Yet this clarification itself blurs the distinction between what *can* be done or what it is *possible* to do, on the one hand, and what *may* be done or what it is *permissible* to do, on the other. As a result of advances in medical science, for example, strictly speaking it is now *possible* for various kinds of personal resources to be moved from one person to another. But presumably the issue at stake here is not what *can* be reassigned but what *may* be reassigned with the person's permission (say). In other words, for reasons of personal liberty we tend *not* to regard personal resources as things that may appropriately be moved around by government agencies; unless, of course, people give their permission with donor cards and the like.[1]

Perhaps, then, the operative distinction here is something like the distinction between *bodily resources*, defined as resources which are to be regarded as falling within the rightful domain of the person and that other things remaining equal may not be reassigned from one person to another – such as skills, talents, body parts, labour power, physical attributes and mental effort – and *non-bodily resources*, where this means resources that fall outside of the protected boundaries of bodily integrity and that other things remaining equal may be reassigned from one person to another – such as land, natural materials, artefacts, commodities, income and wealth. However, this raises a further query over the status of ideas or intellectual property. Should we regard ideas as automatically protected like body parts? How is this possible given the fact that as soon as they are given public expression ideas exist outside of the boundaries of the mind? While I do not intend to delve into this thorny issue here, it seems sensible to regard ideas as bodily resources when they reside in the mind but as non-bodily resources when they are put into the public domain. This does not mean that people may not have rights over their own ideas when made public. Rather, it is that the normal rights that apply to bodily resources may not automatically apply to non-bodily resources.[2]

The desert island auction

Dworkin begins his 'theoretical development of equality of resources' by supposing that the shipwreck survivors 'accept the principle that no one is antecedently entitled to any of these resources, but that they shall instead be divided equally among them'. They also accept the envy test. 'No division of resources is an equal division if, once the division is complete, any immigrant would prefer someone else's bundle of resources to his own bundle' (Dworkin, 1981b, p. 285). The envy test is not static but must be applied over an entire life. So, if Adrian (say) chooses to work on his share of resources with the single-minded ambition of producing as much of what others value as possible, the relevant question is not simply whether other people would envy his net share of resources but whether they would envy his resource output plus the labour it took to produce that output. If no one envies Adrian's bundle of resources and labour, the distribution cannot be said to be unequal on that account (ibid.).[3]

We are then asked to imagine that one of the shipwreck survivors is elected to achieve a division of resources which satisfies the envy test. Initially, the divider tries to achieve this result through a process of trial and error, but it soon becomes apparent that even when nobody would prefer someone else's bundle of resources, some people would prefer that the divider had chosen a different set of bundles in the first place (Dworkin, 1981b, p. 286). So the divider requires a procedure that will register the wishes of the agents concerning how the bundles are to be constructed. Dworkin proposes a modified Walrasian auction in which the divider (now an auctioneer) provides the shipwreck survivors with an equal number of purchasing chips (clamshells) and proposes a set of lots and prices. The auctioneer cries out increasing prices for each lot until there is only one purchaser for that lot. Importantly, everyone has the right to change his or her bids even after the auction is complete and the right to request different lots. Unlike Rawls' veil of ignorance, people know what their personal preferences are when bidding for resources. The auction is run again and again until nobody prefers anyone else's bundle and the survivors come to understand and accept that they cannot do better by further iterations of the auction (p. 287, n. 3). That everyone is in need of food, clothing and shelter may be a practical reason why the envy test is achieved fairly swiftly.

In Chapter 2, I suggested that part of Dworkin's case against equality of welfare is linked to his musings on the motivations of the shipwreck survivors. He claims that they would accept an auction as a fair way to divide the available resources equally rather than attempting to achieve equality of welfare. But why? He indicates that it is because they would reject the core assumption of equality of welfare, namely, that 'people are meant to decide what sorts of lives they want independently of information relevant to determining how much their choices will reduce or enhance the ability of others to have what they want' (Dworkin 1981b, p. 288). While he fails to offer much guidance as to why they would reject this assumption, one explanation might be that they would regard it as unreasonable to make claims against each other on the basis of the tastes, preferences and ambitions they had prior to being shipwrecked. It would be to ignore the fact that their circumstances have radically changed and they are responsible for adjusting their ends to this new challenge. If we were these sorts of shipwreck survivors, perhaps we would accept the auction. Of course, this invites the question why it makes sense to imagine such a scenario in the first place. But I expect Dworkin's response would be to argue that the intuitions implanted in the survivors reflect widely held ideas of fairness.

Even if one accepts these ideas, however, there are a number of potential problems with this procedure. Joseph Heath, for example, questions the need for the auction given the fact that it is perfectly possible for the elected-divider to arrive at a division of resources that is envy-free by persevering with the method of trial and error. In fact, Heath suggests that the main purpose of the auction is to select the most efficient distribution of resources among all the possible envy-free divisions, where this means a distribution which is Pareto efficient. It is important not only that nobody envies other people's actual bundles but also whether or not anyone would be better off and nobody worse off under any other feasible envy-free distribution, and this is what running the auction a number of times helps to achieve. After the auction has been run a sufficient number of times, nobody prefers what he would have had under some alternative division of the available resources. The outcome of all this, according to Heath, is that 'the auction does not appear to be accomplishing much on the equality front' (Heath, 2004, p. 326).

But it is not clear what Heath means by 'on the equality front'. If this means treating the survivors equally, then it is true that there are lots of ways of treating them equally and there is nothing particularly special about the auction. The divider could employ other ways to achieve one of the many possible envy-free results and nobody could complain on that score. However, it is important to bear in mind that Dworkin is interested not in what it means to *treat people equally* but in what it means to *treat people as equals*. So Dworkin would, I suspect, argue that a divider cannot claim to treat people as equals unless he distributes resources in a way that is both envy-free and efficient. In other words, that the outcome is envy-free and efficient is part of what it means to treat people with equal concern under the best interpretation.

In addition to this, however, Heath maintains that it is possible to arrive at an envy-free and efficient distribution without an auction mechanism − for example, by dividing resources in line with *any* envy-free distribution and then introducing a perfectly competitive market (Heath, 2004, p. 326). Of course, Dworkin himself is not ignorant of this possibility: 'Many people will be able to imagine a different set of bundles meeting the no-envy test that might have been established.' Nevertheless, he claims that 'the actual set of bundles has the merit that each person played, through his purchases against an initially equal stock of counters, an equal role in determining the set of bundles actually chosen' (Dworkin, 1981b, p. 287). So the idea is that the divider treats people as equals not only by achieving an envy-free and efficient result but also by giving them an equal input in the process by which that result is achieved. Yet Heath still finds room from criticism: 'Unfortunately, Dworkin does not explain what it means to play an 'equal role' in this context. Clearly, the auction does nothing to influence the *form* that the resources take' (Heath, 2004, p. 326). I find it difficult, however, to see the grounds for claiming that the auction does 'nothing' to influence the form that the resources take. After all, Dworkin makes it abundantly clear that each survivor has the right to notify the auctioneer of his or her desire to bid for some part of an item as a distinct lot (Dworkin, 1981b, p. 286). This means that they do indeed influence the form that the resources take and this is special to the auction: for even in a perfectly competitive market it might not be possible to persuade sellers to chop up certain items as the purchaser wishes.

A second, more powerful line of criticism relates to the ethical standing of the preferences which help to shape the auction result. The criticism is developed by Macleod as follows. Dworkin takes it as read that everyone's tastes and preferences provide a suitable background for measuring the opportunity cost of auction decisions. But in doing so, Dworkin overlooks (so the objection runs) the problem of 'mistaken beliefs': satisfying the envy test does not guarantee an equitable distribution of resources where those involved are mistaken about the kind of life that would be good for them and about what resources they will instrumentally need to live such as life (Macleod, 1998, pp. 28–9). Some people may bid for resources on the basis of malformed preferences in the mould of the contented slave or the tamed housewife. Others may bid in ignorance or misconception of what resources they actually require to fulfil their ends. For this reason, Macleod argues that '[t]he ethical significance which can ultimately be assigned to preferences is partly dependent on their being formed under favorable circumstances' (p. 37). He insists that relevant social structures, such as education and the media, must be organised in advance to guarantee that everyone forms well-adjusted and informed preferences (pp. 38–9).

This is a genuine hurdle, but by no means an insurmountable one. The problem of ensuring an ideal auction based on well-formed preferences is certainly not lost on Dworkin. He acknowledges the objection right from the start (Dworkin, 1981b, p. 290). More generally, he maintains that only 'properly disciplined' markets can measure opportunity costs in a suitably egalitarian way (2004, p. 339). What does he mean by this? It means that a number of background conditions must be satisfied including that each agent enters the market with equal bidding power and that the market is perfectly competitive (pp. 342–3). Elsewhere he also makes it clear that the auction is properly disciplined only if people bid for resources in the absence of coercion and in a fit state of mind so that their preferences are 'authentic'. He writes,

> Personality is not fixed: people's convictions and preferences change and can be influence or manipulated. A complete account of equality of resources must therefore include, as a baseline feature, some description of the circumstances in which people's personalities will be taken as properly developed so that auction calculations can proceed. The baseline needs, that is, some principle defining authenticity.
>
> (1987a, p. 35)

So how might this line of reasoning apply to the desert island thought experiment? Suppose the auctioneer holds some of the resources back for a specified period of pre-auction preparation. During this period the auctioneer gives out information about the lots, works to eliminate coercion and, where necessary, tries to cure malformed preferences through psychological counselling or some other suitable curative method. This may not be enough to ensure that the pre-auction preferences are absolutely pristine. But it may be sufficient to guarantee that preferences are minimally adequate for the purposes of equal distribution. The aim here is not to achieve pre-auction equality of welfare but to ensure that people are in a position to enter into the auction with authentic preferences. Of course, this means that there must be some public use of resources, based on the goal of minimum authenticity, before the auction can get started. But this is not analogous to the radical criticism of equality of welfare: for in that case an antecedent distribution of *fair shares* was required in order to specify equality of welfare.[4]

Emerging inequalities

Having introduced the auction for impersonal resources, Dworkin turns his attention to what is likely to happen on the island after the auction process is completed.

Ambition and endowment

Equality of resources includes two highly abstract requirements. The first is that we must allow the distribution of resources at any particular moment to be ambition-sensitive. This encapsulates the intuition that people's shares of resources should 'reflect the cost or benefit to others of the choices people make so that, for example, those who choose to invest rather than consume, or to consume less expensively rather than more, or to work in more rather than less profitable ways, must be permitted to retain the gains that flow from these decisions in an equal auction followed by free trade' (Dworkin, 1981b, p. 311; see also 1985, p. 207). The second is that we must not allow the distribution of resources to become endowment-sensitive. That is, to reflect 'differences in ability of the sort that produce income differences in a laissez-faire economy among people with the same ambitions' (1981b, p. 311). This speaks to a familiar goal of egalitarian political theory, namely, to mitigate some of the more inegalitarian results of the free market. Even if free markets repay people's different ambitions, they also repay people's different native talents – perhaps even more so – and these talents are matters of birth and upbringing. So the second aim is that no one should have less income 'simply in consequence of less native talent' (p. 327). 'This means that market allocations must be corrected in order to bring some people closer to the share of resources they would have had but for these various differences of initial advantage, luck and inherent capacity' (1985, p. 207).

The obvious difficulty in achieving these two requirements is how to separate that proportion of income which is due to native endowment and that which is due to ambition or choice (Dworkin, 1981b, pp. 313–4). The difficulty stems from the fact that there is interplay between the two. Talents are not discovered full-blown but develop over time. The decision to develop talent is based to some extent on ambition. On the other hand, how much ambition a person has may reflect the amount of talent they have to work with in the first place. Family life can also play a part in determining how much ambition a person has. Consequently, the onus is on the defender of equality of resources to explain how the egalitarian planner should proceed, if at all, in trying to disentangle the inputs of choice and circumstances. Dworkin calls this 'a strategic problem': 'How, in practice, is that distinction to be enforced?' (2000, pp. 324–5).

A natural response to this problem might be to say that if the real distinction here is not metaphysical *per se* but is supposed to track ordinary intuitions and practices, then the problem can be solved with something like the following rule of thumb: in so far as most ordinary people with X amount of talent typically display ambition within a range Y (we might use effort as a proxy for ambition), how much income a person with talent X ought to receive should depend on whether he displayed the amount of ambition we can reasonably expect given his talent (as in, within the range Y). We might say that a fair distributional regime is one in which every person who displays the same degree of ambition relative to talent-type receives the same level of income (cf. Roemer, 1998). However, this sort of proposal leaves unanswered the crucial question of what the appropriate level of income should be. One possible benchmark for redistribution might be the average level of income for people who demonstrate the same degree of ambition across different talent-types. But this benchmark potentially means redistributing vast sums of money from the talented to the untalented. Perhaps if people knew what was involved, they would not bother to develop the most productive talents. Of course, that problem might be avoided by adopting a minimum redistribution goal, that is, to set some kind of minimum income level for people who demonstrate the same degree of ambition across talent-type. But then we need some fuller account of what that minimum should be. There is also an administrative cost at stake here. Even if the egalitarian planner knows how to separate out the different causes of inequality in some tolerably precise way, the more money it spends on doing so, the less money it has to spend on those who are entitled to receive assistance (Dworkin, 2000, pp. 321–2). So, it might be prohibitively expensive to gather evidence on the ambitions and talents of very large numbers of people, to establish certain 'normal' ambition ranges for each talent-type, and then to compare the situation of each individual claimant against that range.

Dworkin's proposed solution to the strategic problem is hypothetical insurance. But before assessing this solution there is a further important distinction to consider.

Option luck and brute luck

Dworkin maintains that people should be held responsible for their 'option luck' but not their 'brute luck'.

> Option luck is a matter of how deliberate and calculated gambles turn out – whether someone gains or loses through accepting an isolated risk he or she should have anticipated and might have declined. Brute luck is a matter of how risks fall out that are not in that sense deliberate gambles.
>
> (Dworkin, 1981b, p. 293)

There are different sorts of option luck, but perhaps the clearest example is an open lottery, where people can choose to buy a ticket or not. To give the winners and losers their money back after the lottery is over is to refuse them the kind of life they would both prefer, a life that contains gambles (pp. 294–5). Another kind of option luck is 'investment luck' (2006, p. 109). If I decide to purchase shares in a company, and the value of those shares rise, then my investment luck is good. But then the price of shares can go down as well as up. So my investment luck could be bad. That we are willing to regard investment luck as a matter of personal responsibility, however, depends on some conditions not made explicit by Dworkin. One is that I am able to live a reasonably comfortable life without having to make the risky investment. To this condition we might add a second: that I am not benefiting from insider dealing. In these instances we may be less inclined to let the results of an investment stand.

Nevertheless, how can we reconcile the results of people's option and investment luck with the envy test? Suppose Adrian works hard with his stock, putting in time that others do not envy, but also gets lucky with the weather so that his stock grows handsomely. Surely others will envy this outcome. On Dworkin's view, however, provided that nobody can envy Adrian's deliberate and calculated gamble to plant where he does, the distribution cannot be said to be unequal on that score (Dworkin, 1981b, p. 295).

Insurance

Returning to brute luck, if equality of resources requires society as a whole to compensate individuals for their brute luck, does this entail that society must compensate for a great many things? Not necessarily. A key plank in Dworkin's theory is that insurance 'provides a link between brute and option luck, because the decision to buy or reject catastrophe insurance is a calculated gamble' (Dworkin, 1981b, p. 293). Being left severely disabled, lacking enough talent to earn a decent level of income, being struck down by illness or disease – these are the sorts of catastrophes that Dworkin believes the shipwreck survivors would wish to buy insurance against.

Dworkin does not, however, think that many survivors would purchase insurance against expensive tastes. Indeed, he goes so far as to say, 'It seems unlikely that many people would purchase such insurance, at the rates of premium likely to govern if they sought it, except in the case of cravings so severe and disabling as to fall under the category of mental disease' (p. 303). But if people with a passion for the finer things in life sincerely believe that not being able to purchase these items would make their existences less meaningful, why is it irrational for them to purchase insurance? Perhaps the idea is that insurance against expensive tastes is irrational either because people identify with their tastes or because they recognise that they are able to adjust their tastes over time. Yet someone might want to buy insurance against rising prices because he identifies with his tastes so much. Even if he knows he could learn to love cheaply priced sparkling wine, he might prefer to buy champagne insurance, assuming that such a thing exists, than have to go through the hassle of readjusting his palate. Nevertheless, the motivational plausibility of a decision to purchase this type of insurance depends crucially on how much the insurance companies would charge. Suppose that a company offered champagne insurance to people worried about sudden shortages of a certain range of commodities. It is difficult to say for sure what the price of such insurance would be. But given the already high cost of champagne, it is likely that such an insurance policy would not be worth the expense for most ordinary people. Most people like a drop of champagne from time to time, but they will take the risk of rising prices and learn to like some cheaper alternative if needs be rather than pay the extra cost of insurance. It is possible that some persons are so enamoured of champagne that even if they are placed under conditions of *ex ante* equality, they would be willing to pay the insurance premiums on top of the existing high price tag. Then again, if someone is willing to do that, then it seems that he has a commitment to champagne tastes that is quite unusual.

This seems to be what Dworkin has in mind when he says that few people would be likely to buy expensive tastes insurance. He is making a point about what the average person would buy. For this reason, however, I think that Dworkin overstates the case against champagne insurance by saying that those people who would choose to spend their equal share of resources on this type of insurance are in the grip of a 'mental disease'. Surely he does not need to go this far. A decision to purchase insurance might be imprudent but need not be interpreted as evidence of some variety of psychological dysfunction or derangement. The real question is whether the choice of a tiny minority of people to purchase such insurance can be fairly used as a guide to redistribution in the real world. Dworkin's answer is that we should rely on what people on average would do, and this, he thinks, is not purchase champagne insurance. (I shall consider below whether or not it is an advantage or a weakness of the hypothetical insurance approach that it justifies patterns of redistribution on the average counterfactual decision in this way.)

Dworkin also makes it clear that we must distinguish between the situation of winners and losers of insurance gambles and the situation of people who were denied the opportunity to purchase insurance in the first place. Under equality of resources, brute luck effects are transformed into option luck effects if and only 'if everyone had an equal risk of suffering some catastrophe', 'everyone knew roughly what the odds were' and had 'ample opportunity to insure', in the sense that everyone has the means to purchase a range of differently priced insurance offering different levels of coverage (Dworkin, 1981b, p. 297). The assumption, then, is that where these conditions obtain a person who chooses to buy very little insurance or to purchase no insurance whatsoever cannot rightly complain of unequal resources *ex post*. This assumption, however, has given rise to a small industry of work, and this is what I wish to explore now.[5]

One strand of criticism has been that an equal opportunity to insure is not always sufficient to transform brute luck into option luck. In his contribution to the 2002 symposium on *Sovereign Virtue* in *Ethics*, for example, Michael Otsuka argues that this

> includes all those cases in which no insurance policy exists that it would be reasonable to purchase and that would fully compensate the harm, where "full compensation" is understood as an amount of money awarded that would make the person indifferent between (1) that amount of money plus the harm and (2) the absence of that amount plus the absence of the harm. No such policy would exist (1) if it were impossible fully to compensate the harm or (2) if, although it is possible fully to compensate the harm, the cost of purchasing such insurance that compensates fully were (2a) beyond the capacity of the individual to purchase or (2b) within his or her capacity to purchase yet unreasonably expensive.
>
> (Otsuka, 2002, p. 44)

Otsuka has in mind cases of severe physical or mental incapacitation where it is very difficult to fully compensate the disadvantage. The suggestion is that in the absence of a reasonably priced insurance policy that provides full compensation differential insurance decisions do not justify unequal outcomes. This means that we should regard as bad brute luck both the situation of someone who goes blind or insane having decided to purchase partially compensating insurance and the situation of someone who goes blind or insane having decided to turn down the same (pp. 45–6).

It seems to me, however, that failing to distinguish the two situations threatens to wipe out the personal responsibility that comes with deciding how to respond to risk. The distinction reflects the choice that each individual would make given the value he or she places on full compensation. Hence the result cannot be entirely unfair because it represents the fact that one person believes full compensation is nugatory in the face of blindness or insanity while the other is more pragmatic (cf. Dworkin, 1981b, p. 296). Moreover, Otsuka's argument relies on the fact that in the absence of full compensation an element of brute luck remains untransformed, and in a way that implies a lack of equal concern. But this depends on a controversial assumption about what it means to show equal concern. In his response to Otsuka in *Ethics*, Dworkin argues that to provide full compensation would carry with it massive opportunity costs that are likely to make everyone worse off (including those who go blind or insane as well as those who do not). This, he claims, cannot amount to genuine concern for the lives of people, since it involves making everyone worse off, and is a decision very few people, if anyone, would wish to make if posed with the insurance question *ex ante* (2002, p. 124). In other words, for society to move in the direction of *ex post* equality − 'to spend all it could to improve the position of those who had become crippled in an accident, for instance' − risks bankrupting an entire community for the sake of rescuing a few and this cannot be what equal concern means (2006, p. 110).[6]

Even so, what about the problem of unreasonably expensive insurance? In a footnote, Otsuka clarifies his position thus: 'If the cost of such an insurance premium entails the impoverishment or indentured servitude of the individual, then such insurance would be unreasonably expensive. Insurance would also be unreasonably expensive across a wide range of less extreme cases' (Otsuka, 2002, p. 44, n. 18). But what are the less extreme cases? Suppose insurance premiums are sufficiently high to mean that people must give up any luxuries and live a fairly basic existence if they wish to maintain cover but not so high that they constitute impoverishment or indentured servitude. Are these premiums unreasonably expensive? I think it useful to draw a distinction here between *modestly priced insurance* and *reasonably priced insurance*. Whereas modestly priced insurance is measured in terms of what people can afford, reasonably priced insurance has to do with what it costs to provide insurance. To mark the difference, then, let us say that modestly priced insurance is insurance which can be purchased whilst maintaining a reasonably comfortable standard of living. In contrast to this, reasonably priced insurance is that which represents *good value for money*, where this means that premiums are proportionate to the likelihood and cost of the dangers involved. Although it might not be possible to offer blindness or insanity insurance that provides full compensation at modest prices, it may be possible to offer a choice between an insurance policy that provides full compensation at a reasonable but not a modest price and an insurance policy that provides partial compensation at a modest and reasonable price. It seems to me that where such insurance is available, it is much harder to complain about the outcomes (as unfair) than if it were not.

Hypothetical insurance markets

The main difficulty that prevents the egalitarian planner from using the model of insurance to deal with inequalities in the real world is the regrettable fact that many people are born with shortfalls on the side of their personal resources, and so never get the chance to purchase insurance. Lack of income will often reflect lack of talent for production, for example. But this tends to materialise early on in life before there is a feasibly insurable risk (Dworkin, 1981b, p. 315; 2000, pp. 333–4). The same can be said for various medical conditions: private insurers will charge more or less on the basis of family medical history or genetic predisposition (1981b, p. 297). Indeed, the problem of medical insurance is compounded by the fact of unequal income, so that people have different amounts of money to spend on insurance (p. 311; 2006, p. 115). Dworkin's solution to these problems is, of course, to invoke the idea of hypothetical insurance.

Consider the case of productive talent (as in, talent that will command economic rent). The reader is asked to imagine that information about the desert island and its group of new inhabitants is fed into a special computer. Using this data the computer projects the income structure that is likely to emerge as a free market for labour develops. Each of the shipwreck survivors knows the projected income structure and his own particular skills and attributes, but is stipulated to be 'radically uncertain what income level his own talents would permit him to occupy'. Some of the survivors will have the talents to command relatively high incomes, others will not, but each person does not know if he or she will be one of the lucky ones and therefore supposes that he or she has the same antecedent chance as anybody else of having the talent to occupy any given percentile. We are then asked to imagine that there are a number of commercial insurance firms on the island who offer insurance policies to the survivors. 'Insurance is provided against failing to have the talent to earn at whatever level of income, within the projected structure, the policyholder names.' Insurance premiums are paid not from initial resources but from future earnings at fixed periods (Dworkin, 1981b, p. 317).

Three aspects of this scenario are immediately puzzling. The first is the assumption that people will be radically uncertain about the value of their own talents. It seems slightly far-fetched to think that nobody could make reasonably accurate predictions about their own talent-wealth. If I pay attention to the auction, then I will have a fairly clear grasp of what sorts of goods are available and how much people will pay for them. If I know that I have the talent to produce the sorts of goods that I know command a high price, then I can be fairly confident that my talent-wealth will be high and that insurance will not be worth its cost for me. It is unclear how Dworkin would respond to this puzzle. He asks us to suppose 'not that people are wholly ignorant of what talents they have, but rather that for some other reason they do not have any sound basis for predicting their economic rent' (Dworkin, 1981b, p. 316). But it is hard to imagine what that other reason might be. Perhaps the survivors find themselves temporarily unable to make clear predictions due to the trauma of the shipwreck. Otherwise it remains a mystery.

The second puzzle concerns the ability of the shipwreck survivors to choose an insurance policy. In order to make intelligent decisions about how much insurance to purchase, people will need to make judgements of how much income they will need on the island. In order to make these judgements, however, they will need to know something about the goods and services available on the island and the market prices thereof. Yet if they know the market prices of specific goods and services, and they know their own talents, then presumably they will be able to work out the market value of their own talents. So there is a tension between two important parts of the imaginary insurance scenario. Perhaps Dworkin would argue that the survivors do not need to know how much income they will require for particular lifestyles. All they will need to understand is that the more income they have the more purchasing power they will enjoy. And that if they are at the bottom of the income structure they are likely to be severely limited in the lifestyles they can afford. So to get a decent standard of living they will probably have to insure higher up the income scale. In other words, the radical uncertainty of the survivors includes both uncertainty about what income level their talents will enable them to command and uncertainty about the level of income required for different sorts of lifestyle. In this way *ex ante* equality can be preserved.

The third puzzle has to do with the commercial insurance companies. We are asked to suppose that there is no monopoly in insurance and that a number of different private insurance firms compete with each other for business in a competitive marketplace. As commercial enterprises the insurance companies will seek to turn a profit of course. That is, they will offer only financially disadvantageous bets because their income must be equal to or larger than not only the expected payments to policyholders but also their operating costs and even their opportunity costs (Dworkin, 1981b, pp. 317–18). But then this raises the question: why not imagine a ministry for social justice on the island whose job it is to make sure that everyone has the opportunity to purchase modestly priced cover as opposed to turning a profit (cf. van der Veen, 2002, p. 71, n. 25)? Dworkin's response to this question is that 'nothing much turns on whether we count insurance company profits in the hypothetical calculation of premiums, so long as we count their costs' (2002, p. 110). The point is that even a ministry for social justice will have operating costs. But this response is somewhat surprising given that, at first glance, it seems inconsistent with the idea of equal concern and respect to ban private insurers given the cost in liberty to prospective insurers and to people who wish to purchase such insurance. I shall have much more to say about commercial insurance in Chapter 7.

Putting these puzzles to one side, however, what is the purpose of the hypothetical insurance question? In actual political communities many people have not had ample opportunities to purchase insurance in advance of risk. Given this strategic problem, it remains unclear what justice demands of distributive institutions. The purpose of the hypothetical insurance question is to turn the theory of equality into practice. That is, having considered what level and type of insurance is worth its cost to people on average under ideal conditions, we can develop an appropriate baseline for judging economic policy in the real world (Dworkin, 1981b, pp. 290, 315; 2002, p. 107; 2006, pp. 115–17).

In fact, Dworkin conjectures that the hypothetical argument for insurance coverage becomes compelling 'well above the level of income presently used to trigger payouts for unemployment or minimum wage levels in either Britain or the United States' (Dworkin, 1981b, p. 321). Similarly, he suggests that no one could think that American health policy satisfies the hypothetical insurance test since a 'great many Americans cannot afford even minimal medical care when they are seriously ill' (2006, p. 118). In 2006, for example, the US Census Bureau estimated that despite the existence of Medicare and Medicaid programmes, around 16 per cent of Americans (roughly 47 million people) live without health insurance (US Census Bureau, 2007). It is scarcely imaginable that the individuals concerned would have chosen not to purchase *any* medical insurance had they had ample opportunity to do so. Britain, by contrast, has a well-established system of comprehensive medical care, the National Health Service. So here the question is whether or not the level and range of care available mimics the average counterfactual insurance decision. Perhaps when it comes to the provision of basic hospital and primary care services the average person in Britain enjoys not much less than the level of health-care provision he or she would have purchased under conditions of *ex ante* equality. Others may take a different view, of course. But I think that the situation is much less clear-cut when it comes to the funding of certain kinds of cancer drugs and fertility treatment. It is certainly possible to argue that by not making these drugs freely available many NHS trusts fail to show proper concern for patients as articulated by the insurance coverage most people would have decided to purchase in conditions of *ex ante* equality. Partial evidence for this hunch comes from the fact that increasing numbers of British people are opting for private medical insurance policies that will pay for many of the expensive drugs currently ruled out by NHS trusts.

Obviously much more could be said in relation to these country-specific questions. However, at this stage in the discussion I want to address two general criticisms of the hypothetical insurance technique. The first is raised by Macleod. He questions the ability of this technique to 'track' the twin requirements of ambition-sensitivity and endowment-insensitivity. His contention is that because Dworkin lights on the hypothetical insurance market in response to the epistemological difficulty of disentangling the influence of differential talent and ambition on people's share of income, his theory is stranded on the horns of a dilemma. Either it is impossible to know (even imperfectly) how much of a person's income is due to talent and how much due to ambition, in which case we cannot know whether the average insured level of income in the hypothetical scenario tracks ambition-sensitivity and endowment-insensitivity. Or we can judge (within a reasonable range of imperfection) how much of a person's income is due to talent and how much due to ambition, in which case this becomes the appropriate standard of justice and there is no need for hypothetical insurance (Macleod, 1998, pp. 148–9).

Dworkin is only stranded on this dilemma, however, if the role of the hypothetical insurance scheme is (as Macleod claims) to track the requirements of ambition-sensitivity and endowment-insensitivity. I do not think that Dworkin is stranded because I reject this description of the role of the scheme. Macleod seems to regard hypothetical insurance as merely an instrumental device for delivering a distribution in line with two well-defined and independently knowable requirements. On Macleod's reading of Dworkin, we already have a firm grasp of what equality means and all we need do is deliver it such that any proposed scheme is judged on how well or badly it serves that end. However, I believe that Dworkin conceives the role of the hypothetical insurance scheme differently. The scheme is not intended to track or imperfectly realise two independently knowable requirements. Rather, it is supposed to offer an interpretation of what two highly abstract requirements mean given the strategic problem. While actual taxation and social expenditure should try to mimic the hypothetical insurance scheme, the scheme itself does not attempt to mimic or stand as a surrogate or proxy for the twin requirements. It is supposed to provide new knowledge as opposed to an application of existing knowledge. To say that the scheme provides a surrogate for these requirements would be to accept a certain amount of injustice out of practical necessity. Dworkin holds the different view that we simply do not know what equality means without the insurance device. So the device plays an interpretive rather than a merely instrumental role in specifying the requirements of equality of resources.[7]

The second criticism is made by Marc Fleurbaey. He argues that Dworkin's method of extracting actual policies from counterfactual choices violates the separateness of persons. He observes that the counterfactual question is one of personal sacrifice: how much would an ideally situated agent be willing to pay for talent insurance? So, for example, an agent may be willing to sacrifice a certain level of consumption to ensure that he is indemnified against the risk of lacking the talent to earn at a decent level of income. Even so, when the many answers to this question are translated into a standard for taxation and social expenditure in the real world, that standard depends on what the ideally situated agents would choose on average. Thus the average level of personal sacrifice will be foisted upon someone who would not wish to make that level of sacrifice under ideal conditions, thereby ignoring his or her separate wishes. In other words, some people will be forced to live in accordance with the terms of a hypothetical insurance policy which they would not have chosen to purchase (Fleurbaey, 2002, p. 90).[8]

I think that we can immediately discount one possible line of reply to this criticism. The reply is that how different people respond to risk and uncertainty is itself a matter of brute luck in the sense that it is influenced by a combination of natural tendencies and family upbringing which people do not control. In so far as the fundamental egalitarian impulse is to eliminate the influence of arbitrary contingencies on people's life prospects, surely it is only fitting that we average out people's counterfactual insurance decisions. In this way the average insurance coverage achieves justice as equal concern after all. The problem with this line of reply, however, is that it makes the controversial assumption that people's attitudes to risk and insurance are a matter of circumstances rather than personality. Arguably this goes against the grain of Dworkin's understanding of that distinction. To respond to differential attitudes to risk and insurance in this way would be to ignore the fact that most ordinary people identify with these features of their personality.

Dworkin's own response to Fleurbaey's criticism is as follows. He concedes that the hypothetical insurance technique provides a general standard of justice at the expense of sensitivity to every individual counterfactual choice. But faced with a decision between doing nothing about the situation of the unlucky and relying on the hypothetical average, he argues that we should favour averaging (Dworkin, 1981b, p. 298, n. 6; 2002, p. 112). We cannot build a tax regime which is fine-grained enough to reflect every individual counterfactual decision because it is extremely difficult, perhaps impossible, to determine such things. Even if such individual determinations were possible – based on in-depth exploration of each person's actual insurance decisions, general attitudes to risk and rewards, preferred lifestyle and so on – they would be prohibitively expensive. Of course,

> some people will turn out not to benefit from the hypothetical insurance redistributive scheme. But none of them can sensibly complain that the community should not have relied on general assumptions about insurance but should have designed individualized tests for deciding who would and who would not have insured at what level. Everyone's taxes, including their own, would have been much higher if the community had done that.
>
> (2002, p. 112)

Although he does not always formally separate out equality and efficiency considerations, clearly both play a crucial part in Dworkin's conception of equal concern. A proper concern for people – including the lucky and the unlucky – requires that authorities do something about the unfairness of unequal insurance opportunities without at the same time bankrupting the society through massive redistribution or squandering vast sums of money on individual counterfactual determinations. No government that was willing to level down in this way could reasonably claim to show equal concern for the lives of all its citizens (2000, pp. 321–2; 2002, p. 126, n. 35). Indeed, Dworkin maintains that 'levelling down is anathema to genuine equality' (2002, p. 123, n. 29).

So Dworkin's argument is that if averaging does amount to ignoring the separateness of persons, it is not unfair because it is better than either doing nothing or levelling down. But arguably this offers a false choice between two courses of action: doing nothing for the unlucky, at one extreme, and basing fair redistribution entirely on individual counterfactual choices, at the other extreme. Perhaps there could be a middle ground such as using existing information on people's insurance decisions – by gathering information from the insurance industry, for example – to place counterfactual insurance choices into broad categories such as high, medium and low. Authorities could then tailor economic policy to these different categories of people in a way that does not mean bankrupting the community or squandering vast sums of money on expensive administration. Dworkin believes that the reason why *ex ante* equality is superior to *ex post* equality is that it gives everyone a hypothetical choice concerning how much they are willing to pay for insurance against certain catastrophes (Dworkin, 2000, p. 342; 2006, p. 110). But if this is true, then surely it would be better to devote at least *some* public funds to investigating individual counterfactual choices rather than none at all.

Notwithstanding this point, I do want to say something in defence of Dworkin's position. I do this by drawing a comparison with Rawls. Dworkin asks us to imagine a situation in which people must choose how much insurance to purchase against the same antecedent risks. Individuals are permitted to choose on the basis of their own personal attitudes to risk. But in the end the differences are averaged out. Rawls, by contrast, places individuals behind a veil of ignorance such that they are ignorant as to their own particular attitudes to risk and uncertainty (or 'special psychologies'). We are to assume that individuals behind the veil of ignorance simply do not know whether they are risk-seeking or risk-averse (Rawls, 1971, p. 530). Yet under closer scrutiny it seems that Rawls *does* make an assumption about people's attitudes to risk and uncertainty. He assumes that it is rational for parties behind the veil to adopt maximin (p. 153). For this to be the case it must be that the parties are risk-averse after all. Hence, Rawls is only able to guarantee that each person would select a certain kind of distributive principle by assuming that everyone is the same. Surely this is to ignore the separateness of persons as well.

At the beginning of this chapter I stressed the fact that on Dworkin's account of equality of resources, the term 'resources' refers to personal or bodily resources (including physical and mental talents and abilities) as well as to impersonal or non-bodily resources of different kinds. The question I now wish to consider is whether or not this enables Dworkin to pre-empt what might otherwise be a devastating objection to equality of resources, the capabilities objection.

The capabilities objection

This objection was first put by Amartya Sen in his seminal article, 'Equality of What?' (1980). He makes the point that making people equal in their share of income and wealth can leave them unequal in other important dimensions, where these dimensions are not reducible to traditional welfare metrics. So, for example, 'a poor person's freedom from undernourishment would depend not only on her resources and primary goods (e.g. through the influence on income on the ability to buy food), but also on her metabolic rates, gender, pregnancy, climatic environment, exposure to parasitic diseases, and so on' (Sen, 1992, p. 33). He concludes from this, and other similar examples, that we should abandon equality of resources and instead adopt equality of basic capabilities as the best reading of the egalitarian ethic (1980; 1985). His core objection to equality of resources is this: 'Of two persons with identical incomes and other primary goods and resources (as characterized in the Rawlsian or Dworkinian frameworks), one may be entirely free to avoid undernourishment and the other not at all free to achieve this' (1992, p. 33).

Dworkin's response to this objection in *Sovereign Virtue* is to insist that his own conception of equality of resources would also distinguish between the two persons.

> I have stressed, beginning in the earliest chapters of this book, that a person's resources include personal resources such as health and physical capacity as well as impersonal or transferable resources such as money, and that though different batteries of techniques are required to correct or mitigate inequalities in these two major domains of resource, both must command the attention of egalitarians.
>
> (Dworkin, 2000, p. 300)

Dworkin, of course, believes that hypothetical insurance markets for illnesses and physical handicaps provide the relevant techniques for addressing these sorts of inequalities. The question is whether or not people would purchase insurance against lacking proper nourishment caused by metabolic rates, gender, pregnancy, climatic environment, exposure to parasitic diseases and so on (p. 301).[9]

There is, however, a residual problem for Dworkin here. It stems from the need to identify the conditions under which an opportunity to buy insurance transforms brute luck into option luck. Suppose one of these conditions is that a person has access to modestly priced insurance, meaning that insurance can be purchased whilst maintaining a reasonably comfortable standard of living. Assuming that this is a necessary condition, it is difficult to see how a reasonably comfortable standard of living could be defined without appealing to measures of capability, such as being clothed, housed, well-fed and so on. At this stage Dworkin is faced with two options. The first is to accept that modestly priced insurance is a necessary condition whilst at the same time rejecting the notion that this must be defined in terms of capability. That is, he must find a way to define modestly priced insurance in terms of resources. The second is to deny that modestly priced insurance is a necessary condition and highlight instead the importance of reasonably priced insurance.

Putting this problem to one side, however, Andrew Williams argues that there are yet further examples of people who lack capabilities which cannot be reduced to questions about either resources or welfare. Consider twins Ann and Bob, who both dream one day of raising families with a member of the opposite sex and pursuing reasonably successful careers. Although they have identical personal and impersonal resources and the same ambitions, they face different challenges in finding a mate to enable them to achieve the functionings they value. This is because the society in which they live demonstrates the following characteristic gendered ambitions: men tend to prefer to be full-time workers, while women tend to prefer to be part-time workers and homemakers. As a result, Ann will find it more difficult than Bob to achieve the amalgamated functioning of home life and career which she desires (Williams, 2002, pp. 30–4; cf. Mason, 2000).

Dworkin, however, contends that the putative difference in capability collapses into another metric, in this case welfare. How so? He urges the reader to reflect more closely on what Ann and Bob will be able to do or not do. To be sure, Ann will find it difficult to find a mate willing to share parenting labour. But Bob will also find it difficult to find a mate willing to let him take on sole parenting should he change his mind and desire that outcome. If we look at the capabilities from this perspective, they appear to have comparable capability sets. 'Why should we assume that her capacity set is overall smaller or less valuable or important than his set?' (Dworkin, 2002, p. 137). Obviously at present Bob does not want to take on sole parenting, and so there is that difference. But from Dworkin's perspective, if *that* is the operative difference between Ann and Bob, then the underlying conception of capability doing the work here is something like 'a capacity to achieve the domestic arrangement that in fact they each want, or that would make each of them happy, or fulfilled, or something of that sort'. In which case: 'we are relying on a welfare metric and have abandoned the idea that the capability metric is distinct from welfare' (ibid.).

In a recent contribution to this debate, however, Roland Pierik and Ingrid Robeyns argue that Dworkin is unable to rule out the possibility of genuine capability inequalities. In the original example, Williams proposes binary preferences. Men tend to prefer to be full-time workers, while women tend to prefer to be part-time workers and homemakers. Pierik and Robeyns ask us to image two more twins, Amy and Ben, who both want to set up a household and raise a family with a member of the opposite sex. In their society, 50 per cent of the men strictly prefer to be co-parents, while the other 50 per cent strictly prefer to be full-time workers, whereas 50 per cent of the women are indifferent between being a full-time worker or a co-parent, 40 per cent want to be either a co-parent or a homeworker and the remaining 10 per cent strictly prefer to be full-time workers. Suppose Amy is one of the 10 per cent of women who would like to be full-time workers and raise a family. She is denied this opportunity, since no men are willing to be homeworkers, whereas there are no options available to Amy that are not available to Ben. Furthermore, they stipulate that these social preferences have been developed in whatever way Dworkin would regard as authentic and therefore just background facts. The result is that there seem to be genuine capability inequalities (Pierik and Robeyns, 2007, pp. 138–9).

I think that this is a legitimate variant of the story but I also think that it ignores the following pertinent question. Suppose it turns out that some of the women in the relevant society, due to the gendered preferences, are unable to have full-time jobs and husbands who are willing to work as homemakers. Nevertheless, presumably there is nothing to stop these women from having full-time jobs, husbands and paid nannies who perform homemaking duties. In this way they can fulfil their dream of raising families with a member of the opposite sex and pursuing reasonably successful careers. This is a capability they do have. So the question is this: why should we assume that Amy's capacity set is somehow impoverished or lesser relative to Ben's capacity set merely because she has the latter capability instead of the former? If the answer is that Amy would prefer it for her husband to look after the children, then once again we have smuggled in a welfare metric. I freely accept that this reply puts a lot of weight on the assumption that 'raising a family' can include paying a nanny to look after the children during a normal working week. But if this assumption is correct, then Pierik and Robeyns have not provided a case of genuine capability differences.

Testing Dworkin's egalitarian credentials

I now wish to consider a far more general question about Dworkin's theory of equality. In what sense can we say that Dworkin is an egalitarian philosopher? This may seem like a perverse question given the title of my book. But the motivation for posing it comes from Chapter 4 of *Is Democracy Possible Here?*, where Dworkin states that '[t]he insurance device *is* a safety-net device: it sets a floor' (Dworkin, 2006, p. 121). Given this description of his project, some might begin to question whether or not Dworkin is really an egalitarian after all. Indeed, many philosophers hold the sceptical view that people who profess to have strong egalitarian convictions are actually exercised not by inequality as such but by the fact that people are badly off or do not have enough (see Raz, 1986, pp. 217, 240; Frankfurt, 1988, p. 146; Narveson, 1998, p. 80). Applying this scepticism to Dworkin, some might think that the average level of insurance coverage is more like a benchmark of sufficiency than of equality. With this thought in mind, what are the hallmarks of a genuinely egalitarian theory and does equality of resources bear those marks?

Scanlon proposes the following two criteria for regarding a reason for reducing material inequality as genuinely egalitarian. The first is that it must be 'comparative', that is, concerned with the relation between the levels of benefits that different individuals enjoy (Scanlon, 2003; 2004). This condition reinforces a point made by Larry Temkin that '[t]he egalitarian has no intrinsic concern with how much people have; her concern is with how much people have *relative to others*' (Temkin, 1993, p. 200). Indeed, Adam Swift observes that '[e]quality has come under fire from political philosophers because it is necessarily concerned with comparisons and relatives' (Swift, 2001, p. 106). The second necessary condition states that a reason for reducing inequality is egalitarian only if it is 'unspecific', in not being concerned with the absolute levels of benefits that individuals enjoy (Scanlon, 2004). The idea is that a genuinely egalitarian reason for tackling inequality does not vanish once the least well-off group have reached a particular level of advantage deemed adequate by some independent normative benchmark. Does Dworkin's equality of resources satisfy these two conditions?

Consider the two key parts of the view: the imaginary auction and the hypothetical insurance scheme. It is relatively simple to see how the auction satisfies Scanlon's first condition. In framing the basic requirements of the auction Dworkin draws heavily on the envy test. This test is avowedly comparative: it demands that everyone have an equal initial bundle of impersonal resources, where this is judged by asking people to compare directly their bundles with those of other people. It also easily satisfies the second condition: the envy test is not concerned with the absolute levels of resources that individuals enjoy but with equal bundles. At first glance, the second part of equality of resources is more equivocal. That each person ought to have the resources he or she would have enjoyed given ample opportunity to purchase insurance does not, on the face it, require direct comparisons between agents. However, it is important for Dworkin not merely that people have ample opportunity to insure but that people face the same antecedent risk and are offered the same terms and conditions as everyone else. Moreover, while Dworkin urges the reader to consider the possibility that the average level of insurance coverage in the case of talent will be below the average income, this does not mean that he is interested in absolute levels of coverage. The average level of insurance has ethical significance not because it somehow represents enough insurance as measured by some independent benchmark. Rather, it reflects the aggregate insurance decisions of equally situated people. Even if the least well-off people in the real world had enough resources to meet their basic needs, the situation would still be unfair if they have less than the average level of insurance in the hypothetical scenario.

For these reasons I believe that it is appropriate to describe Dworkin as an egalitarian despite his use of the language of safety-nets and minimum standards. In which case, why does he use this language? I suggest that this language is best understood as marking the distinction between equality as a set of abstract ideals and equality as a concrete norm. If we could know exactly what proportion of each person's income and wealth is due to choice and brute luck respectively, this would be the standard to aim for. But since we do not know, we require some other way of trying to understand what this standard means in specific terms. So we imagine people shipwrecked on a desert island and we ask a question about counterfactual insurance decisions. Given the further epistemic constraints involved in asking this question individually, however, we must adopt a minimum standard, to wit, 'the minimum we can safely assume that reflective people would have insured to provide for themselves if they were *ex ante* equal' (Dworkin, 2006, p. 118). Perhaps some people will argue that the shipwreck survivors would have insured for much more than Dworkin assumes. This sets a higher standard. But then this assumption is controversial. At any rate, Dworkin hopes that his assumptions will strike most people as less controversial. Furthermore, the hypothetical insurance market sets a minimum standard not only of justice but also of legitimacy. It represents the absolute minimum that is required to display a good faith attempt to treat the poor with equal concern, where this is an appropriate test of the government's claim to the rightful exercise of dominion over its citizens (p. 106).

However, potentially the most powerful line of criticism that has been directed at Dworkin's theory of equality in recent years concerns the luck-neutralising ambition that many associate with equality of resources, and it is this objection that I now want to address.

Is Dworkin a 'luck egalitarian'?

In her 1999 essay, 'What is the Point of Equality?', Elizabeth Anderson charts the emergence of a family of views in contemporary political philosophy which she calls 'luck egalitarian' (Anderson, 1999, p. 289). According to Anderson, luck egalitarians

> place great stress on the distinction between the outcomes for which an individual is responsible – that is, those that result from her voluntary choices – and the outcomes for which she is not responsible – good or bad outcomes that occur independent of her choice or of what she could have reasonably foreseen.
>
> (p. 291)

Citing the work of Dworkin, she adds, 'Luck egalitarians dub this the distinction between "option luck" and "brute luck"' (ibid.). Before turning to Anderson's specific criticisms of Dworkin, however, I want first to consider the preliminary interpretive question: is Dworkin a luck egalitarian?

Anderson is not alone in her characterisation of Dworkin. Samuel Scheffler concedes that luck egalitarianism has different variants but also insists that there is a core idea common to all of these variants, including Dworkin's equality of resources. 'The core idea is that [...] inequalities deriving from unchosen features of people's circumstances are unjust' (Scheffler, 2003, p. 5). Nevertheless, Dworkin explicitly rebuffs the suggestion that equality of resources is luck egalitarian in that sense. In a reply to Scheffler he writes,

> I did not defend that 'core idea' in my book, *Sovereign Virtue*. 'The general ambition of equality of resources,...' I said, 'is to make circumstances equal under some appropriate version of the envy test.' I then argued, over many pages, that the appropriate version of that test requires not, as Scheffler's 'core idea' suggests, that people be fully compensated for any bad luck after it has occurred, but rather that people be made equal, so far as this is possible, in their opportunity to insure or provide against bad luck before it has occurred, or, if that is not possible, that people be awarded the compensation it is likely they would have insured to have if they had had that opportunity. That latter goal is not a compromise or second-best solution that accepts some injustice out of necessity. It is what equality, properly understood, itself requires.
>
> (Dworkin, 2003, p. 191)

In one sense Dworkin is quite correct to emphasise hypothetical insurance rather than Scheffler's core idea as being constitutive of equality of resources. Even so, Dworkin is perhaps ungenerous in his failure to acknowledge the extent to which his own characterisation of equality of resources seems, in places, to support Scheffler's alternative interpretation. For example: 'In principle, I said, individuals should be relieved of consequential responsibility for those unfortunate features of their situation that are brute luck, but not from those that should be seen as flowing from their own choices' (2000, p. 287). Nonetheless, it is crucial to bear in mind the distinction between abstract and concrete levels in Dworkin's theory of equality. Although Scheffler might be correct in his characterisation of equality of resources as luck egalitarian at the abstract level, this does not mean that this characterisation stands up at the lower, concrete level.[10]

Focusing on the lower level, then, I offer two grounds for rejecting the claim that Dworkin's equality of resources is luck egalitarian. The first is that equality of resources does not aim to neutralise brute luck as such. Rather, it aims to convert brute luck into option luck by placing the responsibility for choosing types and levels of insurance with persons placed under equal conditions. In the case of talent insurance, Dworkin avers that persons are unlikely to purchase insurance policies which offer full compensation because of the opportunity cost of doing so and the special disadvantages of such a gamble, namely, the risk of becoming enslaved by one's own talents.[11] This means that the average level of coverage is likely to be below the highest projected income on the island. If the survivors wished to fully neutralise brute luck, by contrast, the average level of insurance would be much closer to the highest projected income (Dworkin, 1981b, pp. 319–20). Likewise, the problem of handicaps is not 'to make people equal in physical and mental constitution so far as this is possible'. Rather, the problem is 'one of determining how far the ownership of independent material resources should be affected by differences that exist in physical and mental powers' (p. 301). Once again, the aim is to give people the resources they would have been entitled to if, contrary to fact, they had enjoyed ample opportunity to purchase insurance, and this, thinks Dworkin, is likely to be less than full compensation because of the opportunity cost of purchasing very expensive insurance policies, even assuming that commercial insurance companies could offer full compensation. Whereas a society of luck egalitarians would undertake to achieve *ex post* equality, that is, to try, so far as is possible, to restore people to the share of material resources or position they would have occupied but for their brute luck, Dworkin proposes instead that a government should try to bring people closer to the shares of resources that are likely to have resulted from conditions of ex ante equality or even try to create conditions of *ex ante* equality, for example, 'by arranging that all citizens have an opportunity to buy on equal terms the appropriate insurance against low productive talent or bad luck' (2006, p. 109).

The second ground for rejection is that Dworkin does not support the mitigation of brute luck across all dimensions of disadvantage. Genuine luck egalitarians take a different view, however. Cohen, for example, writes, 'Whatever number of dimensions the space of disadvantage may have, egalitarianism, on my reading, cuts through each of its dimensions, judging certain inequalities of advantage as acceptable and others as not, its touchstone being a set of questions about the responsibility or lack of it of the disadvantaged agent' (Cohen, 1989, p. 921). This prompts Anderson to suggest that a luck egalitarian would recommend sending compensation cheques to the ugly and socially awkward thereby showing them contemptuous pity (Anderson, 1999, p. 305). Dworkin considers the possibility of amending the distribution of resources on the island to address the fact that some are physically more attractive than others. But he rejects the proposal associating it with equality of welfare rather than equality of resources (Dworkin, 1981b, p. 303). The key point is that he does not anticipate ordinary people wanting to purchase insurance policies against being unattractive. I suspect that given the impact that severe facial disfigurement can have on people's lives this might well be something that a rational person would wish to take out insurance against. Even if I am right about this, however, any compensation that is paid – presumably to fund

plastic surgery – would be something paid under the rubric of equality o
resources rather than one or other conception of equality of welfare. The
insurance device would, in other words, offer an argument for that conse
quence given that assumption.

Nevertheless, let us now proceed to examine Anderson's specific criticisms of Dworkin, of which there are four.[12] The first targets his
methodology.

> The state, says Ronald Dworkin, should treat each of its citizens with
> equal respect and concern. Virtually all egalitarian accept this for-
> mula, but rarely have they analyzed it. Instead, they invoke the for-
> mula, then propose their favored principle of egalitarian distribution
> as an interpretation of it, without providing an argument proving
> that their principle really does express equal respect and concern for
> all citizens.
>
> (Anderson, 1999, p. 295)

The criticism appears to be that Dworkin fails to offer a detailed enough
analysis of the concept of equal concern before he embarks on the project of arguing for his favoured conception of it.

I find two aspects of this criticism puzzling. The first is the charge
that Dworkin fails to provide 'an argument proving that' his principle
really does express equal respect and concern for all citizens. This sets
the bar of political argument very high: for it implies that philosophers can *prove* that one interpretation is better than another. In fact,
Dworkin maintains only that interpreters should try to construct the
best interpretations they can given the available data as a form of inference to the best explanation. Indeed, in what sense does Anderson
prove that her own conception of democratic equality really does
express equal respect and concern for all citizens? The second aspect is
her distinction between *analysing* the formula, which apparently egalitarians rarely do, and *interpreting* the formula, which she accepts as
commonplace. In fact, Dworkin does analyse the concern of concern.
He distinguishes between two different 'modes of concern'. The first
mode of concern is typified by a totalitarian state that attempts to
clone the highest-order interests of all its citizens and then tries to take
over the role of pursuing those interests on people's behalf. Dworkin
thinks that most of us would 'reject that model as unduly, deeply
paternalistic' (Dworkin, 1983, p. 28). The second mode of concern is
characterised by a liberal state that asks what goals it should take up for

all its citizens in virtue of the fact that they have the highest-order interest they do. Here equal concern is shown by adopting goals that are compatible with each citizen's own goals. Dworkin believes that the only political goal that can satisfy this endorsement constraint is equality of resources (pp. 29–30). This analysis severely undermines Anderson's criticism. Either she accepts the first mode of concern, in which case she must answer the challenge of paternalism. Or she accepts the second mode of concern, in which case she cannot plausibly claim to be in disagreement with Dworkin over the core meaning of concern. At any rate, she can scarcely claim that Dworkin has failed to analyse the concept of concern.

Anderson's second criticism has to do with Dworkin's alleged abandonment of imprudent risk takers. She writes,

> Ronald Dworkin has articulated this insurance analogy most elaborately. [...] Where such private insurance is available, brute luck is automatically converted into option luck, for society can hold individuals responsible for purchasing insurance on their own behalf. In its purest form, luck egalitarians would insist that if individuals imprudently fail to do so, no demand of justice requires society to bail them out.
>
> (Anderson, 1999, p. 292)

She offers the example of an uninsured driver who negligently makes an illegal turn that causes an accident in which he is seriously injured (pp. 295–6). She suggests that anyone who would not abandon the uninsured driver has two options. The first is to reject equality of resources outright and to fall back on her preferred conception, democratic equality. The second is to defend paternalistic intervention which coerces people to purchase insurance, perhaps on the grounds that left to their own devices they are too stupid to purchase insurance such that paternalism is justified as a way of mitigating the brute luck of in-born myopia. This, she calls, 'the problem of paternalism' (pp. 300–1).

At this stage, however, I think that Dworkin would simply point out that not all kinds of paternalism are problematic, and that the question of what makes paternalism problematic depends on the deeper question of what it means to show equal concern and respect to all citizens. Indeed, he explicitly accepts the possibility of gamble-limiting paternalism (Dworkin, 1981b, p. 295). In general terms, Dworkin believes that it may be possible to justify paternalism in those instances where it preserves or enhances people's capacity to take charge of their lives, such as limiting people's right to alienate their rights and liberties so as to ensure that they are able to participate in the political process, or where it is rational to accept paternalism because, for example, it helps people to achieve what they actually want in the face of psychological weakness or social pressure, such as forcing a child to do her piano practice. In these instances paternalism is in fact a way of showing equal concern and respect for rational persons (1989, pp. 484–5; 2002, pp. 114–15; 2006, pp. 37, 73).[13] I do not think that it would be difficult to make a plausible case for compulsory medical insurance for drivers on either of these justifications, as we already do in respect of seat belts. If such a justification could be made to work, then a law prohibiting people from driving without adequate medical insurance is not merely compatible with the abstract right to equal concern and respect but is required by it.

The third criticism focuses on putative discrimination among the disabled.

> Dworkin argues that the people who should be compensated for defects in internal assets are those who would have purchased insurance against their having the defect if they were behind a veil of ignorance and did not know whether they would have that defect. It follows, uncharitably, that people who have an extremely rare but severe disability could be ineligible for special aid just because the chances of anyone suffering from it were so minute that it was *ex ante* rational for people not to purchase insurance against it. The proposal discriminates between people with rare and common disabilities.
>
> (Anderson, 1999, p. 303)

Notice, however, that the proposal discriminates against people with rare disabilities *only if* it would be rational not to purchase insurance against such disabilities. Contra Anderson, it seems to me that the rationality of purchasing insurance will have as much, if not more, to do with the *severity* of the disability as with its *rarity*. Take the case of Pelizaeus-Merzbacher disease, which is an extremely rare degenerative disorder affecting around one in 300,000 people; a disorder that causes the deterioration of coordination, motor skills and cognitive functioning. I think that most rational people would be willing to pay for an insurance policy that covers even an extremely rare kind of disablement, such as this, precisely because of the seriousness of the handicaps it involves. Presumably the fact that it is extremely rare will enable insurers to keep the costs of insurance relatively low, thus making it a more attractive proposition. Indeed, it may be that for administrative as well as prudential reasons most insurers will offer, and most customers will wish to purchase, insurance packages which protect people from a range of disorders, diseases and genetic faults which cause certain kinds of disablement up to a given amount of money.

Anderson's final criticism concerns the envy test.

> If pity is the attitude the more fortunate express toward the less fortunate when they adopt luck egalitarianism as their principle of action, what is the attitude the less fortunate express toward the more fortunate when they make claims in accordance with the theory? The resourcist luck egalitarians are explicit on this point: it is envy. Their criterion of an equal distribution of resources is an envy-free distribution: one which is such that no one wants anyone else's bundle of resources. The two attitudes are well suited to each other: the most generous attitude the envied could appropriately have toward the envious is pity. While this makes equality of fortune consistent, it hardly justifies the theory. Envy's thought is 'I want what you have.' It is hard to see how such wants can generate *obligations* on the part of the envied. To even offer one's own envy as a reason to the envied to satisfy one's desire is profoundly disrespectful.
>
> (Anderson, 1999, p. 307)

Anderson seems to think that within Dworkin's theory of equality envy generates obligations to transfer resources. The truth is otherwise. At the heart of equality of resources is an obligation to show equal concern, where this involves finding some tolerable measurement of equal shares. The job of envy is merely to determine what equal shares means within a certain idealised scenario. In other words, it is the goal of the divider to show equal concern to each person and it is this that generates an obligation to equalise shares as measured by envy. This is quite distinct from the idea that human envy generates an obligation to equalise shares (Dworkin, 1981b, pp. 295–6; 2002, p. 123).

Summing up these points we might say that Dworkin's theory of equality of resources is more luck egalitarian when stated at a higher level of abstraction than at a lower, more concrete level. Another way of expressing this is to say that Dworkin is an interpretive luck egalitarian. Furthermore, it should not be forgotten that equality of resources aims to give expression to the abstract egalitarian principle and to the two deeper principles of human dignity on which it is based, and this fact alone may rule out the most radical interpretation of luck egalitarian aims, such as to fully neutralise the affects of brute luck irrespective of whether or not this is in the interests of the average person in society. To put it in Dworkin's own terms, a government that wanted to show equal concern and respect for its citizens would be failing in its task if it attempted to offer full compensation to the victims of brute luck.

The suggestion that the best conception of equality is the one that provides the best interpretation of what it means for a government to treat its citizens with equal concern and respect plays an important role in Dworkin's analysis. Therefore, this abstract egalitarian principle will be the subject of the next chapter.

4
The Egalitarian Plateau

One of the most beguiling claims made by Dworkin in his extensive writings on political values is the claim that the vast bulk of contemporary political philosophy is built upon egalitarian foundations; that virtually every normative theory of social arrangement of the nineteenth and twentieth centuries shares an assumption of equality. His basic contention is that a great many very different political theories can be presented as competing interpretations of the same abstract egalitarian principle, namely, that every citizen has a right to be treated with equal concern and respect by his or her own government. According to Dworkin, this principle can be thought to provide 'a kind of plateau in political argument' (Dworkin, 1983, p. 25).

The idea that there is an egalitarian plateau in modern political argument has been supported by a number of writers in the field (see Nagel, 1979, p. 111; Rakowski, 1991, p. 19; Sen, 1992, pp. 18–19; Swift, 2001, p. 93; Kymlicka, 2002, p. 4). Much less work has been undertaken, however, in exploring the significance of the egalitarian plateau hypothesis. Even if it is true that a great many very different political theories can be presented as interpretations of abstract egalitarian rights, why does this matter? A central plank in Dworkin's answer to this question is that occupying the plateau matters because it provides much needed common ground between the advocates of fiercely opposed political arguments. In this chapter I shall argue that although there are a number of initially plausible reasons for thinking that occupying the egalitarian plateau can make a difference in political argument, on closer inspection some of these reasons turn out to be less powerful and some less applicable than one might reasonably expect. Nevertheless, I believe that there is another kind of abstract egalitarian right that can fill in some of the gaps, and that that kind of right transcends membership of political community.

Equal concern and respect

Dworkin's work contains a number of formulations of the egalitarian plateau hypothesis. For example:

> We might say that individuals have a right to equal concern and respect in the design and administration of the political institutions that govern them. This is a highly abstract right. [...] [This right] is more abstract than the standard conceptions of equality that distinguish different political theories. It permits arguments that this more basic right requires one or another of these conceptions as a derivative right or goal.
>
> (Dworkin, 1977, p. 180)[1]

> From the standpoint of politics, the interests of the members of the community matter, and matter equally. I suggest that this proposition captures the concept of equality, taken to be at least an element in a theory of social justice, in such a way as to embrace various competing conceptions of equality [...] Of course there are some political theories that cannot be presented as conceptions of equality so defined – some racialist political theories, for example – but a great many very different theories can be presented that way, and a great many have.
>
> (1983, pp. 24–5)

> [...] I believe that we are now united in accepting the abstract egalitarian principle: government must act to make the lives of those it governs better lives, and it must show equal concern for the life of each.
>
> (1987a, pp. 7–8)

> Equal concern, as I said, is the special and indispensable virtue of sovereigns.
>
> (2000, p. 6)

Three features of these passages are immediately significant. The first is that in the earliest formulations Dworkin uses the phrase 'the right to equal concern and respect', whereas in later work he often speaks in terms of equal concern alone. Does this mean that he is now *only* interested in equal concern? I think not. He believes that government must show not only equal concern for the lives of all citizens but also equal respect in the sense that every citizen bears a special responsibility for the success or failure of his or her own life (Dworkin, 2000, p. 324). Yet the fact that there are two abstract egalitarian rights raises some difficult questions. How are the two rights to be upheld in cases where they seem to conflict? Must both be given equal weight or is it appropriate to give one lexical priority over the other? What Dworkin actually has in mind, I suggest, is that we must construct two mutually compatible interpretations from the start as opposed to two independently worked out interpretations which are only brought together at a later stage. He gives the example of a government newly dedicated to treating its citizens as equals. At first it only thinks about its obligation to show equal concern to all citizens, and so it envisages a 'radically egalitarian economic policy' in which it collects all of its citizens' resources once a year and redistributes them equally (2006, p. 102). But it soon realises that it must also respect the rights of individuals to be responsible for their own lives, where this implies something other than a radically egalitarian economic policy (p. 103). The lesson behind this example is that

> A theory of just taxation must therefore include not only a theory of what equal concern demands on the best understanding but also a conception of the true consequences of personal responsibility, and it must find a way to satisfy both of these requirements in the same structure.
> (p. 105)

A second feature worth underlining is the suggestion that equal concern and respect is the special and indispensable virtue of sovereigns and of true political communities. The right to equal concern is 'special', as distinct from general, in the sense that it is only held by members of political communities and only against their own particular governments and fellow members. It is 'indispensable' in the sense that no political community can plausibly claim legitimacy that ignores this right. Perhaps also a government cannot realistically hope to maintain social harmony over time if it fails to treat citizens with equal concern and respect. What is most interesting about this claim, however, is that it builds into the very idea of a right to equal concern and respect the feature that this is owed by virtue of a special relationship between citizens and their own governments. It deserves mention that in his *Taking Rights Seriously* Dworkin draws a distinction between *universal* and *special* political rights, where this marks the difference between rights which are held by all citizens within the political community and rights which are only held by a certain sub-section or even a single member (Dworkin, 1977, p. 94, n. 1). But in *both* cases a citizen can only claim these rights against his or her *own* government.

A third feature has to do with the relationship between the egalitarian plateau and its various conceptions. Dworkin characterises the abstract right to equal concern and respect as 'fundamental to' and 'constitutive of' our political morality, in the sense that it is a political end that we value as *an end in itself* (Dworkin, 1977, p. 180; 1978, pp. 116–17, 125–6). Due to the highly abstract nature of this right, however, it 'permits' different arguments about how best to interpret it (1977, p. 180). Although this right sets up some constraints on what an adequate conception would be like, we cannot expect the egalitarian plateau by itself to determine the best conception among the plausible options. Whatever else he believes or does not believe about the abstract egalitarian principle, Dworkin is clear that it cannot in itself rule out substantively non-egalitarian principles as feasible interpretations. This ruling out, so to speak, must be done by a process of constructive interpretation. So, for example, even though he defends equality of resources as the optimal conception of equal concern in matters of distribution, Dworkin accepts the principle 'to each according to his or her merit' as a legitimate rival interpretation along with equality of welfare (2000, pp. 325–7). Indeed, the abstract egalitarian principle does not even have enough content to discount non-liberal theories:

> If, for example, I say simply that it is constitutive of liberalism that the government must treat its citizens with respect, I have not stated a constitutive principle in sufficient detail, because, although liberals might argue that all their political schemes follow from that principle, conservatives, Marxists and perhaps even fascists would make the same claim for their theories.
>
> (1978, p. 121)

It is perhaps surprising that Dworkin is so willing to accept that the egalitarian plateau does not have enough content to decisively favour a liberal egalitarian interpretation given that the central business of his political writings has been to defend just such an interpretation. But surprising or not, this admission places Dworkin on the horns of a dilemma. On the one hand, suppose that abstract rights to equal concern and respect *do* have sufficient content to determine a particular theory of social arrangement using uncontroversial methods of reasoning and inference. We might even suppose that it is some kind of liberal egalitarianism. In which case, he can no longer plausibly claim an egalitarian plateau in political argument. Provided that other people are not making errors in reasoning, what could explain their support for alternative theories? One would be forced to conclude that they are interpreting a different set of abstract rights. On the other hand, suppose (along with Dworkin) that abstract rights *do not* have sufficient content to determine a particular theory. This would make the egalitarian plateau thesis more plausible. But it would also mean that these abstract rights are doing no work in narrowing down the field save for discounting the most extreme theories that we would not count as conceptions of justice at all even though they are sometimes presented as such. So one is left wondering what real purpose the egalitarian plateau is supposed to serve.

In an attempt to respond to this last challenge the next section examines five kinds of reasons for thinking that it matters in political argument whether or not one accepts Dworkin's abstract egalitarian principle. In the end I shall argue that these reasons are less powerful than one might reasonably hope for. But prior to embarking on this evaluation, I need first to briefly mention an additional distinction between three possible versions of the egalitarian plateau hypothesis. The first is that citizens of political communities *only* possess abstract rights to equal concern and respect in respect of issues of individual liberty, such as whether or not it is permissible with regards to social organisation and basic structure to allow discrimination against particular groups of individuals on the basis of their class, gender, race and so on. The second is that citizens *only* have these abstract rights concerning issues of distributive justice, as in, whether the state should try to reduce inequalities, maximise the position of the worst off, satisfy basic needs, uphold historical entitlements, maximise aggregate utility, distribute according to merit, or do something else entirely. The third is that citizens have abstract egalitarian rights in both respects. I suspect that few would be inclined to endorse the second version of the thesis, but perhaps some might think that the first claim is more plausible and less difficult to defend than the third claim. However, in this chapter I wish to try to attack the egalitarian plateau thesis with respect to both individual liberty and distributive justice.

Testing the importance of Dworkin's abstract egalitarian rights

How might accepting or not accepting Dworkin's abstract egalitarian rights make a difference in political argument?

Making the political community more equal

one thought might be that acceptance of these rights matters in the same way that acceptance of a great many large moral ideas matters — in the long run they can make the world a better place. Thus it might be suggested that certain very desirable social and political reforms of the nineteenth and twentieth centuries could not have been achieved without acceptance of these kinds of abstract rights — for example, 'egalitarian' acts of emancipation such as the freeing of slaves in America, 'egalitarian' institutions like the welfare state, and numerous 'egalitarian' principles including equality before the law, one person one vote and equality of opportunity in the competition for offices and positions in society. These changes obviously had a great deal to do with specific historical contingencies and must be analysed on a case by case basis. But how could one plausibly deny the fact that the acceptance of abstract equality was an influencing factor?

In so far as the egalitarian plateau is a thesis about the special rights of citizens to assert their equal freedom in the face of dominion by their own government, then it is clear that this plateau has been pivotal in affecting change in many instances. But there are many other instances where the relevance of *that* thesis is questionable. Take the freeing of the slaves, for example. When the first anti-slavery society in America was formed in Philadelphia in 1775, not surprisingly the political thinker and agitator Thomas Paine was a founding member. Nevertheless, his Essay on African Slavery in America of the same year is worth careful attention: for it speaks not directly to a special relationship between Africans and their own kings (i.e., to the special rights to equal concern and respect held within African political communities) but to more universal human rights. That is, it speaks to the managers of the slave-trade based in America, to the 'desperate wretches' who are willing to steal and enslave men by violence and murder for gain 'contrary to the light of nature, to every principle of Justice and Humanity' (Paine, 1775).

So it is uncertain whether all great 'egalitarian' acts can be explained in terms of a certain form of thinking about the special relationship between a government and its own citizens. Nevertheless, it is not my ambition to contest history or even to contest the history of ideas. What

I do wish to place under the microscope, however, is the continued importance of the egalitarian plateau.

Confronting anti-egalitarians

Perhaps there is something to be said for the importance of these rights in terms of their role in answering the threat to existing egalitarian institutions, ethical principles and practices posed by *inter alia* Neo-Nazis, fundamentalist religious groups that deny women's rights, traditional communities that still practice female circumcision, infanticide and human sacrifice, not to mention government institutions which permit patterns of economic and social inequality to develop along racial lines, and various political leaderships around the word that disregard some and not other people's civil liberties in the name of maintaining social stability or fighting terrorism. Do not special rights to equal concern and respect still have a crucial part to play as a normative bulwark against this sea of anti-egalitarianism?

As with the previous argument, however, these phenomena need to be considered on a case-by-case basis and cannot be assumed to provide a blanket justification for the importance of Dworkin's special rights. One point worth highlighting is that sometimes, very often perhaps, disagreements between proponents of different theories of social arrangement do not turn on fundamental disagreements at the level of value but on differences of judgement about how the world works, who holds power, patterns of social behaviour, the nature of political community and the alleged characteristics of different types of human being. But I begin with a case where the disagreement is about intrinsic value. Suppose we accept that no government could reasonably claim to treat its citizens with equal concern and respect if it permitted racist groups to murder, kidnap and torture certain members of the community who are deemed inferior or wholly devoid of moral worth (Dworkin, 1983, p. 24; cf. Swift, 2001, p. 93). I agree with Dworkin that few morally sensitive people would support such treatment. The question, however, is whether or not the treatment is first and foremost an affront to the abstract egalitarian principle that every citizen has a right to be treated as an equal by his or her own particular government. I do not wish to downplay the moral wickedness of murder, kidnap and torture. Rather, my point is that such treatment is first and foremost an affront to the equal importance of human life as distinct from the special obligations of political communities.

To underline this point, many of the most inegalitarian groups and political agencies *do not* reject the principle that governments must treat every member of the political community with equal concern and respect. What they reject is the principle of equal consideration for those they believe are *not* genuine members of the political community as they see it. Putting the same point another way, if one looks beneath the surface of even the most abhorrent political group or regime, what one finds lacking is not a commitment to equality *per se* but a commitment to equality for *all*. The hard work, therefore, lies in trying to show with uncontroversial evidence and unerring logic that these groups and regimes base their persecution or casting out of certain peoples on erroneous assumptions. Human beings have had a lot of experience of racist governments, through the centuries and the results are far from reassuring. Even when they have acknowledged some morally relevant similarities between people, it can be extremely difficult to get them to relinquish their deeply held belief that certain other dissimilarities are decisive in determining membership of the political community. Needless to say, if a racist government conceded that blacks were equal to whites in all relevant respects but continued to claim that whites were nevertheless owed superior treatment, then it would be violating the well-known ethical imperative that one ought to treat like cases alike. Yet this is rarely the case with actual racists. We might think that racists are by and large deeply ignorant about other races as well as profoundly mistaken about which similarities or differences are morally decisive, but it would be a mistake, I think, simply to assume that they are simpletons incapable of following basic rules of moral reasoning.

Of course, nowhere does Dworkin claim that acceptance of abstract egalitarian rights always makes a difference in politics. Rather, he claims that acceptance of these rights *can* make a difference in *some* important cases. But the crucial point is that in order for abstract egalitarian rights to do the kind of work that we can reasonably expect them to do in important cases it seems necessary that they are rights which, in principle, can be held even by outcasts. Arguably this means that we should refocus our energies on the principal task of trying to dispel prejudice and uncover aspects of human nature and of human interactions which can provide the basis for egalitarian rights that transcend political community. I shall have more to say about this task below.

Oiling the wheels of debate and mutual understanding

In reply to the above, however, it might be countered that the true significance of the egalitarian plateau hypothesis lies less in the contingent histories of actual political groups and regimes and more in the fact that such rights are important in understanding the work of modern political theorists. It is crucial to realise (so the thought runs) that libertarians, utilitarians and liberal egalitarians each defend the policies they do ultimately because they believe that all people are entitled to equal concern from government and because it matters how each person's life goes and it matters equally. How can one possibly subscribe to these doctrines without at the same time endorsing equality in the abstract sense?

Even if this is true, however, it remains unclear what is to be gained by saying that these theories are all egalitarian, abstractly speaking, when we appear to be saying something far more illuminating by pointing out that they have very different substantive implications; as certainly they do.

Perhaps the idea is that abstract egalitarian rights provide an opportunity for effective discourse between mainstream political theorists if nothing else. The fact that libertarians, utilitarians and liberal egalitarians are all trying to understand and interpret *the same* abstract egalitarian rights might help to facilitate meaningful dialogue and mutual critical evaluation between them; something that might not be possible under the rubric of value pluralism. Nevertheless, it is important to bear in mind that an opportunity for effective discourse can be understood in more or less demanding ways. It could mean discourse that has *a good chance of resulting in a winner*. But then it is hard to see how this could be the case. Take the familiar debate among contemporary political philosophers about what it means to treat citizens as equals in the sense of respecting the separateness of persons. Utilitarians, libertarians and liberal egalitarians of different hues all believe that only *their* theories and recommended policies treat people with equal respect in this sense, and so they remain in deadlock (cf. Rawls, 1972, pp. 27, 101–2; Nozick, 1974, p. 214; Kymlicka, 2002, p. 52, n.16; Fleurbaey, 2002, p. 90).

Alternatively, the suggestion might be that occupying the plateau provides a kind of shared vocabulary for debate so that participants are at least able to *understand* one another even if they cannot persuade the other to change sides. The benefit is that disputants will be on the same wavelength and not merely talking passed one another (Kymlicka, 2002, pp. 4–5). For assume instead that utilitarians, libertarians and liberal egalitarians each appeal to a different ultimate value such that their theories are incommensurable in that sense. Surely we invite the dead-end conclusion that one theorist cannot meaningfully comment on or criticise the theory of another. The problem with this suggestion, however, is that the disputants seem to be operating with such different understandings of what it means to show equal concern and respect that the mere fact that they are using the same vocabulary seems weak against the charge of incommensurability. Furthermore, it is quite conceivable that a similar degree of dialogue and mutual understanding between contemporary political theorists could be obtained if the vocabulary of rights to equal concern and respect were replaced with a more simple vocabulary of 'justice', 'fairness' and 'rights'.

Alternatively, perhaps the idea is that by viewing an ethical theory of social arrangement as a conception of abstract equality it is thereby possible to intensify one's appreciation or *approval* of that theory. Now it is certainly conceivable how this is true for some people, especially those who are already deeply committed to abstract egalitarian principles. But it must also be conceded that this may not be the case for people who are not committed to abstract equality in the first place, or who take their fundamental impulse to be something different. Must a libertarian, for example, come to have a deeper commitment to his own theory as a result of his realisation that it can be presented as one possible interpretation of abstract egalitarian rights? Arguably having a deep commitment to libertarianism has more to do with the belief that liberty is supremely valuable or that everybody has a natural right to self-ownership than with the thought that a government has a special obligation to treat its own citizens with equal concern and respect.

To be sure, being able to declare that a great many very different political theories can be presented as interpretations of the same abstract egalitarian principle adds a certain kind of elegance to the description of the current state of play in political theory. But this is beside the point if the hypothesis of an egalitarian plateau, as stated by Dworkin and others, lacks any real clarificatory power and flatters to deceive both in respect of explaining people's deep attachment to their favoured political theories and in terms of bringing out otherwise obscure or hidden implications. Notwithstanding all this, let us now examine why Dworkin himself believes that the acceptance of abstract egalitarian rights matters in political argument.

The impossibility of denial

In his 1983 article, 'In Defense of Equality', Dworkin claims that '[t]he best, perhaps the only, argument for the egalitarian principle lies in the implausibility of denying any of the components that make it up' (Dworkin, 1983, p. 32). Suppose for the sake of argument that equality of resources is the best conception of equal concern and, moreover, that equality of resources demands a programme of subsidised medicine financed from general taxation. How could anyone coherently reject such a programme? He considers three possibilities. First, a person might reject the programme by claiming that whilst it matters what happens to his or her own life and it matters to other people what happens to them, it does not matter from the standpoint of politics whether *any* citizen's life is good or bad. Dworkin insists that this claim is simply not plausible. 'I do not see how we could construct any general justification of political action [...] that does not assume that it is important what happens in people's lives' (p. 33). The reason is that 'this is the assumption on which people are invited to participate in politics, for example, or the only assumption on which it makes sense for them to accept the invitation' (*ibid.*). A second possibility is for someone to reject a programme of subsidised health care on the grounds of some other more important political ideal or interest, such as public culture or low taxes (pp. 33–4). In response to this, however, he argues that since it is not possible to say how much money should be spent on public culture or how much of a person's income ought to be exempt from taxation in general without knowing what resources people are entitled to *ex ante*, these other ideals and interests cannot be regarded as being in conflict with equality (*ibid.*). A third possibility is for a person to reject subsidised medical treatment because they suppose that though it matters how people's lives go from the standpoint of politics, 'it matters more how some lives go than others'. Dworkin claims, however, that it is hard to conceive how members of genuine political communities could ever come to think about other people's lives in this way if those people are 'accepted and treated as members of the community' (p. 35).

I think that these arguments give the egalitarian plateau a new lease of life, but not for long. That there is something suspect becomes obvious as soon as one begins to reflect more closely on Dworkin's response to the third possibility. Even if it is true that one cannot conceive of a member of a genuine political community believing that his or her own life is more valuable than the lives of other genuine members, surely this is to assume precisely what is at stake. One wants to know why we should adopt the plateau and the reason given is that a member of a genuine political community could not coherently view other citizen's lives as having less importance than his or her own and so cannot help but accept the best interpretation of what the plateau is. In other words, Dworkin interprets what it means to be a member of a genuine political community in terms of the idea that one's life is regarded by others as having the same importance. But the question is: why should we adopt this idea of political community?

Surely the more pressing political issue concerns people living within political communities who are not generally accepted and treated as members of the community. Take the case of asylum seekers, illegal immigrants, economic migrants of various kinds and religious isolationist groups. Suppose members of the genuine political community believe that the lives of these other people are less valuable than their own and that as such they have fewer rights. Given the suffering and frustration that is faced by these minorities, and the difficulties caused for the genuine community as a result of tensions between them, might it be more profitable to find a political argument that will convince such people to occupy an egalitarian plateau *with* these other people as opposed to *against* these other people? Would not that be a far more meaningful and important political project in a world of mass migration and pluralism? If the nature of the abstract egalitarian rights conceived by Dworkin are such that they give political communities the right to withhold basic rights and liberties as well as important social services from these vulnerable groups, or even to treat them with general hostility, contempt, prejudice and lack of understanding, then so much for this conception of abstract egalitarian rights.

Holding our politicians to account

Nevertheless, Dworkin has a second reason for caring about the plateau up his sleeve. Given that abstract rights to equal concern and respect are held against a particular government and not governments in general, they provide citizens with a *distinctive* opportunity to hold their own political representatives to account. People can, in other words, call upon their special rights to force their own politicians to explain just exactly how they think current policies treat them as equals and thereby to force those in power to pay closer attention to substantive inequalities within the community. As he puts it,

> Rejecting the principle altogether seems out of the question for us; it is no longer arguable, at least in public, that officials should be more concerned about the lives of some citizens than about the lives of others.
>
> (Dworkin, 1987a, p. 8)

More specifically, Dworkin claims that it would be 'unwise' to abandon the abstract right to equal concern in addressing questions of distributive justice – such as whether citizens should have equal income or merely sufficient income to meet their basic needs – because this would open up the following possibility. Suppose we elect a government that is committed to satisfying minimum needs only. Experience has shown us that such governments tend not to think very generously when considering where the minimum level should be set. So if we permit our politicians to ignore the question of what it means to treat members of the political community with equal concern, we risk allowing them to ignore gross inequalities (Dworkin, 2000, pp. 2–3).

The idea that occupying the egalitarian plateau provides a sharp critical tool for holding our political representatives to account is certainly an interesting one, but it is also rather puzzling. In so far as these are our elected representatives, then presumably they already owe us accountability. If we are already owed accountability by *our* politicians, why do we need to occupy the egalitarian plateau as well? Thus suppose someone believes that his government should, as a matter of justice, act to bring about a redistribution of wealth beyond the point of a bare minimum, where this means a far more generous improvement in the position of the least advantaged than is currently called for by mainstream politicians. Why does such a person need to appeal to egalitarian rights to make his case? Why not simply argue that *justice* demands greater equality, that the poor have a right to live in a just society and that politicians have a duty to deliver justice wherever feasible? On the other hand, suppose someone believes instead that justice demands *no more* of governments than that they satisfy the minimum needs of all citizens. Surely this kind of conviction about justice can feed directly into a person's critical judgement of politicians. On this person's understanding of the demands of social justice, it simply would not be fair for politicians to do more than meet basic needs. Either way, talk of abstract egalitarian rights can be eliminated from the act of holding-politicians-to-account without any genuine loss.

I have now examined five very different kinds of reason for thinking that it matters in political debate whether or not we accept Dworkin's version of the egalitarian plateau. Some of these reasons lacked force in relation to the special nature of abstract egalitarian rights, while others lacked force in relation to the egalitarian nature of abstract egalitarian rights. If I am right, then we are yet to find a strong answer to the question with which we started. Strictly speaking, Dworkin might be quite correct to say that virtually every serious political theory of the past 200 years or so can be interpreted as egalitarian at heart. But it remains something of a mystery what point and purpose the egalitarian plateau is supposed to serve.

However, this chapter is not intended to be purely negative. The goal of the foregoing discussion was not to reject outright the egalitarian plateau thesis. It was not to deny that Dworkin's special rights can

have some value in certain political contexts, especially in those con
texts where it is important to emphasise that governments owe citizen
equal concern and respect. Nevertheless, I believe that some examples
demand a different kind of abstract egalitarian right. More specifically
they demand abstract egalitarian rights that are general as opposed to
special in nature; assuming, of course, that such rights can exist. In
other words, I think that Dworkin has failed to notice an additiona
role that abstract egalitarian rights might play in political argument
because he has failed to recognise different kinds of abstract egalitarian
rights. Hence I believe that a better account can be sought by asking a
more fundamental question.

Equality among whom?

It bears notice that much of the scholarly literature on the idea of equality in the decades prior to Dworkin's own work focused more on the
underlying assumption that there is something shared by *all* human
beings which entitles them to certain kinds of equal concern and respect
from other people than on the issue of how to understand the special
rights possessed by citizens viewed as members of true political communities.[2] This provenance is perhaps not all that unsurprising given the
connection that many philosophers have drawn between the idea of
equality and the idea of humanity. Why bother with equality either as
an abstract right of political society or as a collection of substantive egalitarian aims if you do not think that in some sense all individuals living
in a society are entitled to equal concern and respect *qua* human beings?
So we have every reason to be interested in the question, 'Equality
among whom?'

   The further one proceeds in the direction of discussing what it means
to be a member of a true political community the greater the distance
one travels from the idea of egalitarian rights grounded in humanity.
Why so? If the acceptance of abstract rights to equal concern and respect
amounts to little more than an assertion that only members of certain
kinds of communities are entitled to treatment as equals *qua* members –
to an assertion of the special responsibilities connected with coercive
power and the special status of fraternal association, for example – then
almost inevitably one's political principles become far more concerned
with what some people have in common than with what every human
being has in common. I suspect that if genuine progress is to be made on
the topic of equality, then thinkers need to turn their attention once
again to the question, 'In virtue of what characteristics can we say that

all human beings are equal in a sense that would make them worthy of treatment as equals by the rest of humanity?'

Although there is still much that is unresolved and little that can be regarded as uncontroversial in this debate about the nature of human equality, some answers are more plausible than others. One very crude answer appeals to the fact of equality. It says that because all human beings are equal (in some dimension to be specified) all human beings should be treated as equals. The obvious problem here is that one cannot move from an 'is' to an 'ought' without additional premises. So the difficulty is to provide a plausible account of what it is about human beings that makes them equal in a way that might justify treatment as equals. Focusing on any particular set of physical or mental capacities leaves the field of debate susceptible to malign forces. Focusing on mental capacities, for example, might unwittingly provide material for those who seek to justify the systematic mistreatment of people who are severely mentally ill. An extreme but still relevant example is the Nazi treatment of the mentally ill and handicapped at Hadamar from 1933 to 1945.

Kant, of course, attempted to detach the question of the moral worth of human beings from empirical contingencies through the idea of rational beings, viewed as ends in themselves. Nevertheless, the property of rational nature cannot exist without supervening upon physical properties in some way. Indeed, Kantian ethics rests on the fundamental duties to protect and promote rational nature (Kant, 1785), where rational nature consists in animal instincts, the ability to give oneself the moral law and the mental capacities and physical aptitudes which enable persons to rationally form and pursue different ends (1793). But once we let physical properties back in, we open up the possibility of differing degrees of humanity, and perhaps differing degrees of value.

For these reasons, some philosophers have argued that it is better to concede the point that not all persons are equal in fact, but argue instead that since these differences are often undeserved or a matter of brute luck, there is no justification for certain sorts of unequal treatment. This response embraces the fact that people differ in their possession of human qualities but insists that some shortfalls are not something for which individuals should be held responsible. Herbert Spiegelberg expressed the idea quite simply as 'undeserved discriminations call for redress' (Spiegelberg, 1944, p. 113).

It is, I think, Rawls' brief discussion of Spiegelberg's principle of redress which, amongst other things, leads some commentators to trace the roots of luck egalitarianism back to Rawls. But this is a short-sighted interpretation of Rawls, not least because of his explicit rejection of the principle of redress (Rawls, 1971, pp. 100–1).[3] Rawls himself attempted to sidestep some of the difficulties faced by Kant by appealing to a *political* as opposed to *metaphysical* conception of the person. On this view, citizens are viewed as free and equal by virtue of their possession of two moral powers: the capacity to understand, to apply and to act from principles of justice and the capacity to have, to revise and to rationally pursue a conception of the good. Of course, he justifies this assumption – along with various other assumptions built into justice as fairness – on the grounds that they reflect fixed points of agreement within the public political culture of Western liberal societies (see Rawls, 1980; 1985; 1996).

However, it can be further argued that appealing to any one conception of intrinsic importance – including Rawls' two moral powers – will founder on the rocks of its own particularity. Surely it is possible, and entirely appropriate, for reasonable people to disagree about why it is that human beings have intrinsic value. So, for example, what reason do we have to suppose that religious people should accept a liberal interpretation of moral powers as a basis for political morality? Perhaps some groups will not wish to understand the objective value of each human life in terms of a capacity to form and revise a conception of the good preferring instead an interpretation which says that each human life is valuable in the eyes of God or that all human beings are capable of understanding and living in accordance with the will of Allah. This pluralism of conceptions of the principle of equal human value has obvious implications both for deeply plural political communities and for principles of international justice. I shall say more about the latter in Chapter 7. For these reasons Dworkin takes a slightly different route in answering these tricky questions and this is what I wish to explore now.

Human dignity and wider political debates

In his *Is Democracy Possible Here?* Dworkin attempts to shed further light on the question of how political debate is possible within a divided nation like the United States. He argues that debate is possible because 'almost all of us, in spite of our great and evident differences', share two principles of human dignity. The first is 'the principle of intrinsic value': 'that each human life has a special kind of objective importance' (Dworkin, 2006, p. 9). Faced with the thorny task of explaining what it is about human beings that gives them intrinsic value, Dworkin provides an individualistic answer. It is built into the second principle of human dignity ('the principle of personal responsibility') that individuals possess a special responsibility for identifying what this value is such that nobody else 'has the right to dictate those personal values to him or impose them on him without his endorsement' (p. 10). This does not mean that a person may never defer to the judgements of value offered by political or religious leaders. Rather, the idea is that deference must be the individual's own decision and cannot be foisted upon him or her. The result is that a government cannot claim to uphold the principles of human dignity if it distributes resources or opportunities on the basis that the lives of some citizens have greater intrinsic worth than others. And a government cannot pretend to respect personal responsibility if it routinely constrains liberty and/or distributes resources or opportunities in such a way as to dictate to individual citizens what it means to have an intrinsically worthwhile life (chs. 1, 3 and 4).

If this is right, then what *really* matters in political discourse is not our acceptance of abstract rights to equal concern and respect after all. Rather, it is our acceptance of the even deeper common ground that we share. That is, for Dworkin, it is acceptance of the two principles of human dignity which makes political debate in the United States possible and profitable. Perhaps this is less applicable to non-liberal countries. But even if one focused exclusively on the United States and other like-minded liberal countries, the retreat to the two principles of human dignity invites the following fairly obvious question. If it is necessary in the end to appeal to human dignity in order to facilitate debate or to hold politicians to account, then what is the rationale for defending a theory of political morality that underscores special egalitarian rights? Putting the same question more strongly, why are Dworkin's egalitarian rights still important in a world where people are increasingly calling on their *human rights* as a way of holding *their own* governments to account?

Dworkin's answer to this question is to recommend that we be more careful in the appeals we make to human rights. In fact, a 'core list' of human rights should be reserved for special cases in which acts, such as genocide or torture, are so inhuman that they cannot be interpreted as living up to principles of human dignity on any 'intelligible' interpretation (Dworkin, 2006, pp. 35–6). An appeal to the abstract right to equal concern and respect, on the other hand, is appropriate for more mundane cases, such as when a government permits an unjust distribution of income and wealth (pp. 94–5). If I am right, then Dworkin's model of modern political argument presents us with the choice of adopting, depending on the case, either a discourse of human dignity and human rights, which is universalist yet limited to non-comparative human interests, or a discourse of human dignity combined with equal concern and respect, which is more recognisably 'egalitarian' yet tied to the internal life of true political communities.

I prefer a different model of the point and purpose of principles of human dignity in political argument. It seems to me that principles of human dignity are important in political argument not merely because they force politicians to think seriously about human rights but also because they force politicians to think harder about the *content* and *scope* of the egalitarian plateau and of the concrete egalitarian rights that *it* proclaims. It requires politicians, in other words, to think about a wider class of persons who might have rights to equal concern and respect arising from considerations of human dignity.

There are numerous areas of political life in which this line of thinking about the scope of the egalitarian plateau could make a real difference. But for now I shall limit myself to the case of illegal immigrants who live within a state without full citizenship rights or who are only given full citizenship rights after long difficult periods of residence. Such people are treated − both overtly and covertly − as less than equal by public officials and the wider community. Employers pray on their status to offer them exploitative terms and conditions of employment; landlords cram them into living quarters that few ordinary citizens would accept; the welfare state denies them access to basic housing. What difference would it make if we accepted the idea of a right to equal concern and respect that can be claimed by every human being living within a given territory as opposed to only citizens? Opinions will differ about what these rights demand in practice. But at the very least immigrants will have the same abstract right to equal concern and respect as other resident citizens. Rainer Baubock, for example, interprets Dworkin's abstract rights to equal concern and respect as implying that it is arbitrary for governments to discriminate between individuals within their territories on grounds of place of birth since this is something which lies beyond their control. According to Baubock, this means that minorities are entitled to a catalogue of citizenship, representation, economic and cultural rights, including rights against discrimination of various kinds (Baubock, 1996, pp. 214–15).

In this chapter I have critically examined Dworkin's account of the egalitarian plateau. I have argued that abstract rights to equal concern and respect, as conceived by Dworkin, do not always have the force in political argument that one might reasonably expect them to have mainly because they are tied to membership of a political community.

I have argued that in some instances it could make better sense to posit egalitarian rights borne by human beings rather than citizens. Needless to say, the treatment of immigrants is not the only question to which these rights might be applied. So in Part II, I extend these unbounded egalitarian rights to matters of global distributive justice. The question 'Equality among whom?' is important because it forces an interpreter to consider not merely whether or not every political community has its own egalitarian plateau but also whether there are egalitarian rights which join these plateaus together to make a single, much larger table-land. If he stands on a national egalitarian plateau and looks upwards to the sky, an interpreter will see the overarching principles of human dignity. So he tries to make sense of these principles as best he can. He may even claim that he occupies this egalitarian plateau because of his commitment to these overarching principles. If he looks down at the valley below, he will see different attempts to interpret the meaning and content of the plateau on which he stands. Equality of resources is one such attempt. My ambition in the remainder of this book is to look horizontally into the distance to see whether or not there is an egalitarian plateau that transcends state borders. I shall argue that abstract egalitarian rights can play a role in debates on global distributive justice. But obviously in order to have any significant impact these rights must be given content. So we still need a good answer to the question, 'What is (global) equality?'

Part II

5
Political Community and Beyond

During the same period of time in which Dworkin has been perfecting his theory of equality for life within liberal democracies, another group of political theorists have been arguing that the demands of socio-economic justice are operative not merely within states but also across state borders (see Beitz, 1979, Part 3; Barry, 1982; Shue, 1983; Pogge, 1989, ch. 6; Moellendorf, 2002; Tan, 2004; Caney, 2005). Many of these cosmopolitan thinkers make the suggestion that if every human life has intrinsic worth and equally so – perhaps because all human beings share a capacity for suffering and an ability to form and pursue meaningful conceptions of the good – it remains unclear why the duty to show equal concern and respect is limited only to those whom the government governs and to fellow citizens. If these capacities are shared by every human being and not just by those one regards as fellow members of a narrow political community, then to restrict the scope of economic rights to domestic politics seems arbitrary from a moral point of view. What is more, some scholars of international law now point to the creation of juridical entitlements in the areas of foreign aid, price stabilisation, trade, lending and the global commons based on overarching principles of distributive justice (Franck, 1995).[1]

Thus far Dworkin has been reluctant to make a similar move on the grounds that distributive justice is peculiar to true political communities and not arbitrarily so. The aim of this chapter is to critically examine this assumption. While it may be difficult to interpret current international affairs as displaying the characteristics which Dworkin identifies with a true political community, I intend to argue nevertheless that the two principles of human dignity do point in the direction of global egalitarian rights. I shall argue that these rights apply to various rules, institutions, practices and individual actions, not all of which have received the attention they deserve. Among the sites of global distributive justice that have been discussed at length in the literature are trade tariffs and structural adjustment policies. But I try to show that certain other international practices are also appropriately governed by principles of justice given the profound and pervasive impact they have on people's lives. I have in mind not only the international exploitation of, and trade in, natural resources but also foreign aid including official development assistance and humanitarian aid. Having established these additional sites for the application of global egalitarian rights, Chapter 6 sets out to interpret these rights in terms of the abstract idea of global luck egalitarianism, while Chapter 7 further refines this interpretation by developing a version of global equality of resources.

Three ways of doing normative political theory at the global level

Of the political theorists who grapple with the question of distributive justice at the global level, many subscribe to moral cosmopolitanism: the view that individuals are the ultimate units of moral concern and that the intrinsic worth that attaches to human beings attaches to every human being equally (see Pogge, 1992a, p. 48; 2002, p. 169; Tan, 2004, p. 1). Moral cosmopolitanism dovetails with at least one of the two principles of human dignity upheld by Dworkin, namely, the principle of intrinsic value. The crucial difference arises, however, when we move from the level of deep moral principle to particular domains of social activity. Dworkin subscribes to the view that the principle of intrinsic value does not imply principles of egalitarian justice outside of the context of a true political community. The political cosmopolitan, by contrast, affirms that world affairs are just if and only if equal concern and respect is shown across state borders and not merely within borders. But how can the political cosmopolitan justify this move?

Consider three principal methods. The first begins with *a priori* moral reasoning the purpose of which is to establish independent principles of justice. These principles are independent in the sense that we do not draft them with an eye on the spheres of human life to which they are to be applied (cf. Cohen, 2003). Only when we come to reflect on particular circumstances do we consider making pragmatic compromises. By way of illustration, Robert Goodin starts from the fundamental moral conviction that everyone has a general duty of justice to aid the vulnerable everywhere, where being in a position to help is enough to generate a responsibility to do so, provided that this is not unreasonably burdensome (Goodin, 1985). In the case of international affairs, however, considerations of efficiency and a recognition of people's deep psychological attachments to fellow countrymen come into play and influence how the independent principles of justice are best realised (1988, pp. 681–2).

The second begins with *a posteriori* investigation into the rules, institutions, practices and individual interactions which are intended to be governed by principles of justice. This investigation feeds into the design of justice from the start so that its principles are bespoke. The *a posteriori* method heeds Rawls' dictum that 'the correct regulative principle for a thing depends on the nature of that thing' (Rawls, 1971, p. 29).[2] Examples of this method abound in the literature. In his *Political Theory and International Relations*, Beitz lights on socio-economic *interdependencies* between people living in different parts of the world. He argues from these interdependencies to the conclusion that the wealth generated by 'cooperative activity' among rich and poor countries should be distributed to the benefit of the global poor (Beitz, 1979, Part 3). Pogge's *institutional* argument begins in a somewhat similar way but concludes differently. He looks at the rules governing international trade, the conditions tied to loans to the developing world, and the resource and borrowing privileges given to corrupt rulers across the globe, and argues that they generate *negative rights* on the part of persons not to be harmed by these things. The upshot is that each and every person has a negative duty not to support an global institutional order that leaves people severely poor and is coercively imposed on them in the sense that it is not voluntarily accepted or cannot easily be avoided (Pogge, 2002a; 2005a; 2005b). More recently, Joshua Cohen and Charles Sabel outline a view which they call *weak institutionalism*. According to this view, 'the existence of an institution with responsibilities for distributing a particular good (education, or health, or decent wages and working conditions, for example) is necessary and sufficient to require that institution to meet the obligation of equal concern in fulfilling its responsibility' (Cohen and Sabel, 2006, p. 153). By way of illustration, in his 2008 book, *Just Health: Meeting Health Needs Fairly*, Norman Daniels argues that organisations such as the WHO must show equal concern in the distribution of public health expertise and technology (Daniels, 2008, p. 352).

I think that there is much we can learn from both of these methods and illustrations thereof. But I also think that neither method quite captures the kind of enterprise in which we ought to be engaged. The third method I have in mind is that of *constructive interpretation*. As outlined in Chapter 1, this method also begins by asking questions of the form, 'What kinds of institutions, rules, practices and individual actions are we engaged in at the global level?' but it also asks, 'What is the real point and purpose of these things?', 'When are these things at their best?' and 'What out ought to be the point and purpose of these thing given the deeper common ground that we all share?' Putting these questions together, one possible justification for thinking that principles of egalitarian justice apply at the global level is that to think that they do would offer the best interpretation of the principles of human dignity within that domain given the best interpretation of the things to which these principles of justice apply.

One of the virtues of this methodology is that we are not beholden to what the authors of international agreements think. To illustrate, many writers find Rawls' characterisations of a just liberal society or a just society of peoples unattractive. But some find these characterisations unattractive not in the sense that they do not regard them as accurate presentations of what are in fact widely held beliefs within the public political culture of the societies or the society of peoples in question. Rather, they find them unattractive in the deeper sense that they believe that these characterisations do not show these societies or the society of peoples in the best possible light. They claim that although Rawls may have expressed rather well our current state of thinking about justice domestically and globally, he has not expressed what justice could or should be. For example, many people reject Rawls' picture of a society of peoples as a society of mutual recognition. Evidently some people reject it on the grounds that it fails to reflect how the authors of international law and institutions intended these things. They argue that it ignores certain egalitarian features of core international documents such as the Universal Declaration of Human Rights (Hayden, 2002, p. 136). But others make the different criticism that Rawls' characterisation of mutual recognition (a matter of keeping the peace, respecting sovereignty, upholding basic human rights and assisting burdened peoples) neglects to show the society of peoples in its best light given a deeper understanding of what it means to respect human value, either because it eschews principles of distributive justice altogether (Beitz, 2000) or because the duty to assist burdened peoples is not demanding enough (Tasioulas, 2005). I believe that constructive interpretation is better placed to account for these more fundamental criticisms.

Of course, it is one thing to take up the attitude of constructive interpretation, quite another to use this attitude to identify sites of global egalitarianism in a way that is convincing. Before showing how I think this can be done, I want first to address Dworkin's reluctance to apply justice as equal concern and respect globally.

On the assumption that equality is peculiar to true political communities

This is best explained by the fact that Dworkin interprets the right to equal concern and respect as a special as opposed to general egalitarian right. Citizens of a true political community can possess egalitarian rights against *their own* political communities but not against other political communities around the world. That is, citizens can possess (special) *domestic* but not (general) *global* egalitarian rights. But what, more exactly, is a true political community?

Dominion and legitimacy

According to Dworkin, a 'bare' political community is characterised in part by the dominion of its government over its citizenry, but one of the hallmarks of a true political community is legitimate government, where legitimate government depends on showing equal concern for all citizens. As he puts it,

> No government is legitimate that does not show equal concern for the fate of all those over whom it claims dominion and from whom it claims allegiance. Equal concern is the sovereign virtue of political community – without it government is only tyranny – and when a nation's wealth is very unequally distributed, as the wealth of even very prosperous nations now is, then its equal concern is suspect.
>
> (Dworkin, 2000, p. 1)

The term 'dominion' can be read, I think, as meaning political communities that form or acquire governments which claim a monopoly on the exercise of coercive power over all citizens within a given terrain (cf. Dworkin, 1986, p. 188). That the exercise of dominion creates a special responsibility to treat citizens with equal concern and respect is clear enough. Otherwise there would be no requirement for prejudiced, discriminatory or tyrannical rulers to treat their citizens as equals. Much less clear is whether dominions are the *only* entities that we can or should say this about. Michael Blake argues that issues of distributive justice, in the sense of concern with relative deprivation, only arise among those who 'share liability to a coercive system of political and legal institutions' (Blake, 2001, p. 264). On this view, coercion 'expresses a relationship of domination, violating the autonomy of the individual by replacing that individual's chosen plans and pursuits with those of another' (p. 272). This has important implications for global justice debates. For if there is no such thing as a global sovereign which exercises dominion over all nations on Earth, then, according to one reading, the members of poor nations have no right to expect equal concern from the members of wealthy nations. This appears to be Dworkin's view.

In what follows I shall have much more to say about the possibility of global dominion, but at this stage I wish to stress the fact that although equal concern is an important dimension of legitimacy, and legitimacy is one of the things that distinguishes bare political communities from true political communities, it is not the only thing. Dworkin also wants to highlight a range of other political virtues as being characteristic of a true political community. So in that sense legitimacy is merely part of what is needed to complete a set of sufficient conditions for something's being interpreted as a true political community, and it is to these other conditions that I now turn.

Democracy

Dworkin argues that something can be considered a true political community only when its political processes live up to a democratic ideal.

> A political community that exercises dominion over its own citizens, and demands from them allegiance and obedience to its laws, must take up an impartial, objective attitude toward them all, and each of its citizens must vote, and its officials must enact laws and form governmental policies, with that responsibility in mind.
>
> (Dworkin, 2000, p. 6)

In other words, as a true political community is one that accepts the abstract egalitarian principle so the most appropriate form of democracy is one that affords equal voting rights and other forms of equal participation to all citizens (1987b; 2006, ch. 5). The intimate connection between being a member of a true political community and democratic involvement is summed up in the following passage from *A Matter of Principle*:

> If people are asked to sacrifice for their community, they must be offered some reason why the community which benefits from that sacrifice is their community; there must be some reason why, for example, the unemployed blacks of Detroit should take more interest

in either the public virtue or the future generations of Michigan than they do in those of Mali. [...] He can identify himself with the future of the community and accept present deprivation as sacrifice rather than tyranny, only if he has some power to help determine the shape of that future, and only if the promised prosperity will provide at least equal benefit to the smaller, more immediate communities for which he feels special responsibilities, for example, his family, his descendents, and, if the society is one that has made this important to him, his race.

(1985, p. 211)

The issue of democratic involvement is pertinent to the present discussion about global distributive justice for this reason. In his 'The Problem of Global Justice', Nagel argues that there is something normatively peculiar about the state, only this peculiarity is not captured by the mere existence of dominion or coercive power. To speak sensibly of the demands of justice as equal concern 'requires a collectively imposed social framework, enacted in the name of all those governed by it, and aspiring to command their acceptance of its authority even when they disagree with the substance of its decisions' (Nagel, 2005, p. 140). What creates the special presumption in favour of treating all citizens as equals, in other words, is 'that we are both putative joint authors of the coercively imposed system, and subject to its norms, i.e., expected to accept their authority even when the collective decision diverges from our personal preferences' (pp. 128–9). According to Nagel, it is because of the fact that the active engagement of the will of each member of a society is crucial for appropriately raising questions of justice as equal concern and because of the fact that this engagement is peculiar to states that we can say the state is the largest social system in which it makes sense to raise questions of justice as equal concern. For similar reasons, Dworkin seems to be saying that part of what creates and then sustains the special presumption in favour of equal concern within a true political community is that a democratic government acts in the name of all its citizens. In a context where this ideal of egalitarian democracy is unattainable or inappropriate for some reason, the special case for equal concern starts to vanish.

Integrity

Integrity is another important dimension of true political community. Dworkin believes that legal integrity is a matter of the consistent application of substantive legal principles seasoned with larger considerations of justice, not least the consideration that each member 'is as worthy as any other, that each must be treated with equal concern according to some coherent conception of what that means' (Dworkin, 1986, p. 213). Clearly legal rules ought to be applied in a consistent, even-handed manner and in accordance with a single vision of justice rather than being swayed by narrow self-interest, discrimination, prejudice, fear or weakness of will. But to qualify as integrity there must also be 'a concern by each for all that is sufficiently special, personal, pervasive, and egalitarian to ground communal obligations according to standards for communal obligation we elsewhere accept' (p. 216). Since integrity is defined, in part, by relations of equal concern, Dworkin affirms that '[i]ntegrity holds within political communities, not among them' (p. 185).

According to Dworkin, a government that displays the virtue of integrity can claim moral legitimacy for its use of coercive force (Dworkin, 1986, p. 188) and can do so in the name of fraternity (p. 214).[3] But he also makes it clear that this is not the only advantage of integrity. If the government of a true political community shows integrity, there is the possibility of continuity between the fundamental public conception of justice and the formal legislation that characterises political life. When there are conflicts of interest between members of the political community, for example, each party *qua* citizen can look to the vision of justice of his community as the appropriate arbiter (pp. 189–90). This aspect of integrity is especially relevant to international affairs. One barrier to applying Dworkin's ideal of integrity to this domain is the fact that international disputes (on trade, for example) often involve sovereign states who are not committed to a common scheme of justice. Even where common principles of justice can be found, they tend to be based on good faith and fair play rather than equal concern. I shall say more about these problems below.

Fraternity

Whereas the virtues of legitimacy, democracy and integrity focus on the relationship between those in power and those who are governed, fraternity has much more to do with the relationship between members of the community. The basic thought is that a true political community is characterised, in part, by a certain kind of fraternal relationship between its members. But what is the nature of this relationship? Dworkin rejects the idea that membership of a fraternity must be based on consent. Nor does it depend on emotional attachments which presuppose that each member of the group has some kind of acquaintance with all of the others (Dworkin, 1986, pp. 196–7). Nevertheless, he insists that not every political community will involve associative obligations which are rightly described as fraternal. One must be careful to distinguish between the accidental genetic, geographical or historical conditions that cause people to become members of bare political communities from the normative conditions that are necessary to transform a bare political community into a true political community, where true political communities are those with fraternal obligations (pp. 196–8). According to Dworkin, in order to count as a fraternity it must be possible to interpret the members of the group as holding certain attitudes about the responsibilities they owe one another. Specifically, they must 'share a general and diffuse sense of members' special rights and responsibilities from or toward one another, a sense of what sort and level of sacrifice one may be expected to make for another' (p. 199).

What is this shared sense of sacrifice? Dworkin identifies four essential features. First, members of the political community 'must regard the groups' obligations as *special*, holding distinctly within the group, rather than as general duties its members owe equally to persons outside it' (Dworkin, 1986, p. 199). Second, they must accept that the obligations are owed to each member of the group rather than to the group as a collective entity *(ibid.)*. Third, 'members must see their responsibilities as flowing from a more general duty each has of *concern* for the well-being of others in the group' (p. 200). (Note, even though Dworkin describes this as 'a more general duty', it is still a special duty in the crucial sense that it is owed to co-members only.) Fourth, they must suppose that the duty of concern is a duty of equal concern for other members, meaning that no member's life is seen as intrinsically more valuable than any other member's life. Dworkin thinks that it is relatively uncontroversial that any deeply discriminatory or hierarchical society is unlikely to satisfy this last condition of fraternity (pp. 200–1). Although the members of a political community must hold these attitudes in order for them to be considered members of a fraternal political community, Dworkin argues that it is unnecessary for these attitudes to be conscious or explicit (pp. 199, 215). The possession of these attitudes is 'an interpretive property'. So it is enough that we can interpret their actions as though they had these attitudes as opposed to saying that the attitude must be 'a psychological property of some fixed number of the actual members' (p. 201).

This account leaves unanswered the question of what proportion of the community must be treating each other in ways that can be plausibly interpreted as fraternal for that community to be considered a true community. But putting that question to one side and returning to the question of global justice, Dworkin might say that a lack of fraternity in the world of states provides a further barrier to the extension of principles of domestic justice into the global sphere. In other words:

> We suppose that we have special interests in and obligations toward other members of our own nation. Americans address their political appeals, their demands, visions, and ideals, in the first instance to other Americans; Britons to other Britons; and so forth. We treat community as prior to justice and fairness in the sense that questions of justice and fairness are regarded as questions of what would be just or fair within a particular political group.
>
> (Dworkin, 1986, p. 208)[4]

Dworkin does not, I think, wish to suggest that sovereign states are not entitled to enter into larger political groups which might incur fraternal obligations. But neither does he want to suggest that they have a duty to strive toward such ties. States are at liberty, in other words, to avoid entanglement in obligation-generating relationships just as two friends might concentrate on the obligations they have to each other resolutely avoiding new attachments. He also insists that no political community can be considered fraternal unless it is also a bare political community. Someone who shares no actual association with the members of a group through shared territory, shared history, common jurisdiction or blood line, for example, cannot be regarded as a member of a genuine political community even if others are disposed to treat him as such (pp. 201–2). This might throw up a physical barrier to the existence of a true global political community.

Weighing the prospects for a global political community

So far we have this much. A statist who rejects the idea of applying egalitarian rights or principles of egalitarian justice to the global domain can point to dominion, democracy, integrity and fraternity as necessary conditions for making this application.[5] This argument, however, is by no means unanswerable. Two strategies are worth noting. The first tries to motivate the proposed extension by insisting that the aforementioned characteristics are present in global politics. A second strategy is to deny that these characteristics are necessary existence conditions for global egalitarian justice by pointing out alternative sites of justice.

In this book I shall pursue the second strategy, but I shall begin with the first strategy since it clears the way for the second.

Global dominion and legitimacy?

Looking beyond Dworkin's particular usage, the word 'dominion' was originally employed as an official title for an overseas territory or province of the British Empire. If identifying plausible sites of global egalitarian justice depended solely on the existence of dominion in this old historical sense, the results could scarcely be more discouraging. Why should a sovereign state wish to regard itself as a dominion of another, even as a way of claiming a right to economic redistribution?

A more promising strategy is to look at international rulemaking bodies. The genre of trade dispute settlements is an interesting example because it involves agencies with the authority to make juridical prescriptions backed up by the threat of sanctions. Consider the procedures and penalties used by the Dispute Settlement Body of the World Trade Organisation (WTO). This body consists of all the WTO members and has the authority to establish panels of experts to judge cases, consider appeals, monitor the implementation of its rulings and authorise economic penalties where countries fail to comply with rulings. To take one example, in 2003 the WTO Dispute Settlement Body made a ruling against President Bush's manoeuvre to protect the American steel industry by imposing 30 per cent tariffs on steel imports from Japan, South Korea, China, Taiwan, Germany and Brazil. Its ruling resulted in the Bush administration having to lift the tariffs, demonstrating that unilateral protectionism can be hard to sustain under the rule-based regime of the WTO. From the fact that the WTO claims authority to impose sanctions it might be argued that it has an obligation to treat all members as equals.

International trade disputes are one thing, but what about the global redistribution of income and wealth? Presented with what appear to be sustained and predictable patterns of official development assistance (ODA) a growing number of legal theorists interpret this behaviour as reflecting not mere habit but *opinio juris*. This means that assistance is given on the basis of obligations grounded in international law including UN resolutions and various multilateral aid treaties (Zamora, 1997, p. 264). Inamul Haq, for example, interprets the modern practice of development assistance as demonstrating 'the emergence of a norm of customary law which makes it obligatory for the affluent countries to assist the poor nations in their development' (Haq, 1979, p. 420). The term 'customary law' incorporates both ethical and legal dimensions. In the ethical sense it implies that countries ought to fulfil self-imposed obligations of aid in accordance with basic principles of justice as acting in good faith. From a legal perspective it means that it should be in some sense binding on countries to fulfil their obligations.

Even if it can be said that rich states are liable to customary law in respect of commitments on foreign aid, however, the present question is whether this system is coercive enough to make it appropriate to apply the standard of justice as equal concern to it. Some commentators proffer the view that current practices of ODA and humanitarian aid were made possible by the rise of the domestic welfare state which provided both an impetus and a model for practices of international redistribution (see Lumsdaine, 1993, pp. 216–17; Noël and Thérien, 1995). Nevertheless, this does not establish that such practices can be meaningfully interpreted as being on a par with a domestic welfare state. Of course, it would be short-sighted to overlook the role played by bodies such as the Organisation for Economic Co-operation and Development (OECD) in recruiting donor countries and putting pressure on existing donors to keep giving. Yet it remains the case that if rich countries do not fulfil their aid obligations to poor countries, they do not at present face the economic sanctions they would face if they imposed illegal import tariffs. Nor do they face the penalties that citizens and corporations within states face if they neglect to pay their taxes. Given the voluntary nature of foreign aid, it is hard to interpret this as a form of activity undertaken because of state-like intervention (Schachter, 1976, pp. 249–51).

It is, of course, a matter of controversy whether we should regard a sanction-based framework as a necessary condition for applying standards of equal concern to any given practice. It is also open to question what counts as coercion. It might be argued, for example, that ODA can be extremely coercive when considered from the perspective of recipients. While rulemaking bodies such as the EU and UN do not impose sanctions against countries who fail to meet aid targets, the development programmes of the EU, UN, OECD, the World Bank and IMF can make offers of monetary assistance to poor countries the terms of which are nigh-on impossible to refuse. In many instances the terms of these offers are nigh-on impossible to refuse precisely because recipient countries desperately need monetary assistance in order to fight poverty, disease and economic stagnation, and are unable to access the money from other sources. For this reason it may be possible to interpret development assistance as falling within the more general class of coercive offers (cf. Steiner, 1974–5; Day, 1977; Gorr, 1989).

Even so, I suspect that Dworkin may want to insist that this is a different *form* of coercion and that each form of coercion gives rise to its own distinct kind of morality. He would not be alone in doing so. Blake, for example, argues that there is a pertinent difference between the form of coercion used by the IMF or World Bank when they tie conditions to loans and the form of coercion that is characteristic of domestic law and taxation, namely, the former relates to states or entire nations whereas the latter relates to individual citizens (Blake, 2001, p. 264). For this reason, 'Material equality becomes relevant only in the context of certain forms of coercion, forms not found outside the domestic arena' (p. 284). Similarly, Dworkin might argue that even if the practice of ODA is tantamount to a sanction-based system because of the substantial burden of refusing assistance, it remains the case that these are coercive offers rather than coercive threats, where this distinction is directly relevant to the kinds of principles of regulation that are appropriate.

The claim is not that we cannot make sense of the concept of legitimacy outside of the domestic case. Clearly we have a concept of international legitimacy which is conventionally understood in terms of state sovereignty and *inter alia* the right to territorial integrity, the right to non-interference in internal affairs, and the right to sign or not sign international treaties including treaties on international aid. Rather, the claim is that the existence of state sovereignty makes it much harder to raise meaningful questions about global redistribution. That is to say, if states have the right to withhold their consent from international agreements on official development assistance (and the right to refuse humanitarian aid from entering their borders), it becomes much harder to evoke the language of global redistribution which seems to imply the existence of an entity that has the right to force rich countries to redistribute their wealth. Allen Buchanan, for example, raises serious doubts over the capacity of existing global institutions to play a *direct* role in making authoritative pronouncements of what distributive justice requires globally, enforcing those pronouncements and monitoring compliance (Buchanan, 2004, ch. 4).

Global democracy?

Consider next the suggestion that the duty to show equal concern does not arise in the global setting because in order to speak sensibly of such a duty there must be not only a coercive framework but one that implicates the wills of all those governed by it. Here the problem faced by the political cosmopolitan is to first identify the site of global democracy. To this end he might point to the existence of transnational democratic bodies such as the UN General Assembly. As the principal deliberative organ of the UN each representative has one vote and all of these votes feed into resolutions on a range of issues from international peace and security onto the admission of new members and targets for international aid. The General Assembly also elects members of the UN Economic and Social Council (ECOSOC) which is tasked with the responsibility of coordinating and guiding the policies of a family of executive organisations including the UN Commission on Human Rights (UNCHR) and the UN Development Programme (UNDP). The political cosmopolitan might also point to the first biennial Development Cooperation Forum which took place at UN Headquarters, New York in June 2008. This was instituted to provide a forum for global dialogue and policy review not least with respect to the amount of aid given each year and its allocation. Moreover, it can be noted that there is a well-established system of transnational political movements and organisations who attempt to contest, challenge and hold to account decisions and activities of these organisations and programmes (Cohen and Sabel, 2005, pp. 764–5).

However, there remain significant question marks over the democratic credentials of this framework. One difficulty stems from the fact that the ECOSOC is made up of only 54 members, some distance short of representing every member of the UN. This puts a lot of pressure on the processes by which representatives are elected to this council and to the various executive boards that operate under its authority. There are also legitimate concerns over the considerable real-world influence that ministers from powerful financial institutions exert over the council's decisions. How can poor countries regard this council as democratic given the fact that since 1998 it has held a special annual meeting with finance ministers from the World Bank and the IMF? Another reason to be dubious about the democracy of this system relates to the lack of accountability that these political bodies and executive organisations have to the governments and citizens of poor countries. This is something that applies as much to the UNDP as to the OECD (cf. Goetz and Jenkins, 2002). There are also grounds for scepticism concerning the possibility of democratic accountability of international aid NGOs. Not only are NGOs not accountable to shareholders or to democratic assemblies for providing good projects but they are not even accountable to the beneficiaries of their aid. As discussed at the end of Chapter 4, the main tool of accountability is for governments to refuse entry to or expel NGOs from their country. But this is a sanction only open to political leaders, not to local people on the ground. This means that the effective power of a collection of poor people to scrutinise, reform or even reject the actions of NGOs is vanishingly small (Wenar, 2006, pp. 13–14).

The question here is not the degree to which development assistance and humanitarian aid promote democracy, although these are important questions, but whether the organisations in control of this money could be considered democratic in Dworkin's sense. This is one instance of a general problem for democracy at the global level. How could it be possible for all individuals around the world to have something approaching an equal chance to influence global decisions, to help set the agenda for those decisions, to make informed choices between candidates for office and to have radically diverse interests properly catered for when this is something that rarely occurs even at the domestic level? To use the words of Robert Dahl (a leading global democracy sceptic), we must be 'wary of ceding the legitimacy of democracy to non-democratic systems' (Dahl, 1999, p. 33). With this scepticism in mind, we might ask, if individuals around the world can regard a system of global redistribution as legitimate only if they have equal power to help determine the shape of that system, what hope is there for regarding the present system as legitimate given the absence of a global people's assembly at the UN?[6]

Global integrity?

What would it take to interpret international law under the ideal of integrity? Obviously the fullest possible answer to this question would consider various parts of international law including the conduct of war, the treatment of foreign detainees, border controls, international declarations on human rights and human rights law, the treatment of refugees, diplomacy, agreements on the law of the sea or climate change, international trade agreements, dispute settlement procedures, the rules and practices of international lending and debt negotiations and so on. To make things a fraction simpler, however, I propose to concentrate on the case of dispute settlement procedures.

In his book, *Third Party Dispute Settlement in an Interdependent World* (1995), Marcel Brus tries to make the case for third-party dispute settlement in international law. Although he does not claim to be applying Dworkin's theory of integrity to this case, he does use it as the inspiration for a theory. Examining dispute settlement procedures used by the WTO Dispute Settlement Body as well as the procedures established by the UN Conference on the Law of the Sea and the UN Conference on Environment and Development (UNCED) he argues that there is evidence that states are beginning to transform themselves from what Dworkin calls a 'rulebook community', which seeks to forge a compromise between competing interests as a *modus vivendi*, into a 'community of principle', which is built around virtues of legitimacy and integrity. Brus points to the emergence of substantive legal norms (such as principles of *jus cogens* and obligations *erga omnes*) and of the virtue of legitimacy and integrity:

> Legitimacy from a social system point of view in this respect requires the states involved to participate fully in the procedures, whereas the rule system perspective requires the principles and rules of the community to be upheld in accordance with the principle of integrity.
>
> (Brus, 1995, p. 180)

There are, however, three factors which limit this project. The first is that at present there is only a patchwork of different dispute settlement procedures around the world. So even if there is a case for interpreting this aspect of international law under the virtue of integrity the case may not extend globally. Perhaps we would lose something of regional value by creating truly global third party dispute settlement procedures. The second complicating factor is the need for coherence within the entire scheme of international law. Would transferring integrity to international law with respect to dispute settlement procedures – assuming it is even possible to build fidelity to a single vision of justice among diverse states – be coherent in principle with the rest of international law including parts where a transfer of integrity is not made and domestic integrity remains intact (cf. Dworkin, 1986, p. 186)? Finally, when Brus speaks of the virtues of legitimacy and integrity he seems to have in mind justice as acting in good faith and justice as impartiality. With respect to agreements on import tariffs and trade areas, for example, parties are called upon to interpret and fulfil prior agreements and to negotiate any disputes in a reasonable manner and in such a way that the original agreement can be realised. As for the WTO Dispute Settlement Body itself, we might say that it has an obligation to treat the parties concerned in an impartial manner, where this involves adopting an even-handed attitude, treating like cases alike, following procedures and so on. Even if these qualify as forms of showing equal concern and respect, they are different from the more substantive forms of equal concern and respect associated with distributive justice. Brus also alludes to the fact that parties to these dispute settlement procedures accept the duty to bear in mind the interests not only of those people directly involved in the dispute but also of the members of other states whose stability might be affected by these disputes. But nowhere does he mention the kind of equal concern for all that Dworkin identifies with true political communities.

Even if there is greater hope for interpreting certain aspects of international relations under the ideals of democracy and integrity than I have imagined here, however, the essential ingredients of fraternity laid down by Dworkin provide an even stiffer test.

Global fraternity?

What scope is there for interpreting international affairs under a fraternal ideal? One initially promising story begins with the Declaration for the Establishment of a New International Economic Order (NIEO) adopted by the UN General Assembly in 1974. The aim was to restructure the global economy to promote greater participation by, and benefits to, less-developed countries. Although this initiative ultimately failed, in 1986 the General Assembly adopted the Declaration on the Right to Development, a fundamental commitment to cooperation in solving international problems of an economic, social, cultural and humanitarian nature. Allied to this Declaration are various executive organisations which operate under the ECOSOC and UNDP. These are joined in the field by the development agencies of the EU, the OECD and various other regional development schemes and NGOs. Reflecting on all this it is difficult to avoid the conclusion that some degree of concern for the well-being of citizens of other states is widespread. But the present issue is whether or not this amounts to the kind of concern that could be interpreted under a fraternal ideal.

The realist tends to interpret such arrangements in terms of greed or fear rather than flowing from any genuine sense of mutual sacrifice or fraternity between states (see Morgenthau, 1962; Hayter, 1971; Waltz, 1979; Desch, 2003; Kamminga 2006). He will say that development assistance is really designed to create a climate conducive to worldwide private investment, to maintain international peace and security, to sustain export markets, and as a means of advancing liberal ideology. Hence the true purpose of unconditional aid is to ensure the stability of vulnerable states on the frontlines against communism and now religious fundamentalism, for example, while money offered by rich countries on the condition that beneficiaries agree to purchase goods from the donor and to remove trade barriers is aimed at protecting foreign exports.

But not everything lends itself to this sort of interpretation. Western governments often withhold development money from countries where human rights abuses are taking place even when this is not in their own best interests (Donnelly, 2003, pp. 164–5). Nor can self-interest fully explain the significant sums of money donated to humanitarian aid programmes like the World Food Programme (WFP) or the billions of dollars of external debt that were written off by the G7 group of countries and international financial institutions as a result of the Jubilee 2000 campaign. The realist might persist in arguing that such things only happen because the well-being of people in poor countries somehow enters into the utility functions of people in rich countries through a desire to avoid feelings of guilt or emotional distress. But it remains the case that far greater benefits accrue to the poor countries. Moreover, a growing number of political theorists interpret the practices of development assistance, humanitarian aid and Jubilee debt relief as reflecting a 'moral vision' of what we owe to each other around the globe. They argue that this moral vision has had a significant transforming power over foreign aid over the past 50 years or so because it is based on a shared sense of justice, compassion or even virtue (see Lumsdaine, 1993; Opeskin, 1996; Hattori, 2003; Busby, 2007).

So what is to stop us from interpreting these practices as displaying the virtue of fraternity? Why not say that they reflect a general and diffuse sense of what sort and level of sacrifice people are expected to make for one another? These are fair questions. But there remains an insoluble difficulty in applying Dworkin's conception of fraternity to the above practices conceived globally. Recall that Dworkin's first condition of fraternity is that members must regard the obligations that are owed to each other as *special* in the sense that they are obligations owed exclusively to members of the group as opposed to non-members. This allows us to make sense of a regional fraternity in which a group of countries club together and recognise special obligations within the group. Nevertheless, who are the relevant non-members when we are thinking about fraternity from a truly global perspective? In the case of the UN, with its 192 member states, these obligations can only be special in respect of excluding the citizens of a tiny number of non-member states. The distinction between special obligations and general duties disappears altogether if one reflects on a possible future in which every nation on Earth is a fully-fledged member of the UN. If this is a global fraternity, then who are the relevant non-members? Some people might be tempted to say that the non-members are other animals or even extra terrestrials. But then the putative distinction between an associative obligation and a general obligation collapses into a more familiar distinction between the moral duties we owe to fellow human beings and the moral duties we owe to other species. In the absence of other human beings who can plausibly play the role of non-members, the idea of a global political community that is fraternal in Dworkin's sense starts to look like a contradiction in terms.[7]

A different strategy: equal concern without a true political community

We have seen that Dworkin regards the virtue of equal concern as being idiosyncratic to a true political community. But this raises the spectre of a status quo objection. The theory of equal concern is biased in favour of those who already happen to be members of this kind of association to the detriment of those who do not find themselves so positioned.[8] Now it might seem logical to conclude from this that what has gone wrong here is Dworkin's methodology. Yet it seems to me that what has gone awry is not the methodology but the way Dworkin uses it. After all, he does not commit himself to the strong claim that questions of justice cannot arise outside of a true political community. On the contrary, 'An association of principle is not automatically a just community; its conception of equal concern may be defective or it may violate rights of its citizens or citizens of other nations' (Dworkin, 1986, p. 213). Thus it is perfectly legitimate for us to condemn as unjust a political community which utilises war for the purposes of national self-interest. We can repudiate the idea that its members have genuine obligations to support unjust wars because we take the view that 'any conflict between militant nationalism and standards of justice must be resolved in favor of the latter' (p. 206). So it is not the case that when assessing international institutions, rules, practices or even individual actions as just or unjust the attitude of critical interpretation is no longer relevant. It is that when looking at these things Dworkin has hitherto been attracted to only one sort of interpretation, a sort that leaves no space for concern with relative deprivation or socio-economic inequalities. This, I think, is where he goes wrong.

With this in mind, I now wish to adopt the second strategy mentioned above, which is to argue that egalitarian rights and principles can be applied to aspects of the global domain even if that domain fails to exhibit the characteristics of a true political community as defined by Dworkin.

Dworkin views dominion as one of the preconditions for applying justice as equal concern to a domain. However, this sort of condition has been challenged in the recent literature on global justice. Andrea Sangiovanni asks us to imagine an internally just society whose ordinary means of law enforcement (as in, the police and army) have been temporarily disabled by a terrorist attack.[9] Even though the ordinary means of coercion have disappeared, this society does not descend into a war of all against all. Most laws continue to command a reasonable degree of obedience, public services continue to be provided, the legislature meets and writes new laws, property is transferred in accordance with the law as normal, disputes are settled, and by and large citizens continue to pay their taxes. But suppose that a small group of very rich gentlemen start to protest that norms of egalitarian justice no longer apply to them because they object to heavily progressive taxation. If one intuitively believes that this group does not have a right to avoid the present tax burden, then it seems to follow that coercion is not a necessary existence condition for egalitarian rights (Sangiovanni, 2007, p. 20).

My own intuitions track those of Sangiovanni on this limited point: the absence of ordinary means of coercive law enforcement need not forestall claims of distributive justice. Some people might argue that because the terrorist attack has only 'temporarily' disabled law enforcement in Sangiovanni's society it is unclear whether coercion or something like it is no longer the operative factor. Perhaps most people obey the rules because they consciously or subconsciously think that law enforcement will shortly be reinstated and that as soon as this happens they might be punished for what they have done. Sangiovanni supposes that the conditions continue for several years, but this is no guarantee that people do not continue to have one eye on the re-instigation of the police and armed forces. So maybe the existence of coercion or vulnerability to coercion remains operative despite the intention of the example. Nevertheless, suppose that the authorities make it absolutely clear to everyone that although they are working hard towards reconstructing ordinary mechanisms of law enforcement, for practical reasons there will be no retrospective punishment once things are up and running again.

Where I depart from Sangiovanni, however, is in not sharing his further claim that what is driving intuitions in this case is the fact that the post-attack society exhibits a sense of *solidaristic reciprocity* (Sangiovanni, 2007, p. 20). I do not intend to enter into a detailed discussion of this argument save for making the following point. Sangiovanni appeals not merely to the concept of justice but to a particular conception of justice, namely, justice as reciprocity in the distribution of mutually created benefits and burdens. Nevertheless, I think that an equally sound interpretation of the continuing relevance of considerations of justice in this society can be sought from justice as equal concern and respect. Notice that the group of rich gentlemen believe that only they should not have to pay taxes or should pay lower taxes because they object to progressive taxation. I agree with Sangiovanni that this attitude is objectionable, but note that this objection can be put by saying that these gentlemen are not entitled to more concern and respect than anyone else and to allow them to avoid their tax burden would be to treat them as though they were more important or nobler than other people. Moreover, that they should pay a progressive tax is the result of a coherent interpretation of the right to equal concern and respect under conditions of *ex ante* equality (Dworkin, 1981b, pp. 325, 337; 2006, pp. 123–6).

My suggestion is that even in the absence of coercion people can be subject to claims of justice as equal concern. I need to make it clear, however, what does and what does not trigger claims in this case. It might be thought that justice is triggered only if people already share a sense of equal concern for one another as a form of fraternal feeling. But I refute that hypothesis. By analogy, Mathias Risse argues that even if Sangiovanni has shown that coercion is not a necessary condition for justice, he has failed to show that solidaristic reciprocity is a necessary condition because we can imagine situations in which such reciprocity is absent yet questions of justice still arise. Risse offers the case of a society in the grip of mass lethargy (Risse, 2007). I believe a similar line of argument applies to fraternity. Imagine a society in which a new and highly effective folk story has caused the majority of the population to believe that a group of rich gentlemen are superior to them and therefore should be permitted to pay lower taxes. Suppose the story begins to take a hold of officialdom such that tax collectors are no longer minded to enforce the existing progressive tax laws against the rich gentlemen and although there is a reasonable chance of exit from the society most ordinary people choose to stay because they are in awe of this group of men. In these circumstances people no longer regard one another as equals and in that sense it is not a fraternal community. Of course, one could simply bite the bullet and concede that questions of justice no longer apply here. But surely it makes more sense to say that we can raise questions of justice about what is going on here even if the society does not actually exhibit a sense of fraternity.

So what does trigger questions of justice in this case? I think that it is possible to make sense of why justice is relevant by looking at the consequences of the rich gentlemen's actions, that is to say, at the profound and pervasive impact that their actions are likely to have on the life chances of other people. If these gentlemen decide to stop paying a proportional tax, this is likely to have severe repercussions for the life prospects of the poorer members of the society. Without this tax revenue, they will no longer have access to an equal share of resources with which to pursue their own ends. It is these severe repercussions, as judged by the standards of equal concern and respect, that I believe make it plausible to call the actions of the rich gentlemen unjust (cf. Cohen, 1997; 2000; Murphy, 1998). So my claim is that pervasive impact can be a sufficient trigger for asking questions of justice, and that as such neither coercion nor a sense of fraternity are necessary existence conditions. But in saying this, I do not mean to claim that pervasive impact is itself a necessary condition, not least because sometimes other things, including coercion, can trigger questions of justice.

Returning now to issues of global distributive justice, looking to the impact of rules and practices is by no means a novel approach (cf. Rawls, 1971, p. 96). In the opening pages of *The Law of Peoples*, for instance, Rawls argues that domestic and foreign policies can be viewed as subject to the law of peoples because they have caused the 'the great evils of human history' (1999, pp. 6–7). Much is made in the literature of the profound and pervasive impact of international agreements covering trade, international finance and private property rights (Buchanan, 2000, pp. 205–6). In his *Justice without Borders* Kok-Chor Tan also shines a torch on the ways in which domestic policies regarding tax laws, consumption, border controls, immigration and the protection of the environment can potentially have 'grave implications' for individuals living in foreign countries.[10] According to Tan, the fact that these sorts of decisions can cause deprivation in other parts of the world means that the decisions must be such that they can be reasonably accepted by those who stand to be impacted by them (Tan, 2004, p. 174).

Although these insights are correct and valuable, I believe that certain other types of decisions have so far not received the attention they deserve in this debate. Momentous decisions concerning whether or not to provide ODA and humanitarian aid, to whom, at what level and on what conditions are taken by individuals, groups, governments and various sorts of regional and international organisations. Along with the aforementioned policies, I suggest that such decisions also satisfy the proposed basis for asking questions of justice, to wit, that they can have a profound and pervasive impact upon the life chances of people across the globe. There is a considerable literature that examines the impact of foreign aid on economic growth, poverty and human well-being at both the micro- and macro-levels. This material explores aid in the form of loans, grants, debt relief as well as cash and aid in kind. It also delves into the conditions tied to aid as well as the consequences when aid is given and when it is not (see Morrissey, 2001; Burnside and Dollar, 2002; Easterly, 2003; 2007; Addison et al., 2005; Riddell, 2007). Looking at the findings of this painstaking work it is hard to avoid drawing the conclusion that foreign aid has a profound and pervasive impact on the lives of individuals all over the globe and that on this basis it makes sense to consider what, if any, principles of justice ought to govern the rules, practices and individual actions which constitute it.

To clarify, I believe that there are a number of different features that can make it appropriate to raise questions of distributive justice: social cooperation, a sense of reciprocity or fraternity, coercion, profound and pervasive impacts, and even humanity. Moreover, it seems to me that our ordinary grasp of the concept of justice is sufficiently loose to mean that no single feature can definitively claim to be the essential ground of justice, that is, to be a necessary condition for talking about justice across all contexts. Of course, these features are not coextensive such that they will not always obtain in the same context or at the same time. Furthermore, positions taken about which feature is operative in any given context, if more than one feature is present at the same time, will shape the content of the relevant principles of justice. If, for example, one concentrates on humanity, then one might be more likely to interpret justice in terms of human rights. My suggestion is that profound and pervasive impact is the operative ground in the case of foreign aid, although I freely admit that an interpretive case could also be made for each of the other aforementioned grounds. So identifying the grounds of justice is as much a matter of constructive interpretation as spelling out the contents of justice.

Before spelling out some general principles of justice to govern foreign aid, however, I need first to make three general points about the interpretation of foreign aid. The first is that it is not enough from the perspective of constructive interpretation merely to show that it makes sense to raise questions of justice about these things. The task must be to make the best sense of the purpose or value of the subject matter at hand. Pogge, for example, suggests that we should stop looking upon the individual donations we make to the global poor as well as various international development initiatives as 'helping the poor' but as compensating action undertaken to protect others from an unjust world order of our making (Pogge, 2002a, pp. 23, 144). The question I wish to ask is slightly different: would it be profitable to interpret foreign aid as being at its best (or most just) when the agents involved, individual and collective, treat with global equal concern and respect those persons affected by what they do or do not do?

The second, related point is that there is likely to be more than one way of seeing the real purpose of foreign aid. Perhaps some people will insist that the only feasible way to interpret such activity is in terms of the twin aims of protecting human rights and providing a humanitarian minimum. Nagel, for example, takes the view that in the absence of a global state there is no question of socio-economic justice but there can be a global morality which calls on us to fulfil basic human rights and to assist all human beings who are threatened with starvation, disease or lack of basic shelter (Nagel, 2005). However, I think that this ignores an important truism about human behaviour: that it is often possible to see it as fulfilling more than one purpose or being valuable for more than one reason. It would be strange to think that sporting activity, for example, has a sole purpose or can only be interpreted in the light of a single value. Some people concentrate on the idea that the aim of sport is to foster competition and they work to provide the best interpretation of competition they can. Others focus instead on the idea that the purpose of sport is to improve people's health and they work to develop an interpretation of healthy engagement in sport as their interest dictates. Like sport, I believe that rules, practices and activities relating to the giving and withholding of foreign aid can serve more than one purpose or be valuable for more than one reason. My own interest is with justice as global equal concern and respect, and so I interpret these things accordingly. I shall argue that foreign aid is at its best when it goes beyond the decency threshold implied by humanitarianism and reaches out for egalitarian justice.

This feeds into my third point, which is that there are many different ways of interpreting the concept of global justice. In his 'Humanity and Justice in Global Perspective', for example, Brian Barry draws a useful distinction between *justice as reciprocity* and *justice as equal rights* (Barry, 1982, p. 226). I expect that if justice as reciprocity were the only viable idea of justice, then it would be more difficult to make sense of the idea of global justice. It might be thought that justice as reciprocity requires for its application the existence of a certain kind of institutional reciprocity that is characteristic of domestic politics, whereby members contribute their money to a common pool on the understanding that they and others can draw upon this pool should they fall into dire straits (Miller, 2002b, pp. 82–3). Yet I do not accept this narrow picture of justice and so deny that such institutions are necessary preconditions for questions of socio-economic justice to arise. I have much more sympathy with Barry's idea of justice as equal rights, which he interprets in terms of 'the principle that natural resources are the joint possession of the human race as whole' (237–8). Nevertheless, my own interpretation appeals to the more inclusive idea of *justice as global equal concern and respect*. In the remainder of this book I intend to argue that various rules, practices and individual actions – not least international exploitation of, and trade in, natural resources and foreign aid – are at their best (or most just) only if they strive towards justice as global equal concern and respect as distinct from the state-biased ideal of justice as reciprocity. I shall return to the question of natural resources in Chapter 7. But for now I wish to focus on foreign aid.

Equal concern and foreign aid

The aim of this section is to try to meet the challenge of a sceptic who claims that justice as global equal concern and respect would not merely be an unattractive theory of foreign aid but would be incomprehensible as such a theory because no competent preinterpretive account of foreign aid could support this.

Development assistance

According to World Bank figures from 1998, the world's rich, developed countries have transferred around $1 trillion to poor, less-developed countries in unilateral, bilateral and multilateral ODA transfers since the 1940s (World Bank, 1998, p. 2). While $1 trillion is undoubtedly a vast amount of money, it must be put into context. It has been widely reported that the recent credit crunch alone has cost the world economy around $1 trillion. Relative figures tend to be far more revealing. Between 1955 and 1960 total public and private capital flows to poor countries increased from around 0.5 per cent to 0.83 per cent of GNI (UN, 1968, Vol. IV, Table 8). In 1960 the UN General Assembly adopted Resolution 1522 (XV) which states that 'the flow of international assistance and capital should be increased substantially so as to reach as soon as possible approximately 1 per cent of the combined national incomes of the economically advanced countries' (UN, 1960). This target was later reduced to 0.75 per cent at the Second Session of the UN Conference on Trade and Development in New Delhi (UN, 1968, Vol. I). Since that time the figure of 0.7 per cent has stuck and there is now a widespread expectation and commitment among developed countries that they should, if they have not done so already, reach that level or else develop a reasonable timeframe in which to do so.

I do not mean to suggest that all developed countries actually meet this target at any given time. According to OECD figures for 2007, Norway, Denmark, Sweden and Holland are among a small minority of countries who do meet the 0.7 per cent target. In absolute terms the United States is by far the largest donor giving $21.8 billion in net ODA. But in relative terms this only amounts to 0.16 per cent of its GNI. The United Kingdom does not do much better at 0.36 per cent. It is also possible to chart the ebb and flow of total development assistance over the past 30 years or so. ODA increased fairly steadily throughout the 1970s and 80s but fell dramatically in the 90s. It then recovered again during the early 2000s and reached a peak in 2005–6 as a result of large Paris Club debt relief operations in Iraq and Nigeria. But since then it has dropped off again reflecting a narrowing of these operations and an international economic downturn affecting Europe and North America (OECD, 2008). Consequently, the UN has issued a 'wake up call' to the world's richest countries to the effect that they must increase their development assistance by $18 billion a year between now and 2010 so as to meet the pledges they made at the 2005 G8 Summit in Gleneagles (UN, 2008, p. viii). However, these fluctuations need not be interpreted as countries rejecting or changing the fundamental terms of their moral duty to less-developed countries. Rather, it can be seen as a readjustment of the feasible achievement of their responsibilities in the face of economic pressures at home.

There have also been some interesting trends in ODA. During the 1970s Robert McNamara advocated a basic needs approach to the Board of Governors of the World Bank. Partly as a result of this the World Bank (along with the UN and OECD) started to take more seriously the importance of targeting assistance towards people at the bottom even if this meant a short-term loss in growth for the recipient population taken as a whole. It also attempted to provide for social needs in the areas of agriculture food, health, education and housing. By the 1980s, however, the basic needs approach had been usurped by national governments who were intent on pushing development money in the direction of developing countries willing to adopt market-friendly policies. In addition to this, a new emphasis was placed on increasing economic growth in the economy as a whole rather than focusing on the satisfaction of basic needs (Leys, 1996, ch. 1). Some scholars suggest that the 1990s witnessed the fusion of the priorities of the two previous decades (Thérien, 2002). Evidence for this can be seen in a key OECD policy statement from 1996 which speaks of a strong moral imperative among the industrialised nations 'to respond to

extreme poverty and human suffering' whilst at the same time acknowledging 'a strong self-interest in fostering increased prosperity in the
developing countries' (OECD, 1996, p. 1). The latest trends in development assistance are linked to the UN Millennium Development Goals
(MDGs). Since 2000, 189 UN member states and roughly 25 international organisations have agreed to the eight MDGs, which include a
commitment to halve extreme poverty and hunger by 2015.

The purpose of constructive interpretation, however, is not simply
to mirror current practices much less to plot the trends in practices
over time but to develop an account of what it would mean for these
practices to be as good (or just) as we can reasonably expect them to
be. Development assistance constitutes a vast and unprecedented
redistributive practice. Not surprisingly, then, it may be subject to
the dictates of more than one form of justice. One is that countries
have an obligation to fulfil their previous undertakings. So when the
member states of the UN agreed in the 1960s to attempt to provide a
minimum of 0.7 per cent of their GNI in development assistance,
an undertaking which most states have reiterated subsequently,
this generated a special obligation of justice to do so. In so far as the
figure of 0.7 per cent was the product of an international agreement
among free and democratic countries this confers *pro tanto* weight on
that target from a contractarian perspective.[11] In addition to this,
arguably there should be fair play in the burden of ODA such that
members of countries who stand to benefit from a cooperative
scheme of ODA must contribute their fair share and not free ride on
the efforts of others. I think that both of these reasons lend support
to recent efforts to ensure that countries fulfil their undertakings.
At the 2008 G8 summit in Hokkaido, Japan, for example, member
states reaffirmed their 2005 commitment to the 0.7 per cent target,
which equates to an additional $50 billion in ODA by 2010. Arguably
fair play requires larger contributions by BRICK countries (Brazil,
Russia, India, China and Korea) which, despite their emerging
economies, have thus far not been taken to task for their relatively
low provision of ODA in the same way and to the same degree as
G8 countries. Nevertheless, I do not think that these exhaust the
forms of justice which are appropriate for ODA. On the contrary, to
restrict obligations of justice to the fulfilment of existing undertakings and fair play could allow countries to rest on their laurels
as far as assistance is concerned. Of course, the mere failure to sign
up to a treaty is not automatically unjust. Then again, the mere
achievement of signing the treaty is not automatically just either. So

the question I want to address is whether it is appropriate to evaluate ODA against justice as global equal concern and respect.

Consider three aspects of ODA in this regard. First, the MDGs include halving extreme poverty and hunger, reducing child mortality rates, improving maternal health, combating HIV/AIDS, malaria and other diseases, and improving gender equality. The question here is whether or not it is plausible to interpret these goals as being at their best only if they flow from the acceptance of a general duty to show equal concern and respect for the life of every human being on the planet. Furthermore, in the past a great deal of development assistance has been devoted not merely to tackling poverty but also to fostering increased prosperity in the recipient country as a whole. It seems right to ask whether these aims are as just as they could be.

Secondly, the UN has recently expressed its concern that progress towards the MDGs has been unequal between different countries (UN, 2007). Whereas many parts of Asia have made substantial progress towards achieving all of the MDGs, a large number of countries in sub-Saharan Africa are not on track to meet a single MDG by 2015. The question is how best to interpret this renewed commitment among nations to achieve more equal progress towards the MDGs worldwide (see Fukuda-Parr, 2004; Pogge, 2004; Vandemoortele, 2005; Daniels, 2008, ch. 13; Franklin, 2008).

Thirdly, it is appropriate to consider the targeting of ODA through the use of terms and conditions. As suggested above, during the 1980s and 90s conditions were increasingly tied to aid programmes, first as economic conditions and then conditions of a social and political nature. The consensus among participants at the 2002 UN Conference on Financing for Development in Monterrey, Mexico, was that ODA is most effective when it is targeted at countries with sound economic policies and good governance including strong property rights and the rule of law (Dollar and Levin, 2006). But is this sort of targeting just?

Although I will not be in a position to provide full answers to these questions until the end of Chapter 7, I can make some general remarks now. First, one of the chief benefits of adopting the method of constructive interpretation is that it becomes possible to call into question existing ODA targets and goals. To do otherwise would be to endorse a glass ceiling on levels of assistance, meaning that states are under no obligation to increase the level of their undertaking after 2010. In so far as it is appropriate to judge such targets against the requirements of global equal concern, and to interpret those requirements in terms of global equality of resources (say), it becomes highly unlikely that the current target of 0.7 per cent of GNI treats recipients with equal concern. This does not mean, however, that it is right to aim for flat equality. Take the MDGs relating to reducing child mortality rates, improving maternal health and combating HIV/AIDS, malaria and other diseases. In recent years the WHO has been criticised for its over-use of cost-benefit analysis thereby neglecting issues of equity in the distribution of health care. But it is right to ask whether a programme of health development that stopped at nothing to eliminate health inequality, even if it meant making everyone within the local population less healthy than they might be under an alternative arrangement, could be interpreted as treating people with equal concern (cf. Daniels, 2008, p. 352).

Secondly, in addition to measuring absolute levels of ODA against the requirements of justice as global equal concern it is fitting to apply this standard to the relative progress towards existing development goals across the world. In this way it might be said that progress towards the MDGs is not just unless those responsible for that progress demonstrate equal concern for everyone. If there has been a tendency to progress far more swiftly towards the MDGs in some parts of the world than in others, for example, this may be interpreted as contrary to the right to global equal concern. Drawing on the deeper principles of human dignity, there may come a point at which the progress is so uneven that it can only be interpreted as though those who are responsible for achieving the MDGs presuppose the intrinsic inferiority of some peoples.

Thirdly, I propose that it is possible to interpret the terms and conditions of ODA in the light of justice as global equal concern and respect. Arguably injustice occurs if development funds require recipient countries to radically reduce much-needed social welfare programmes as a condition of receiving development money or if recipient countries have little or no say in identifying their own development needs. In this event concern becomes unduly paternalistic trying as it does to clone the highest order interests of the recipients of aid in the mode of a totalitarian state attempting to clone the highest order interests of its citizens.

Obviously, I have outlined very different aspects of ODA ranging from aims and rules to procedures and practices and on to individual actions. But I think that it would be wrong to exclude any of these things as potential sites of global justice on merely formal grounds, especially if they have a profound and pervasive impact on people's life chances. More importantly, it should be clear from the above that justice as global equal concern and respect is intended to apply as much to the targets that countries set or fail to set in assisting persons around the world as to how they treat people when fulfilling their targets. Of course, some people might assume that one can only meaningfully apply the concept of justice to the latter and not the former. I reject such a restricted interpretation.

However, in saying that justice as global equal concern and respect applies to agents who provide foreign aid, in no way do I seek to overlook the responsibility of recipients. Money is given by state actors directly to other state actors or indirectly through international agencies or from non-state actors to other non-state actors, and then this money is put into the hands of local officials and (hopefully) into the hands of ordinary individuals. But at each point in the chain an agent, individual or collective, can fail, whether intentionally or negligently, to make the best use of that money or to pass it along. Given the potentially disastrous consequences of ODA diversion by NGOs, local officials, armed militia groups and ordinary individuals, the requirements of global equal concern and respect must apply as much to these persons as to the original donors.[12]

Nor do I wish to say that this form of justice is the only thing we can reasonably demand of foreign aid. Another important standard for successful ODA is effectiveness. This agenda is now being set by the 2005 Paris Declaration on Aid Effectiveness, with members of the OECD agreeing to increase efforts towards aid harmonisation and mutual accountability. That being said, these two kinds of standards for successful ODA are connected. After all, it is possible to interpret the fundamental tenet underpinning the Paris Declaration – to change the current system in which accountability requirements are harder on developing countries than on donors and to ensure that developing countries exercise strong and effective leadership over the development policies and strategies within their borders – as a way of showing equal concern and respect to recipient communities.

Humanitarian aid

There is, a whole raft of problems to which aid agencies try to respond in the wake of catastrophes. Among them are: the inability of people to maintain clean water supplies and sanitation; lack of access to basic food supplies; limited opportunity to sustain livelihoods and earn income; the inability to rebuild homes and schools; lack of money to pay for drugs and medicines to ward off illness and diseases. Aid can be provided by national governments and international aid NGOs, of course, but increasingly humanitarian aid is being organised by the United Nations Office for the Coordination of Humanitarian Affairs (OCHA). The OCHA solicits donors to the UN Central Emergency

Response Fund (CERF) both directly and through the Consolidated Appeals Process (CAP). Established in 1992, the CAP brings together governments, donors, aid agencies, the Red Cross Movement, NGOs and local organisations to raise funds for humanitarian action as well as to plan, implement and monitor activities. In January 2008 Secretary-General Ban Ki-moon kick-started the 2008 UN Humanitarian Appeal, which requested $3.8 billion to assist 25 million people in more than 20 countries, with the following declaration: 'We are here today on behalf of people the world has all too often forgotten: the weak, the disadvantaged, those suffering the effects of climate change, violence, disaster and disease' (Ban, 2008).

In accordance with what particular obligations is humanitarian aid currently provided? Close scrutiny of Resolution 46/182 of the UN General Assembly (UN, 1991), the statement of values and principles of the European Commission Humanitarian Aid Office (ECHO, 2005), the International Federation of Red Cross and Red Crescent Societies' Code of Conduct for Disaster Relief (International Federation of Red Cross and Red Crescent Societies, 2004) and the Sphere Project's Humanitarian Charter and Minimum Standards in Disaster Response (Sphere Project, 2004) reveals a number of particular obligations. An obligation to provide humanitarian assistance wherever and whenever it is needed; an obligation to respect state sovereignty (for states to recognise the independence of other states); an obligation of neutrality (that NGOs will not taking sides in hostilities); an obligation of independence (that NGOs will act autonomously from the will of state donors); an obligation of selflessness (to organise relief not prompted in any manner by desire for gain); an obligation of non-discrimination (that assistance will not be dependent on the race of the recipients and without adverse distinction based on the adherence of the recipients to the particular political or religious standpoints of aid agencies); an obligation of universality (that all donors share not only an equal status but also equal responsibilities and duties in helping others); an obligation of respect for local customs (that assistance will be sensitive to local wishes).

I interpret many of these particular obligations as flowing from a more general duty to show global equal concern and respect to the victims of poverty, violence, natural disaster, disease endemics, food shortages and so on. This duty is manifest in many of the particular obligations listed above. First, the obligation to provide humanitarian assistance can be interpreted as flowing from the general duty to show equal concern for those in dire straits wherever they happen to be. Secondly, the obligation of non-discrimination can be viewed as reflecting a duty to show equal concern for people in different countries regardless of differences of race, religion or political viewpoint. Thirdly, the obligation of selflessness is interpretable as flowing from a more general duty to show equal concern to those belonging to different nations according to some minimally adequate conception of what that means. Finally, the obligation of respect for local customs arises from the general duty to show equal respect for the recipients of aid. The obligation of universality, by contrast, speaks to justice as fair play, so that agents act fairly by taking on an equal share of the burden of foreign aid.

In this way the right to global equal concern and respect places demands both on the substantive goals of humanitarian aid and on the ways in which aid is allocated and delivered. The rationale of aid, the concentration of aid in some parts of the world, the way aid is put into effect – none of these should escape evaluation (cf. Barnett and Weiss, 2008). The overall amount of foreign aid given is a matter of global equal concern in the sense that everyone is entitled to a decent life no matter into which country they are born. The allocation of foreign aid among recipients and potential recipients aims at equal concern in the sense that assistance must be evenly divided. Furthermore, there must be equal respect for the right of the local community to be fully involved in decisions about the way aid is delivered and used in the field. As an example of inequality, compare the response to the 2004 Asian tsunami aid appeal with the response to appeals made in the wake of the 2005 food crisis in Niger. In the year immediately following the 2004 tsunami more than $6 billion in humanitarian aid was pledged (including $4 billion from private donations) to help the estimated 5 million Tsunami survivors facing disease and starvation. This dwarfs the amount of money donated to the Niger crisis and in a way that was disproportionate to the numbers of people affected. In May 2005, the UN appealed to international donors for a mere $16 million in emergency aid to keep alive 2.5 million people in Niger. The response was meagre. In August 2005, Jan Egeland, the United Nations under-secretary-general for Humanitarian Affairs and Emergency Relief coordinator pointed out that even though Niger donated $250,000 to the victims of the 2004 tsunami, the world capitulated as millions of people in Niger faced starvation (Egeland, 2005).

To be clear, my view is not merely that rules and practices of humanitarian aid ought to be subject to principles of global justice but also that the individual actions taken against this background ought to be so subject. This claim is vague, so let me say a bit more about its main terms. 'Practice' is understood here to mean the customary activities of a number of agents who share at least some similar knowledge, goals, interests and values. A practice is not merely an accidental repetition of actions over time but an ongoing disposition to act in accordance with a norm. (Pogge, of course, believes that global poverty is a structural problem and as such we have duties not to support institutions which do harm, where 'institutions' is used inclusively to mean both formal rules and informal practices in the above sense.) Practices can condition individual action in the sense that they create expectations and condition the set of costs and benefits. For this reason they are appropriate sites of principles of justice. But it also seems to me that particular choices (whether of individuals or collectives) should not be immune from considerations of justice. Choices − about whether to give or withhold aid and about whether to make good or bad use of aid, for example − also have severe repercussions for people's lives and as such agents cannot abdicate responsibility for individual actions. Of course, sometimes individual actions may be so constrained by background rules and practices that attaching responsibility is impossible.

No theory of foreign aid would be complete, however, without addressing the issue of humanitarian intervention and human rights. In December 1991 the General Assembly passed a resolution stating that state sovereignty 'must be fully respected' and that in this context 'humanitarian assistance should be provided with the consent of the affected country' (UN, 1991). However, a number of high-profile cases including the Rwandan genocide of 1994 and the ethnic-cleansing of Kosovo Albanians in 1999 have spawned a vital debate between those who seek to justify humanitarian intervention and those who err on the side of state sovereignty.[13] In chapter 2 of *Is Democracy Possible Here?* Dworkin acknowledges the important role that the concept of human rights plays in such debates.

> The United States and other nations invoke the idea to justify extreme sanctions; we refuse financial aid or economic advantage to countries that we accuse of human rights violations, and we try to stop other nations or agencies from helping them. We believe that in some circumstances we are justified even in invading those countries to prevent such violations.
>
> (Dworkin, 2006, p. 28)

In line with the rest of his political theory, he adopts an interpretive attitude to human rights: to understand human rights is to understand the role they play in the international arena. But he also draws a distinction between legal disagreements about what human rights currently exist and moral disagreements about what human rights ought to be respected and ratified. He claims that 'the second, moral question must be our question now' (p. 29). Furthermore, his own particular interpretation of human rights is that something qualifies as a denial of human rights only if it amounts to an egregious denial of the two principles of human dignity. He takes it as read that human dignity only grounds what he call 'baseline' human rights where this does *not* include social and economic rights. Baseline human rights are 'the concrete rights, like the right not to be tortured, that set limits to how any government may act' (pp. 35–6) According to Dworkin, these baseline human rights 'forbid acts tha could not be justified by any intelligible interpretation of the ideas tha people's lives are of equal intrinsic value and that they have a personal responsibility for their own lives' (p. 36).

There is plenty in this picture of baseline human rights to comment on I begin by comparing it with Rawls' position on human rights. Rawls' prin ciples of international justice include a duty of non-intervention, but they also include an exception to that duty in the case of outlaw states engaged in 'grave violations' of human rights (Rawls, 1999, p. 37). For Rawls human rights 'are a class of rights that play a special role in a reasonable Law of Peoples: they restrict the justifying reasons for war and its conduct and they specify limits to a regime's internal autonomy' (p. 79). Although Dworkin agrees that human rights can play a justificatory role in the case of armed intervention, he also argues that they can justify economic sanc tions such as refusing financial aid or other advantages such as trade or preferential loans (Dworkin, 2006, p. 28). To return to the issue of humani tarian intervention, these were the sorts of questions that came to the fore in the case of cyclone Nardis in 2008 where the military junta initially refused entry to representatives from the UN and other internationally recognised aid agencies. Similar questions have been asked in connection with the crisis in Zimbabwe where President Robert Mugabe's governmen has banned Care International from giving further aid to hungry villagers.

Of course, Rawls argues that any adequate list of basic human right must not 'depend on any particular comprehensive religious doctrine or philosophical doctrine of human nature' (Rawls, 1999, p. 68). He avers that only certain human rights (or 'human rights proper') can sat isfy this constraint: the right to life (including the right to the means of subsistence), the right to freedom from slavery, the right to a sufficien measure of liberty of conscience, the right to private property, the righ to formal equality (as in, the right to have like cases treated alike) and the rights of ethnic groups against mass murder and genocide (pp. 65 79). Although Dworkin does not cite *The Law of Peoples*, he echoe Rawls' conviction that if human rights are to justify intervention or economic sanctions, then they cannot be 'parochial or drawn from a single cultural tradition' (Dworkin, 2006, p. 34). He also endorses some of the human rights on Rawls' list, including the right to a sufficient measure of liberty of conscience and the right against torture (p. 38). Furthermore, Dworkin points to the fact that people in the international arena disagree about whether universal human rights include economic rights and subsequently excludes such rights from the class of baseline human rights (p. 37).

What should we make of these baseline rights? There is, of course, a sense in which acknowledging the existence of baseline human rights does amount to the recognition of every person's right to equal concern and respect, namely, it is to show equal concern and respect through the recognition of baseline human rights. But this falls short of equal concern in another sense. So, for example, if the government of country A acts to uphold and protect the baseline human rights of both its own citizens and the citizens of country B, then there is a sense in which it treats both groups of people with equal concern. But if in addition to baseline human rights it routinely provides its citizens with a range of social and economic rights which it does not protect for citizens of country B, then clearly there is another sense in which it does not show equal concern. So the question is, what is the absolute minimum standard of human rights that is required to display a good faith attempt to treat all human beings with equal dignity? Moreover, when is the failure of a country to provide for its people economically and socially a failure of human rights and thereby grounds for intervening in that country including imposing financial sanctions against it?

'The fundamental human right', according to Dworkin, 'is the right to be treated with a certain *attitude*: an attitude that expresses the understanding that each person is a human being whose dignity matters.' What is more, any 'government can respect that human right even if it makes mistakes in identifying which more concrete political rights it must respect, so long as its mistake is honest' (Dworkin, 2006, p. 35). But who is to judge whether a government has made an 'honest' mistake? Presumably the first port of call must be the mechanisms and procedures for addressing humanitarian intervention and human rights abuses already present in the UN. But as constructive interpreters our task must be to show how practices can be as just as we can reasonably expect them to be. This will mean that we can condemn governments that invade or impose sanctions against countries on the basis of procedures which are unfair or fail to show integrity. More substantively, what constitutes an honest mistake in relation to identifying the list of baseline human rights that must be respected? Although Dworkin has things to say about the bottom limit of human rights, he is strangely silent on the upper limit. So there is an important yet unresolved issue here concerning the possibility of an interpreter who claims, as I wish to claim now, that no agent can claim to respect human dignity that does not recognise social and economic human rights.

My interpretation starts with the following simple thought. If one accepts that every human life has intrinsic value – that it matters from an objective point of view whether that life goes well or badly and it matters equally for the life of each person – it is hard to see how the importance of showing equal concern for that life only matters with respect to issues of liberty and bodily integrity and not for other issues, such as the distribution of income and wealth. After all, issues of distribution can have as much bearing on whether a life goes well or badly as liberty and bodily integrity. This interpretation is intended to have implications for how states may treat their own citizens if they wish other states to respect their sovereignty. Put simply, a state that systematically fails to discharge its duties with respect to its citizens' basic economic and social rights can be called not merely unjust or illegitimate but also a human rights violator, where this may justify the imposition of sanctions against that state and in some instances even military intervention. That being said, it is imperative, in order to show equal concern and respect, that any punitive measures directed at a state or its government do not worsen the situation of individual citizens who may bear little or no responsibility for state actions, especially in cases of undemocratic states. So, for example, it is one thing to say that individual states or international organisations such as the EU should impose economic sanctions against Iran for allowing the public stoning of women or against Burma for not helping the victims of cyclone Nardis or against Zimbabwe for banning NGOs, it is quite another to say that the sanctions should involve withholding foreign aid. To undertake the latter could in fact undermine or impede the fulfilment of duties of global equal concern for individuals.

Why justice rather than charity?

I have now outlined two main kinds of foreign aid and tried to show how each might be interpreted as raising particular questions of justice as global equal concern and respect. Two general questions we can ask about foreign aid are as follows. First, what is the level and kind of foreign aid that is required to achieve the optimum or gold standard of treating all human beings with equal concern and respect? Secondly, what is the level and kind of foreign aid that is required to count as a good faith attempt to achieve a minimally adequate standard of treating all human beings with equal concern and respect? I try to answer these questions in Chapters 6 and 7 respectively. But even as they stand the foregoing claims are controversial and face a number of objections.

One objection relates to the suitability of global equal concern as a model for foreign aid. How can foreign aid realistically be interpreted under this ideal given that the sums of money involved are dwarfed by the money which governments devote to their own people year on year? If a Western liberal democracy spends 25 times more (say) on its own health care system than on foreign aid to the global sick, how can the real purpose of foreign aid be said to be egalitarian in nature? I understand the scepticism that stands behind this objection, but I also think that it needs to be handled with caution. I offer two grounds for this caution. The first is that the objection seems to presuppose that global equal concern means something like equal treatment as opposed to treatment as equals. But prior to establishing what treatment as equals means in this global context, one cannot merely assume that it means something akin to flat equality. The second reason to be cautious is that the objection overlooks the possibility of a nuanced normative picture that includes the general demands of global equal concern and respect alongside a set of special obligations to fellow compatriots. From the mere fact that a country spends far more on welfare programmes at home than on foreign aid it cannot be concluded that this is because of an outright rejection of the demands of global equal concern. I shall have more to say about this in the next chapter, but for now let me say that I think a more relevant question is this: do Western liberal democracies currently spend on foreign aid an amount that reflects the coverage offered by a hypothetical insurance policy that it is reasonably safe to assume an average of persons around the globe would have decided to purchase under conditions of *ex ante* equality?

Another objection relates to the interpretation of foreign aid under the rubric of justice rather than charity. I have suggested that foreign aid can be interpreted as having more than one kind of purpose or value. Yet some interpreters will say that foreign aid is at its best when it embodies the idea that charity begins at home but does not end there. An important dimension of the ideal of benevolence or charity is that someone voluntarily chooses to transfer resources that are rightly his or hers to people in order to ameliorate problems that are lamentable. Since my goal is to interpret foreign aid in the light of justice as global equal concern and respect, I posit a different interpretive property. In Chapter 7, I shall argue that foreign aid is at its best when it embodies the idea that we have a duty to transfer resources that are *not* rightly ours to people whose disadvantages are not rightly theirs. No doubt some people will think that it stretches the idea of foreign aid to breaking point to describe it in such terms. But this response relies on a conventional understanding and I do not think that we must be wedded to this sort of understanding. That we could come to see ODA and humanitarian aid in terms of what we owe to other people as a matter of justice does not, it seems to me, fall beyond the limits of our imagination, especially given the various dimensions of foreign aid outlined above.

Of course, the sceptic might insist that ODA and humanitarian aid are practices or activities of charity rather than justice because many people who give this money do not regard themselves as seeking to address the injustices of global inequality. At best the money is a gift of beneficence. Now I do not contest that 'official development assistance' and 'humanitarian aid' are labels conventionally used to describe the money, technical support and basic commodities that donors from rich economically developed countries voluntarily provide to poor less economically developed countries in response to severe poverty, lack of development and humanitarian crises of various kinds. This conventional understanding of the point of these practices is reflected in international agreements on ODA and in the mission statements of aid agencies around the world. In the words of James Orbinski, former president of Médecins Sans Frontières, 'Humanitarianism occurs where the political has failed or is in crisis. We act not to asssume political responsibility, but firstly to relieve the inhuman suffering of failure' (Orbinski, 1999). Nevertheless, I think that it is legitimate to ask the question, 'What is the real point of foreign aid?' If foreign aid were mere charity, then other things remaining equal it would be the giver's moral right to decide whether, to whom and how much to give. But this overlooks two important points. The first is that there is a way of interpreting the resources that people in rich countries have 'at their disposal' to give or not give to people in poor countries as of uncertain status from the perspective of just distribution. As Charles Jones puts it, 'without that prior assessment, individuals or states could give "generously", thinking they were acting charitably, when their giving actually constitutes merely what justice *already* demands' (Jones, 1999, p. 13). So it is conceivable that the real purpose of foreign aid is to honour global equality of resources. The second point is that there is a way of interpreting practices of foreign aid as generating their own requirements of equal concern and respect. After all, when agents are engaged in giving or withholding foreign aid their actions have serious repercussions for other people. So arguably they have a duty to show equal concern and respect to those affected by their actions.

Notwithstanding these points, the fact that it is possible to interpret foreign aid under more than one kind of norm is supported by the results of a number of social attitude surveys conducted in various countries around the world. These show a range of attitudes about the moral justification for aid including both norms of humanitarian compassion and norms of justice (see Lumsdaine, 1993, pp. 149–51; McDonnell et al. 2003; Fransman et al., 2004). This observation, however, invites the following question. If it is possible to interpret foreign aid in the light of different kinds of norms, why endeavour to interpret them under the umbrella of justice as global equal concern and respect?

I proffer two reasons. The first is that it is not merely a terminological issue whether we have duties of justice towards distant others or we have instead duties of humanitarian compassion, loving kindness, benevolence, philanthropy or even Christian grace. It is widely accepted that duties of justice have a force that these other kinds of duties lack. Put crudely, when we entreaty people to be more compassionate we do so with less moral force than when we demand them to be more just or to do the right thing. Similarly, the use of the words 'right' and 'justice' can have a special significance in both domestic and international political debates. I have already discussed the question of intervention to compel states to accept foreign aid. But consider now the question of intervention to compel states to give aid. If a group of like-minded powerful states opted to use economic sanctions against states who systematically failed to meet just ODA targets, using the language of 'justice' would lend a kind of support to such action that would not be present if they acted in the name of duties of beneficence. Perhaps this may not be decisive in the end to justify punitive measures against sovereign states, but the possibility that it could must be taken seriously nevertheless.

The second reason draws on Dworkin's own distinction between goal-based and rights-based political theory. He suggests that when we are talking about homogenous societies united by a single urgent goal such as self-defence, it is natural that we should interpret rules, practices and individual actions under goal-based ideals. When societies are marked by cultural differences and divergent aims, by contrast, this becomes a much less feasible project and rights-based ideals appear more suitable. In so far as any plausible political theory must not propose as a fixed goal of distribution anything that a large number of individuals could not endorse, then we see that a rights-based theory is more appropriate for certain kinds of societies (Dworkin, 1973; 1983). Applying this line of reasoning to the present case, I do not wish to deny that there may be instances where large numbers of people across the globe are united around a single goal, such as assisting the victims of a natural disaster. The 2004 Asian tsunami may be a case in point. But in other circumstances people will disagree about many things: whether a country merits financial assistance given its democratic record, social and economic institutions, or even political culture; whether to provide large-scale financial assistance or food aid; how much assistance is morally fitting and to what end. When there are these sorts of deep disagreements about what the relevant goals should be, it may be more appropriate to construct a rights-based political theory (cf. Barry, 1982, pp. 204–5).

By way of summary, in this chapter I have scrutinised the claim that justice as equal concern and respect only applies to the circumstances of a true political community. I concede that it is difficult to interpret current global affairs as living up to Dworkin's narrow definition of such a community, but I reject the further assumption that this constitutes the only plausible site of egalitarian justice. On the contrary, I believe that constructive interpretation throws up numerous possible sites of global egalitarian justice. Perhaps it would be a good thing if the world could be transformed into a true global political community. But where this is not possible, there is nothing to be gained by ignoring global injustice. This is to throw up our hands. So if we can find a way to interpret a range of rules, practices and actions under a plausible conception of justice as global equal concern and respect, we might have one less reason to lament the absence of a true global political community.

6
Global Luck Egalitarianism

In Chapter 5, I argued that it is possible to identify a range of things which are appropriately governed by principles of global justice including though not limited to official development assistance and humanitarian aid. If there is a justice component to these things, however, what does that component look like? I try to make some progress in answering this question by exploring the abstract idea of global luck egalitarianism. For the present purposes I take examples of global bad luck to include being born into a country with limited natural resources, shortfalls on the side of development talent, a long and continuing history of bad government and civil war, poor climate, disease epidemics and natural disasters. The final step in developing a complete theory will be undertaken in Chapter 7, where I interpret the abstract idea of global luck egalitarianism in terms of the more concrete conception of global equality of resources. But the main focus of this chapter is the more abstract idea.

I begin by offering a critical assessment of Pogge's work on global poverty as a way of motivating the need for global luck egalitarianism. Many people have been attracted to Pogge's theory of negative rights, but an equal number find it deeply problematic and for good reasons. I shall argue that some of the inadequacies of Pogge's system of ideas point in the direction of global luck egalitarianism. I try to advance our understanding of the latter by distinguishing three alternative conceptions and by presenting reasons in favour of the third conception, which I call *interpretive global luck egalitarianism*. I then compare and contrast interpretive global luck egalitarianism with two additional accounts of the duties of international justice found in the work of Beitz and Rawls respectively (the duty to maximise the position of the worse off at the international level and the duty to assist burdened peoples). Finally, I shall outline and respond to two main objections that are typically laid at the door of cosmopolitan theories of global justice and that might be laid at the door of interpretive global luck egalitarianism. On the one hand, the agency objection states that such theories are inadequate because they fail to ground the right kinds of duties and to specify a clear agent who must perform these duties. On the other hand, the nationalism objection declares that since most people identify strongly with their own national communities it is a mistake to believe that people could have a moral duty to show the same degree of concern and respect to foreigners as to their co-nationals. I argue that the first objection over-eggs the significance of perfect duties in a theory of global justice and fails to notice an important distinction between *global agents of justice* and *agents of global justice*. Furthermore, the second objection defeats a *strong* version of global luck egalitarianism (which claims that its principles exhaust the demands of global justice), but leaves a *weak*, more plausible version intact.

Learning some lessons from Pogge

Few in the field of international political theory can boast a larger, more sophisticated body of work than Pogge. His considerable literary corpus looks at issues of international justice, human rights and poverty and explores an array of institutions and states of affair around the world. One such institution is loans offered by the IMF and World Bank on the condition that recipient countries privatise state-run industries, reduce spending on health and education services and devalue the local currency. According to Pogge, in so far as these conditions harm the poor of that country, there is a case of global justice to answer (Pogge, 2002a, p. 24). Another example is the protectionist trade policies and pricing monopolies pursued by rich, developed countries, in so far as this is permitted by the WTO, especially in the fields of agriculture, textiles and pharmaceuticals (2007, p. 135). Generalising from these illustrations, Pogge's vision of global justice asserts that being badly off, in both absolute and relative terms, is a problem of justice not merely when it is caused by or associated with crimes such as colonialism, enslavement or genocide but also when it is the result of a coercively imposed institutional order (2001; 2002a; 2004; 2005b; 2005c; 2007).

Among the numerous objections that Pogge's vision has attracted are: that it places a great deal of weight on an under-analysed concept of coercion; that it offers a contested account of the sense in which persons are responsible for world poverty merely because they support the global institutional order; that it devotes insufficient attention to the responsibility of international corporations for poverty as compared to individual agents; that it fails to specify appropriate duty-bearers in respect of world poverty since few individuals are in a position to be able to make continual adjustments to distribution and to foresee the long-term consequences of their actions; that it requires a robust baseline from which to measure the impact of the world order on people's lives but offers instead a controversial account of absolute poverty; that it ignores the extent to which even negative rights rely on positive acts for their realisation; that it attempts but fails to capture the idea of global justice by relying on negative rights alone (see Ravallion, 2003; Buchanan, 2004, ch. 4; Gilabert, 2005; Robeyns, 2005; Risse, 2005; Brooks, 2006; Ashford, 2007; Caney, 2005; Gould, 2007b; Mieth, 2008; Meckled-Garcia, 2008).

No doubt there are things which could be said on Pogge's behalf regarding each of these objections, but my own intention is to put yet more pressure on his rationale for assuming merely negative rights. His claim is that this enables him to accept a minimalist libertarian constraint on the nature of human rights 'without disqualifying social and economic human rights' (Pogge, 2002a, pp. 66–7). Even if Pogge can avoid objections from libertarians by occupying the higher ground of negative rights, however, this does not mean that he can avoid objections from egalitarians. Occupying the higher ground will only succeed on both counts if he can convince egalitarians that negative rights are sufficient to capture social and economic rights. But this, I think, is a big ask. Pogge's retreat to this higher ground restricts our attention to negative duties, namely, the duty not to support a coercive world order which is such that persons do not have secure access to basic necessities through institutional denial or deprivation (*ibid.*). This way of expressing what the duty is, however, may work to undermine his own position. Consider misfortunes caused by natural disasters. If Pogge argues that global institutions do *not* have a positive duty of justice to assist the victims of natural disasters, then his position will seem unattractive to those people who believe in social and economic rights of the kind that do impose such duties. On the other hand, if he argues that global institutions *do* have a positive duty of justice to assist, then not providing assistance will amount to official denial or deprivation and the negative duty not to support unjust global institutions ultimately relies on the existence of positive duties. It is interesting to note that *World Poverty and Human Rights* contains four mentions of natural disasters, but nowhere are earthquakes, tropical storms, hurricanes, tidal waves, draughts, wildfires and floods recognised as possibly generating positive duties of assistance. In this way Pogge ignores the global luck egalitarian who believes that nobody should have to suffer the bad luck of being born into a region prone to natural disasters any more than they should have to suffer colonialism, theft, slavery or even severe poverty caused by unjust global institutions.

Perhaps Pogge would claim that if persons suffer a tropical storm or hurricane and global institutions do nothing to assist them, then we as individuals have failed in a duty of justice (as opposed to beneficence) only if the tropical storm or hurricane was caused by global warming which itself resulted from a coercively imposed world order and the violation of a negative duty not to support such a world order. But my own view is that even if the tropical storm or hurricane is a purer case of brute luck than this, then it may still be the case that agents have failed the requirements of justice if they do nothing. Here the injustice is located in how agents deal with the misfortune as opposed to in the misfortune itself.

The wider point is that for many millions of people around the world it is not *merely* trade protectionism, structural adjustment policies or even international resource and borrowing privileges which cause them to lack the opportunities others take for granted. How the human race responds to natural catastrophes, disease epidemics, lack of proximity to natural resources and shortfalls on the side of the talents required for effective development also plays a part. That inequality can be caused by different factors has not been lost on writers in the field of domestic justice. In his 1998 article 'Choice and Circumstance', for example, Hiller Steiner avers that 'the causal factors contributing to a person's incurring adverse (or benign) consequences can be exhaustively consigned to a threefold classification: (1) her own doings; the doings of others; and (3) the doings of nature' (Steiner, 1998, pp. 102–3). It seems to me undeniable that global inequalities can also be the products of a complex mixture of three kinds of factors: (1*) local doings; (2*) the doings of foreign peoples; and (3*) the doings of nature.[1]

Natural lotteries have a deleterious affect when unlucky people live among lucky people. This is compounded when unlucky people find themselves in a country full of other unlucky people. Consider the bad luck of being born with a level of talent which commands a low economic rent as compared to other people in a country where average talent commands a lower economic rent relative to the rest of the world or where the average level of talent would not be especially low were it not for a brain-drain to other countries; in being born into a country whose climate is such that most of the population are at high risk of certain insect-borne diseases not suffered in other parts of the world; in being born into a country which faces a high probability of natural disasters; in being born into a country whose general population suffers from a poor genetic endowment with respect to health. This is bad luck upon bad luck and it is something that international aid agencies end up responding to every day and on a massive scale. That being said, the proper measure of global inequality from the perspective of ethical individualism, with its focus on individuals rather than countries, is not in terms of inequalities in average incomes or health levels between different countries but rather in terms of inequalities in incomes and health levels between individuals across the globe.

However, the most common 'bad luck' argument found in the literature is that in the absence of any antecedent claim to natural resources no population has a right to possess more than its equal share of resources or the value thereof (see Barry, 1982; Steiner, 1999). Beitz has even gone so far as to suggest that the distribution of natural resources across the surface of the globe is 'a purer case of something being "arbitrary from a moral point of view" than the distribution of talents' (Beitz, 1979, p. 140). It is a purer case because any presumptive entitlement a person might claim to have over his own natural talents or personal resources by virtue of a right to self-ownership is absent in the case of natural impersonal resources. What is more, Beitz insists that this distribution is a matter of egalitarian justice quite apart from the existence of any social cooperation between resource-rich and resource-poor countries pertaining to this natural bounty. While I do not seek to defend the claim that the distribution of natural resources is a *purer* case of moral arbitrariness than the distribution of human talents, I do think that Beitz is right to widen the field of egalitarian concern. Then again, if we are going to widen the field of (luck) egalitarian concern, surely we have reason to reflect on other causes of deprivation besides the distribution of natural resources.

My proposal, then, is to apply principles of egalitarian justice to various rules, practices and individual actions concerning many different causes of deprivation including not merely the distribution of natural resources but also the distribution of talent, genetic endowment, climate and natural disasters. In saying that principles of justice apply to these things, however, I do not overlook the fact that the global institutional order itself exacerbates the doings of nature because, for example, it can create changes in climate which increase the incidence of natural disasters in certain parts of the world and prevents people from being able to purchase insurance against such disasters or move to safer areas. Thus we need to consider what rich, industrialised countries owe to poor, less-developed countries in terms of reducing greenhouse gas emissions and paying compensation for their past emissions (see Shue, 1999; Caney, 2006; Moore, 2008). I am also in full agreement with Pogge about the urgency of preventing crimes such as slavery and genocide, of reforming international rules on trade and lending so that individuals are not pushed into deprivation, of rethinking the resource and borrowing privileges given to corrupt and undemocratic rulers in foreign climes, of encouraging leaders in developing countries to introduce constitutional amendments forbidding new governments from selling natural resources seized illegitimately by preceding governments, of taxing the extraction of raw materials such as gas and oil, and so on (see Pogge, 2002a; 2005b; 2007). Nevertheless, I do not regard it as somehow trivial to attempt, in addition to these things, to make the giving or withholding of foreign aid as just it can be, and not merely *qua* compensation for harm in Pogge's sense.

So what we need, I think, is a compound approach to global distributive justice which identifies a range of possible sites of justice, recognises positive as well as negative rights, and acknowledges both absolute and relative deprivation. Having said that I endorse a compound approach to global distributive justice, in what follows I intend to concentrate on the global luck egalitarian component of the position. However, I do this *not* because I assume that the injustices it highlights are in some sense worse from a moral point of view. On the contrary, we often look more harshly upon or punish more severely the person who intentionally sets out to harm other people than the person who is aware of his own good luck but fails to lift a finger to assist those who are less fortune than himself. For this reason I want to leave conceptual space for the possibility that there are degrees of global injustice in the sense that although theft of land, slavery, human exploitation, closed borders, trade protectionism, structural adjustment policies, international resource and borrowing privileges and failures to properly mitigate the affects of brute luck are all unjust, they are not equally unjust. This implies that in an imaginary set of circumstances in which we must choose between ending one of two unjust practices that have similar effects, it may be right to end the practice dealing with the doings of other people rather than the practice dealing with the doings of nature. Obviously the difference between these two kinds of doings can be represented as a matter of degree, and we may be uncertain how to describe a particular doing.

Nor do I wish to imply that injustices associated with how we respond to the doings of nature are the single biggest cause of global inequality. I expect that a compelling case could be made for other factors being more significant. Some people will argue that national factors such as civil war, political corruption, economic mismanagement and so on are responsible for a higher proportion of global inequality. Others will say that most global inequalities can be traced to the fact that developed countries have controlled international markets, monopolised industrial development and new technologies. Yet others will say that the single biggest cause of global inequality is structural adjustment policies prescribed by international monetary institutions such as the IMF and World Bank. (Of course, for those individuals affected by these factors they might be experienced as so many more instances of bad luck.) Rather, I focus on the doings of nature because I think that this component has thus far received much less attention than other causes of global inequality and has been widely misunderstood as a consequence.

Three conceptions of global luck egalitarianism

As the name implies, global luck egalitarianism is a view about the status of inequalities caused by brute luck at the global level. I believe that a great deal of work still needs to be done in order to understand the precise nature and implications of this view and that without this work any attempt to evaluate or criticise its usefulness is likely to be at best premature and at worse prone to error and misinterpretation. In this section I take the first few steps in this direction by contrasting three possible conceptions.

A priori global luck egalitarianism

The first conception, *a priori global luck egalitarianism*, starts with the fundamental intuition that the aim of everyone everywhere must be to try to eliminate inequalities which reflect brute luck but at the same time uphold inequalities that reflect voluntary choices. Having established the bedrock moral duty independently of particular contexts of application, the luck egalitarian then considers the realm of global affairs and prescribes a set of political, legal and economic arrangements which best realise that duty. At the extreme, he might argue that nobody should be worse off than anyone else because of the vagaries of nature and therefore the world needs a radical economic mechanism to eliminate inequality such as a 100 per cent tax on any wealth generated through close proximity to natural resources. More vaguely, and therefore perhaps less radically, he might simply say that our goal must be to create a world in which as far as possible every person enjoys equal opportunities at the start of adult life (see Caney, 2005, p. 122; cf. Wenar, 2008, p. 404).

Three main criticisms can be laid at its door. The first is that it is overdemanding. Even with a tax rate closer to 50 than 100 per cent, anyone who is even moderately adept at exploiting natural resources will have to pay a significant global tax in addition to any taxes he already pays to his own government. Quite apart from the creation of a global wealth tax, if persons are to follow the spirit of global luck egalitarianism then presumably they will be bound to try to mitigate a great deal of brute luck everywhere and this could potentially require a life almost entirely dedicated to the alleviation of deprivation and misfortune. Now in reply to this the *a priori* global luck egalitarian can try to argue that justice is but one of a number of legitimate claims on people's time and effort and must exist alongside other ethical obligations and personal projects. A life that is dedicated entirely to mitigating brute luck inequalities both at home and abroad is certainly not what is suggested. However, he is then faced with the difficult task explaining on principled grounds the precise limits of any reasonable *a priori* global luck egalitarianism. How much achievement of luck egalitarian aims is reasonable?

A second criticism is a version of the levelling down objection. Suppose we discover tomorrow an inaccessible planet populated by intelligent human-like creatures. Satellite communication reveals that they are much worse off than us and not because of anything we or they have done but because of accidents of nature. As things stand we can do nothing to reduce this inter-planetary inequality except by levelling down at our end. The *a priori* global luck egalitarian thinks that this situation is unfair and that if we could do something about it, to wit, make ourselves worse off, then we have a reason of justice to do so. Of course, the standard response to the levelling down objection is to insist that levelling down is only something we consider doing *all things considered*. We are likely to have other (stronger) reasons not to level down, not least the fact that generally speaking it is bad to make some people worse off without making anyone better off. But once again we need a fuller account of what is reasonable given this value conflict. Would there come a point at which a small amount of levelling down is justified? How do we determine the right sort of concern for the different lives involved?

A third – and in my view more powerful – criticism is that *a priori* global luck egalitarianism fails to respect a commonly held intuition about natural lotteries and social justice. This intuition is famously expressed by Rawls in *A Theory of Justice*:

> The natural distribution is neither just nor unjust; nor is it unjust that persons are born into society at some particular position. These are simply natural facts. What is just and unjust is the way that institutions deal with these facts.

(Rawls, 1971, p. 102)

Rawls does not condemn the distribution of natural endowments as such but the way in which basic institutions allow it to be converted into material inequalities. In other words, 'the most obvious injustice of the system of natural liberty is that is permits distributive shares to be improperly influenced by these factors so arbitrary from a moral point of view' (p. 72).

Institutional global luck egalitarianism

The second conception, *institutional global luck egalitarianism*, takes very seriously Rawls' point about natural lotteries and justice. It says that global natural lotteries are not in themselves just or unjust. What is just or unjust is the way in which global institutions deal with these facts. Among the relevant institutions are legally enforced borders, internationally recognised private property rights, rules governing international trade and monetary arrangements, and international laws relating to sovereignty and non-intervention. Included within the scope of how institutions deal with natural facts are both actions and omissions. In addition to this, some defenders of institutional global luck egalitarianism argue that the view is not intended to be constitutive of global distributive justice. Rather, its role is merely to justify or motivate the choice of distributive principles. This means that it does not by itself stipulate that those distributive principles must be egalitarian in nature (Tan, 2008).

I think that this version is partly right, but not fully right. It has two weaknesses or potential weaknesses. The first is that some activities raise questions of justice even though they are not constituents of the basic structure of the society of peoples. Consider the actions of ordinary citizens and heads of government in deciding whether or not and how much to respond to relative deprivation in other countries. To be sure, citizens are obligated to pay their taxes, some of which goes to development assistance, just as their political leaders are responsible for honouring previous international commitments. But they also make decisions everyday about whether or not to get involved in much higher levels of assistance, where these decisions are not dictated by current institutional structures. Citizens may decide whether or not to donate money directly to NGOs and in some instances whether or not to move their money to countries with a different tax burden, while heads of government decide whether or not to sign up to new treaties. It is, I think, dogmatic to insist that these decisions, which can have equally serious repercussions for other people's life chances, cannot fall within the purview of justice merely because they are decisions about how to behave within the basic structure as opposed to the basic structure itself.

The second potential weakness is that institutional global luck egalitarianism sees an abridged role for its own requirements. The suggestion is that the requirements of global luck egalitarianism are not constitutive of global justice but merely provide justifications for other, perhaps non-egalitarian principles. It might be argued, however, that to posit this limited, justificatory role is to misconstrue the real point of luck egalitarian thinking in contemporary political theory. After all, many egalitarians have been attracted to luck egalitarianism precisely as a description of what distributive justice is or what justice demands of us as opposed to what it can be used to justify where this may not be equality (see Cohen, 1989, p. 908; Roemer, 1993, p. 147).[2] I call this a 'potential' weakness for the simple reason that it is open to interpretation what the real point of global luck egalitarianism is.

Interpretive global luck egalitarianism

The third conception, *interpretive global luck egalitarianism*, says that various rules, practices and individual actions are at their best (or most just) only if they aim to mitigate global brute luck whilst at the same time upholding the consequences of personal responsibility around the world. It says that the appropriateness of applying these two requirements is the result of interpreting certain rules, practices and individual actions in the light of the concept of egalitarian justice and in terms of deeper principles of human dignity. What is more, both the content and the purpose of these requirements is subject to further constructive interpretation.

Of the three, I find this conception of global luck egalitarianism most attractive. It has two principal benefits. The first is that it is well placed to identify other sites of egalitarian justice besides institutional regimes. It does not deny that rules and practices are important sites of egalitarian justice, but it does recognise that particular actions which either fall outside of or within a social framework can also be interpreted as subject to principles of global luck egalitarianism. So, for example, by choosing to do something but not enough to help the victims of natural disasters elsewhere in the world, agents who are engaged in institutional foreign aid, a rule or practice, must account for why *they* have failed to satisfy the demands of global luck egalitarianism. They must do so because justice applies to the decisions they make within the current institutional structure to which principles of justice also apply. Justice applies to their decisions for the same reason it applies to the institutions, namely, that they have serious repercussions for the lives of those affected.

The second principal benefit of interpretive global luck egalitarianism is that it successfully walks the line between being too luck egalitarian and not being luck egalitarian enough. On the one hand, the aim of *a priori* global luck egalitarianism is to fully compensate brute luck and uphold choice and responsibility as much as possible. But there are occasions when this aim comes up against the inappropriateness of levelling down. Interpretive global luck egalitarianism, by contrast, incorporates the twin requirements of mitigating brute luck and upholding choices within a larger interpretive framework of understanding what it means to show equal concern and respect at the global level. So there is less suggestion that it requires levelling down even in principle. On the other hand, institutional global luck egalitarianism merely provides a justificatory device for defending other, perhaps non-egalitarian, principles of distributive justice. Interpretive global luck egalitarianism offers a different way of understanding the point of luck egalitarian requirements. So, for example, an interpretive luck egalitarian is able to say that the twin requirements are constitutive of what justice means at a high level of abstraction. Of course, these requirements cannot be taken at face value but must be interpreted at a lower level of abstraction.

To expand on this last point, Dworkin draws a useful distinction between abstract egalitarian rights, on the one hand, and the more substantive right to equality of resources, on the other, where the latter interprets the former. I think that a similar distinction applies here. One might say that global luck egalitarianism is an abstract statement of the right to global equal concern and respect, whereas global equality of resources provides a more concrete interpretation of that right. Global equality of resources does not attempt to fully compensate brute luck but to respond to it appropriately by transforming it into option luck. It requires only that people receive the resources they would on average have received under conditions of *ex ante* equality, where this is likely to be much less than full compensation given that most people would not choose to purchase full compensation given how costly the relevant policies would be. By developing this theory I hope to go some way to assuaging the objection put by anti-egalitarians that principles of global equality must be hopelessly over-demanding.

But how can global luck egalitarianism plausibly be said to capture the real point of foreign aid given that current patterns do not, and perhaps could not, exemplify its two basic requirements? The history of ODA has not been one of eliminating entirely the gap between the lucky and the unlucky, and most humanitarian aid goes to the very poorest of the poor because of the severity as opposed to the genesis of their situation. People who walk into refugee camps are by and large given food and shelter not philosophical investigations into their brute luck versus personal responsibility. To be sure, rich, industrialised countries may be more reluctant to give aid to corrupt or illegitimate governments and they sometimes demonstrate sensitivity to the moral distinction between the responsibility of a country's leaders for the poverty of its people and the responsibility of ordinary individuals. But this is not the same as saying that foreign aid is an attempt to compensate brute luck and to hold governments responsible for their choices.

Obviously, then, there are difficulties in trying to characterise foreign aid as a practice whose sole purpose should be to satisfy global luck egalitarian requirements. Even so, I think that these difficulties merely underscore the point that practices can be valuable for more than one reason. It also highlights the incompleteness of the abstract idea of global luck egalitarianism and the need for further interpretation. To this end, in the next chapter I shall argue that it is appropriate to interpret foreign aid as being adequately just when it mimics the payments that would be made by hypothetical insurance companies to their individual policy-holders if, contrary to fact, persons around the world faced the same antecedent chance of disaster, destitution and lack of development and enjoyed ample opportunity to purchase insurance against such risks. I shall argue that these sorts of policies are much closer to capturing what the real purpose of foreign aid should be. To use Dworkin's own phraseology, this is not a compromise or second-best solution but an attempt to understand what equal concern truly requires of us.

Global luck egalitarianism as distinct from Rawlsian justice

An alternative strategy for trying to understand what equal concern truly requires of us globally has been to plunder the work of Rawls. Consider the familiar suggestion that Rawls' difference principle could be applied to international socio-economic inequalities (see Barry, 1973, pp. 128–32; Scanlon, 1973, pp. 1066–7; Beitz, 1975, pp. 362–3; 1979, pp. 150–3). Beitz, for example, suggests that an appropriate role for a global difference principle would be to specify what a fair distribution of the benefits and burdens of international economic cooperation would be (1979, p. 152). Two factors militate against this strategy. The first has to do with implementation. Although open to debate and dependent on circumstances, it is quite possible that the amount of redistribution required would be enormous, perhaps even more than under global luck egalitarianism, which is sensitive to the principle of special responsibility. Robert Amdur conjectures that implementing the global difference principle is likely to require 'monetary and trade reforms, debt cancellation, and, more important, massive development aid' (Amdur, 1977, p. 455). Now the mere fact that the global difference principle requires massive development aid need not be decisive against it. Yet a principle of redistribution which calls on the world to give money to the worse off group and to keep on giving irrespective of the responsibility of that group for the position they are in and the impact this will have on economic growth both in the target economy and in the global economy may not stand the test of equal concern. For it is far from obvious that the average person would choose the difference principle at such a price if placed under conditions of *ex ante* equality.

The second militating factor is that Rawls himself rejected the global difference principle (Rawls, 1999, pp. 115–18). His reason for rejecting it, however, is not the absence of an effective implementing authority or even the possible negative impact on economic growth but the conviction that doing so 'would fail to express due toleration for other acceptable ways [...] of ordering society' (p. 59). For Rawls, it is integral to the law of peoples that decent peoples must respect the decisions made by free and responsible peoples in other parts of the world regarding such things as the trade-off between production and leisure time and even population size (pp. 115–19). In so far as these decisions contribute significantly to global inequalities it would not be acceptable to transfer resources from wealthier countries to poorer countries in order to undo such inequalities (p. 118). Rawls also gestures at the further argument that the 'relations of affinity' that characterise life within well-ordered political societies, and which make the difference principle psychologically palatable for its members, are absent between different peoples 'with their separate languages, religions, and cultures' (pp. 112–13).

I think that Rawls is correct but only up to a point. The drawback with his particular conception of what it means to show due toleration is that it ignores the way in which individuals living within poor countries are often hostages to the fortunes of the countries in which they live. I shall have much more to say on this intricate subject in the next chapter. For the present moment I want to consider Rawls' preferred conception.

Although Rawls rejects the idea of a global difference principle, in *The Law of Peoples* he defends the following duty: 'Peoples have a duty to assist other peoples living under unfavorable conditions that prevent their having a just or decent social political regime' (Rawls, 1999, p. 37). Rawls clarifies that these 'burdened societies' lack, amongst other things, 'the human capital and know-how, and, often, the material and technical resources needed to be well-ordered' (p. 106). The duty of assistance is a transitional duty. The idea is not to assist the worse-off in perpetuity (as per the difference principle). Rather, 'the duty of assistance holds until all societies have achieved just liberal or decent basic institutions' (p. 118).

What are the similarities and differences between the duty of assistance and global luck egalitarianism? Arguably there is one respect in which Rawls' duty of assistance marches in step with global luck egalitarian. In so far as burdened societies characteristically suffer shortfalls in human capital and material resources, not to mention susceptibility to natural disasters such as drought or flood, on the surface this could be presented as a principle of compensation for bad luck. But this would be a false interpretation, since the similarities are only on the surface. Rawls makes it clear that even a society 'with few natural resources and little wealth can be well-ordered if its political traditions, law, and property, and class structure [...] are such as to sustain a liberal or decent society' (Rawls, 1999, p. 106).

It is also important to recognise that Rawls' duty of assistance is not a principle of global equality. That is, the objective of the duty of assistance is not to reduce socio-economic inequalities between peoples. Rather, the aim is to use assistance, conditions of relief and persuasion to encourage outlier countries to join the society of well-ordered states (Rawls, 1999, p. 108). So, for example, when Rawls discusses the duty of assistance in respect of famine he emphasises the need for well-ordered states to put pressure on governments of burdened societies to develop effective back-up arrangements (p. 109). He cites Sen's example of the 1943 Bengal famine in which a sudden shift in the exchange value of fish and other foods meant that fishermen were unable to buy enough food to survive. Both Sen and Rawls point the finger at a national government that did not care enough for the well-being of its citizens to make proper arrangements for these fluctuations, such as through a scheme of safety-net entitlements (Rawls, 1999, p. 109; Sen, 1999, pp. 163–4). An interpretive global luck egalitarian, by contrast, will try to look at deprivation from the perspective of the individuals concerned. To hold this view is not to eschew attempts to promote good governance either as an end in itself or as an instrument for tackling global inequality. Instead it is to affirm that this cannot be all there is to global equal concern and respect. So, for example, global equal concern and respect could mean using development money to assist individuals who are the victims of both crop failure and bad governments as compensable forms of brute luck.

The agency objection

I now turn to two main objections that might be laid at the door of inter-pretive global luck egalitarianism. I begin with the agency objection. This has two parts. The first is that global luck egalitarianism is inadequate because it fails to set out the right kinds of duties. The second is that global luck egalitarianism is inadequate because it fails to specify a clear agent who must perform those duties.

To begin with the first part, this starts with a simple question about what kinds of duties are properly called duties of justice. Suppose that duties of justice must be both strong in the sense that they generate urgent demands to transfer resources to other people and perfect mean-ing that they specify whom the duty is owed to and do not afford too much leeway in how and when the duty is performed. Onora O'Neill, for example, argues that rights-based accounts of what we owe to distant others are inadequate as theories of justice because such things as 'the right to food' are mere 'manifesto rights' in the sense that they generate only imperfect duties. The duty to feed people who are starving is an imperfect duty because it does not by itself determine which particular starving persons are to be fed and, what is more, it provides too much room for manoeuvre concerning how and when the duty is discharged (see O'Neill, 1986; 1989; 1998; 2000; 2001). Can global luck egalitarian-ism satisfy these constraints any better?

When governments decide upon their aid budgets and where to send the money earmarked for aid it is likely that a number of factors will enter into their deliberations. But according to interpretive global luck egalitarianism their decisions are only just if they take special note of the urgency of the claims made upon their money. The urgency stems from the requirement to mitigate the impacts of brute luck. This means that agents should endeavour to respond to every case of brute luck which has a devastating impact on people's lives. Of course, if the relevant con-ception is *a priori* global luck egalitarianism, then the implication might be that every government has a *prime facie* duty to give and keep giving up to and beyond the point of bankruptcy. But this is certainly not what interpretive global luck egalitarianism demands. At first glance, global luck egalitarianism is also clearer in stipulating to whom the obligation is owed and provides less room for manoeuvre than the theories O'Neill criticises. This is because it implies not a generalised duty to feed the hungry but the more specific duty to assist individuals, at home and abroad, who suffer relative deprivation as a result of brute luck and to do so at every available opportunity.

Nevertheless, it might be pointed out that the duty to assist the victims of brute luck is still an imperfect duty because it fails to specify what the duty to mitigate the affects of brute luck is exactly and for whom it must be performed in the likely event that an agent cannot assist everyone. Of course, at this stage I could try to fall back on the interpretive dimension of global luck egalitarianism. The abstract requirements of global luck egalitarianism are exactly that, abstract. This means that the requirements stand in need of further interpretation. The specific interpretation I shall develop in Chapter 7 is that of global equality of resources. But even here it is unclear that the duties involved could be described as perfect duties. Alternatively, one could try to argue that agents have a duty to turn imperfect duties into perfect duties by making or establishing institutional arrangements for fairly specifying, distributing and enforcing duties of assistance (see Buchanan, 1987, p. 570; Tan, 2004, pp. 50–2). Yet this response merely postpones the original point: for it is likely that the immediate duty to make institutional arrangements is itself an imperfect duty not least because it remains unclear to whom the duty is owed or what exactly it means to perform the duty. Inevitably there will also be leeway in how and when the duty is to be performed.

For these reasons I think that the correct response to O'Neill is to put pressure on the interpretive assumption that something is an adequate theory of justice only if it specifies perfect duties. One strategy is to draw an analogy with other duties that we think are duties of duties but which would not qualify as perfect duties on O'Neill's understanding. Pogge, for example, offers the example of a manufacturer's duty to repair faulty watches. Here the content of the duty and the person for whom it is to be performed remain unspecified until such time a customer comes forward with a faulty watch (Pogge, 1992c, pp. 241–2). Another strategy is to show that O'Neill's own alternative theory of duties of assistance towards the global poor appeals to Kantian-type duties to protect and promote rational nature, some of which, by her own lights, are imperfect duties (see Jones, 1999, ch. 4). In what follows I shall assume therefore that duties of justice need not be perfect duties.

The second part of the agency objection goes even further, however. It claims that global luck egalitarianism is inadequate because it fails to specify a clear agent who must perform the duties. By analogy, Samuel Freeman questions the capacity of independent countries to manipulate global inequalities so as to satisfy a global difference principle. According to Freeman, it is not feasible for individual countries to calculate the effects of its many decisions upon the worst off members of the world. So a country has no way of telling whether what it is doing in the name of the difference principle is actually having the desired effect (Freeman, 2006, pp. 61–2). In a similar vein, Saladin Meckled-Garcia doubts whether any agent could produce the kind of continuous adjustment to distributive effects that would be required to bring those effects in line with, and to sustain over time, a just distribution. Agents who give foreign aid, individual or collective, are inherently unable to judge whether any single effort, or even series of efforts, will produce egalitarian effects overall. 'Well-intentioned donations to a group who are disadvantaged might lead to their economic domination of another group, or to market effects which disadvantage others' (Meckled-Garcia, 2008, p. 256).[3]

Although I think that these sorts of arguments also have the potential to be damaging to global luck egalitarianism, I do not think that they are devastating against it. The key thing to note about interpretive global luck egalitarianism is that it is an attempt to understand what it means to treat persons with equal concern. If this means that each agent has a duty to mitigate brute luck around the world as an end state, then obviously it would be nigh-on impossible for any single agent to fully achieve and sustain this end state over time or even to know, with absolute assuredness, that their actions were actually working. But suppose that the duties set out by interpretive global luck egalitarianism were not of this order. Suppose instead that they amounted to doing one's bit towards realising the requirements of global luck egalitarianism along with other agents. If so, then perhaps it makes sense to relax the conception of agency that we associate with the idea of global justice. Relaxing the conception of agency means that it is no longer necessary for each agent to have knowledge of, and the ability to produce continuous adjustments to, the global distribution. Rather, the more modest constraint on an adequate theory of global justice is that the agents it specifies can do their bit towards promoting a just global distribution, where the exact nature of that bit is to be specified through interpretation. We might call this the distinction between being a *global agent of justice* and being an *agent of global justice*. As a rough approximation, an agent of global justice is an agent that can and ought to contribute to the requirements of global justice even if that action falls short of being a decisive contribution to global justice. So the hope is that even if global luck egalitarianism is unable to specify global agents of justice, it may be able to specify agents of global justice.

How can agents of global justice have knowledge of whether their actions amount to treating others with equal concern? A preliminary step here is gaining knowledge of the impact of actions. This is a difficult step and one that is also difficult for governments in the domestic sphere. But it is, I think, not inconceivable that agents could know and understand the impact of their actions even in the context of lots of other independent agents attempting to do likewise. Consider the work of the MDG Gap Task Force which was created by Ban Ki-moon in May 2007 to provide monitoring of MDG fulfilment at the international and country level and includes more than 40 major regional and international organisations. The reports of the Task Force provide countries with a clear indication of how far they have left to go (see UN, 2008). The second step is knowledge of what is and what is not due to brute luck. In many respects this problem is not idiosyncratic to the international domain. Even so there may be additional problems for agents on one side of the globe gaining knowledge over the brute luck being suffered by agents elsewhere. Yet technology may hold the key to solving some of these problems. Internet news organisations such as the Disaster News Network and other agencies like the EM-DAT International Disaster Database, the Global Disaster Information Portal and the Global Disaster Alert and Coordination System currently provide a wealth of up to the minute information about the experiences of persons in far-flung places and what is or is not being done to help them. With this information to hand, agents do not have the excuse of not knowing that their acts or omission are permitting brute luck to ruin people's lives.

Naturally when agents come together to coordinate their effort against global inequality in ways that can make continual and effective interventions possible the entities they create will attract secondary duties. After all, the history of foreign aid is a long history of complex and multilayered cooperation between individuals, associations, corporations, national governments and international organisations of various kinds who themselves attract duties. But it does not follow from this that these secondary duties are duties of justice only because they are generated by agreements or special relationships. They can be duties of justice by virtue of the primary duties of those who contribute to them. Although it is quite possible to take a different interpretive stance, my own is that individuals can be both primary holders of global egalitarian rights and primary bearers of global egalitarian duties. I shall provide a list of these duties at the end of Chapter 7.

However, I accept that there are some kinds of actions, harms and externalities – such as wars, human rights abuses, protectionism and pollution – concerning which it makes better sense to regard nations, states or even corporations as primary duties bearers. In the case of international human rights law, for example, it is states rather than individuals who are customarily understood to be the primary duty bearers. (Of course, this in itself does not preclude an alternative interpretation of the relevant duty-bearers.) To take a different example, perhaps pharmaceutical companies have a moral duty not to bring lawsuits, individually or collectively, against national governments when the latter are attempting to offer affordable medicines to their citizens under the compulsory licensing provision of the WTO's Trade-Related Aspects of Intellectual Property Rights Agreement (TRIPS) signed in Marrakesh, April 1994. To bring such lawsuits, it might be argued, not only goes against the spirit of TRIPS but is a dereliction of a collective duty to the global sick. These are just two illustrations. There are many other kinds of collective responsibility.[4]

The nationalism objection

I now turn to the nationalism objection. It states that nationality constitutes a necessary condition for including persons within the scope of egalitarian justice. In other words, it is only against the backdrop of ties of nationhood that persons can have obligations to treat other people with equal concern and respect. And this means that persons may show more concern for fellow nationals than for foreigners. One way to articulate the nationalism objection is to say that national sentiments have been and continue to be necessary existence conditions for the development and maintenance of the modern welfare state and not inappropriately so (Tamir, 1993). This does not mean that in pursuing a national interest persons are permitted to act as they please towards members of other nations. But it does imply that they are entitled to put their nation first in deciding whether or not to contribute to something like a global welfare state.

A common reply to the nationalism objection is that it presupposes a set of circumstances which are for the most part matters of brute luck. It is in this attitude that Pogge writes, 'Nationality is just one further deep contingency (like genetic endowment, race, gender, and social class), one more potential basis of institutional inequalities that are inescapable and present from birth' (Pogge, 1989, p. 247). Likewise, Simon Caney argues that 'people should not be penalized because of the vagaries of happenstance, and their fortunes should not be set by factors like nationality and citizenship' (Caney, 2001, p. 125). 'If one thinks that, as egalitarian liberals do, that it is unjust if persons fare worse because of their class or ethnic identity one should surely also think that it is unjust if persons fare worse because of their nationality' (2005, p. 123). Although I have some sympathy with this reply to the nationalism objection, I also think that it is important to acknowledge its limitations. Merely highlighting the fact that membership of a national community is happenstance is not the same as showing that it is unfair to allow this feature to influence how we treat non-members. Even if one regards membership of a nation as a matter of contingency — as opposed to consent, for example — this does not automatically make it morally arbitrary. Cosmopolitans, that is, global luck egalitarians, must do more to motivate the view that global socio-economic inequalities based on nationality are unjust.

To expand on this last point, David Miller — one of the most sophisticated defenders of the special demands of nationhood — maintains that it is simply bogus to claim that membership of a nation is morally arbitrary in the context of international relations *in the same* way that natural talent, class, ethnicity and so on are morally arbitrary features in the context of domestic justice (Miller, 2007, p. 32). The fact is that members of nations do not typically regard membership as a morally arbitrary feature (2000, pp. 25–6). Even if one finds regrettable some aspects of nationalism, it is hard to refute that national identifications are felt to give rise to extra obligations (2002b, pp. 80–5). After all,

> the great majority of people continue to identify strongly with their national community, most significant political decisions are taken at nation-state level, and nations to a greater or lesser extent constitute themselves as mutual benefit schemes in which people who suffer from certain types of loss – disability, ill-health, unemployment, and so forth – are compensated by those who enjoy better fortune. To show that all of this is morally irrelevant when assessing the opportunity sets enjoyed by people belonging to different national communities would require a great deal of argument.
>
> (2005a, p. 70)

This may strike some people as a devastating line of response to the cosmopolitan. But notice how conservative it is. Miller quite rightly points out that national communities often *do* give priority to people living within their own borders. Yet this is not the same thing as showing that they act justly in doing so. Why should we take these particular views as decisive when they are often the product of the sort of nationalistic political arrangement which they are supposed to justify?[5]

Miller tries to add rhetorical force to the assumption that equality is the special preserve of nations with examples of the following sort.

> In an encounter with a stranger from another community, there are certain things that I may not do – if he is ill or in pain I must do what I can to help him – but it makes no sense for either of us to try to apply comparative principles – for instance to insist on equality in some respect.
>
> (Miller, 1998, p. 171)

Perhaps both Miller and Dworkin would say that this is an example of what it means for a political theory to be continuous with our conventional personal ethics. But is it really true to say that in the example it makes *no sense* for either of us to insist on equality in some respect? That I owe anything to the stranger presumably has to do with the fact that we share at least a moral universe if not a national community. So we must treat each other as equal members of that universe at least. It might be said that we have a duty to treat each other in accordance with principles of human dignity. Evidently there are different interpretations of what this means in relation to our encounters with strangers from other countries, but suppose this particular stranger sincerely believes that individuals should work to mitigate the influence of brute luck on other people's lives whoever they are. Given this assumption, arguably it *does* make sense for the stranger to insist on equality. To assume that it cannot make sense is to beg the question against the cosmopolitan.

Of course, showing that it can make sense for the stranger to ask for equality is not the same as showing that this is actually what justice demands. And it is here where the argument becomes difficult. Suppose a region has been hit by a powerful hurricane leaving many thousands of desperate souls spread across its coastal areas. Can it really be right to think that persons living in a wealthy, developed country with its own problems of relative deprivation would not be justified in giving more assistance to fellow nationals than to perfect strangers whether directly through voluntary transfers or indirectly through government aid?

At this stage, the cosmopolitan has two main options. The first is to adopt Caney's line of response which is to insist that even if there are moral reasons to show more concern to those at home than abroad, we should not assume that these are reasons of *justice* (Caney, 1999, pp. 128–33; 2005, p. 134). This response acknowledges the moral relevance of patriotic ties in determining how we ought to behave towards fellow nationals and foreigners all things considered but does not grant that this moral relevance is of the order of justice. This response seems dogmatic, however. To suppose that all of our associative obligations (including those based on national-ity) are obligations of general morality rather than justice flies in the face of what many people take these obligations to be. For this reason I accept that associative obligations can be obligations of justice. Whereas obligations of nationality rest on the contingencies of con-quest, geographical proximity, racial decent, language, shared his-tory, culture, fraternity, reciprocity, solidarity, mutual trust and so on, duties of global equal concern and respect rest on other grounds. But both are rightly called justice.

The second option – the one I find more intuitive – is to adopt what Miller dubs 'weak cosmopolitanism'. According to this view, 'morality is cosmopolitan in part: there are some valid principles of equal consider-ation with a universal scope, even though there may also be indepen-dent, nonderivative principles with a more restricted scope' (Miller, 1998, p. 166). Drawing on this distinction we might say that in contrast to strong global luck egalitarianism, weak global luck egalitarianism is the view that even though the aims of luck egalitarianism have global application, they do not exhaust the demands of global justice. In this way weak global luck egalitarianism *does* recognise the existence of spe-cial obligations such as obligations arising from the ties of nationhood (cf. Schemmel, 2008, p. 63).

There is nothing inconsistent about claiming both that we have spe-cial obligations towards members of our own national communities and that we have general egalitarian duties towards everyone. Pogge famously argues that national relationships can *increase* what we owe to co-nationals in terms of positive obligations, but they cannot decrease what we owe to everyone else in terms of *negative* duties (Pogge, 2002b, pp. 90–1). I think that there is truth in this argument, but I also think that there is truth in the further argument that special relationships can increase what we owe to co-nationals in terms of some positive obliga-tions but cannot decrease what we owe to everyone in terms of general positive duties. This could entail, for example, that there are certain minimum levels of assistance that we must give to everyone affected by natural disasters wherever they happen to be in the world if our actions are to qualify as showing an adequate level of global equal concern and respect, but that we may have other reasons to provide higher levels of assistance to our fellow nationals if our actions are to qualify as showing equal concern and respect interpreted under the ideal of national community.

Nevertheless, some people might insist that even weak cosmopoli-tanism is wrong, especially when it pertains to aid. To take one example,

Richard Miller argues that the kind of mutual trust which is necessary for tax-financed aid is *only* possible among compatriots of national communities. As he puts it,

> A plausible comprehensive morality of universal respect produces a strongly biased duty of special concern for compatriots in matters of tax-financed aid, largely because it dictates a special interest in leading a social life based on mutual respect and trust and a special commitment to provide adequate incentives for compatriots to conform to the shared institutions that one helps to impose on them.
>
> (Miller, 1998, p. 204)

Yet it remains unclear why comparable arguments do not apply to non-compatriots. Do not we also want to be able to rely on non-compatriots to act in ways that we can trust given an uncertain future and the risks we share? And does not this also require incentives? If so, then Miller's own argument would seem to suggest a need for duties of special concern for compatriots *and* duties of concern for foreigners that are sufficiently egalitarian to produce the necessary incentives (cf. Arneson, 2005, pp. 141–2).

Once we recognise special obligations to fellow compatriots alongside general duties of global equal concern and respect, however, this inevitably raises a question about relative importance. The temptation will be to establish a principle of lexical priority according to which one kind of demand should only be sacrificed for itself and never for the other kind of demand – to assert, for example, that national obligations must always take precedence over the relevant global duties. It seems to me, however, that such a rigid principle would require a very special form of argument: for there may be cases where it seems intuitive that duties of global equal concern and respect should take precedence over national obligations. Sometimes it might be right, for example, to provide more of the available assistance to people in a foreign county hit by a natural disaster that has caused terrible devastation than to people at home struck by a natural disaster that has wreaked much less damage by comparison. Of course, these sorts of examples do not show that it is never fitting to give priority to associative obligations. But at the very least the onus of proof would fall on the defender of a rigid order of priority to show why national obligations always take precedence over general duties (cf. Miller, 2007, p. 44; 2008, pp. 562–5; van der Veen, 2008).

Finally, the nationalist might persist in claiming that national identities and sentiments make up a significant part of moral life and therefore deserve pride of place in a theory of global justice. But we must also appreciate the fact that moral life has many different dimensions. Whilst some conventional beliefs and practices at the global level might point in the direction of strong nationalism, a great many other beliefs and practices do not. If we focus on the ordinary ethical beliefs and practices of relatively nationalistic political communities, this will make continuity take one form. But if we focus on the ordinary ethical beliefs and practices of some member states of the EU and UN, of the large number of international NGOs, of various cosmopolitan intellectual communities and of the many thousands of individuals around the world who campaign, pay their taxes and donate additional money in the belief that foreign aid should be very high up on the list of priorities, the picture of continuity is likely to take a different form. This means that when people read about starving individuals across the globe and exclaim 'There but for the grace of God go I!' or 'How can it be fair to sit back and do nothing?' this is part of the tapestry from which the critical interpreter can construct a theory of global equal concern. Any act of interpretation must identify some data as important and other data less so. The present enterprise is no different.

In this chapter I have attempted to clarify the idea of global luck egalitarianism, to distinguish this idea from Poggean and Rawlsian approaches to global justice, and to respond to two standard objections that are laid at the door of cosmopolitan theories. At certain points in the discussion, however, I relied on the abstract nature of this idea and promised a more complete account. The main aim of the next chapter therefore will be to provide such an account in the form of global equality of resources. More specifically, I develop a version of global equality of resources which remodels key aspects of Dworkin's own account of equality of resources suitable for sites of global justice.

7
Global Equality of Resources

Every day we make decisions about whether to consume or invest our resources, we rely on international trade which enables us to buy and sell products with people living in other parts of the world, we purchase shares in companies with interests in oil, gas, metals and precious stones, and in some cases donate money to countries who are struggling. But all of these choices are for naught from the perspective of global justice unless we know what shares of resources we fairly have at our disposal in the first place. It is tempting at this stage to evoke the principle that every individual on Earth is entitled, upon reaching the age of majority, to an equal share of the planet's natural resources or to the value thereof. This helps us to evaluate the plight of people living in resource-poor countries such as Armenia, Belarus, Benin, Burkina Faso, Comoros, French Polynesia, Guam or the Cook Islands whose poverty may stem in large measure from a lack of proximity to natural resources. Nevertheless, the principle of equal entitlement is not enough by itself to capture the full demands of justice as global equal concern. There are two reasons for this. The first is that it overlooks the situation of people faced with the 'resource curse': a paradoxical state of affairs in which a country with abundant natural resources in fact enjoys lower economic growth than a country without that gift. This can happen in different ways. One is that the good luck of being born into a country with abundant natural resources is meaningless without development capacity. One need only compare the fortunes of Japan and the Pacific Islands to see this point. Japan is one of the richest countries in the world despite having meagre natural resources, whereas inhabitants of the Pacific Islands are among the globe's poorest people in the face of abundant natural resources. Nor can we overlook the situation of millions of people living in countries across Central and Eastern Europe, the Caucasus and Central Asia where life chances are hindered by a lack of the development expertise required to make use of their average or above average compliment of natural resources. Another version of the resource curse occurs when the good luck of being born into a country with abundant natural resources is ruined as a result of weak property rights and/or prolonged periods of political mismanagement, corruption and civil war. This particular form of the resource curse has befallen a great many countries in sub-Saharan Africa not least Sierra Leone, Nigeria, Angola, Equatorial Guinea and the Democratic Republic of Congo. The second reason why equality of entitlement is insufficient for global distributive justice is that it fails to take account of other kinds of brute luck factors which can affect people's life chances such as poor health endowment, bad climate, crop failures and natural disasters of various kinds. In this chapter, I try to develop a theory of global equality of resources that is appropriately sensitive to all these inequalities.

But the devil, as they say, is in the detail. A complete statement of global equality of resources must address the following questions. What would it mean for there to exist an equal distribution of the planet's natural resources? What would global equality of resources demand over time once an equal distribution of natural resources had been achieved? Finally, what kinds of things are rightly governed by principles of global equality of resources? In what follows I develop a Dworkinian answer to these questions. I call this a Dworkinian answer because it proceeds on the basis of a similar thought experiment involving shipwreck survivors, employs a comparable conceptual framework including distinctions between ambition and endowment, option and brute luck, and employs equality of resources as the standard of egalitarian justice, where this is defined in terms of the familiar tools of the envy test, an imaginary auction and hypothetical insurance markets. These various components are reinterpreted, however, to take account of distinctive aspects of the global political arena. Things are not plain sailing here. Significant cultural differences at the global level raise questions over the appropriateness of the auction method and the use of insurance. Not only do many people wish to be treated as members of nations and not merely as individuals but there is also tremendous diversity in cultural attitudes concerning the value of different kinds of natural resources, what people may or may not do with resources, the relative importance of common versus private ownership, the moral standing of commercial insurance and what ought to count as option or brute luck. This pluralism can make it difficult to articulate, apply and implement equality of resources at the global level without favouring some groups of people over others. Even so, I shall argue that with the right amendments it is possible to develop a tolerably complete statement of the view that can operate at the global level without unfair discrimination. More specifically, I shall argue that global equality of resources provides a fitting conception of justice to govern international exploitation of, and trade in, natural resources as well as foreign aid.

The desert island thought experiment remodelled

How do we measure whether or not individuals living in different parts of the world have equal shares of the Earth's natural resources? At this stage my question is theoretical rather than practical. I am not interested just yet in asking how we could feasibly bring about equality of such a large amount of resources. Rather, I want to examine the more fundamental question of what global equality of resources means given the bewildering array of different kinds of natural resources up for grabs and tremendous diversity in the value placed on different resources by people around the world.

I believe that significant progress can be made in answering this theoretical question by recasting Dworkin's desert island thought experiment as follows. Suppose that at some time in the near future the people of Earth are forced to abandon their planet after an unforeseen and unprovoked alien onslaught. The destruction of the human race is only partial, however, as small numbers of people from every nation manage to evade capture and make their escape using spaceships seized from the alien invaders. After travelling aimlessly in space for a period time they find themselves space-shipwrecked on a small planet which has abundant natural resources. The planet, call it Mini-Earth, bears an uncanny resemblance to Earth, only it is much smaller in size. Although it was once inhabited by an industrialised and technologically developed human-like species, they were all wiped out in a devastating flu pandemic. At present there are no well-developed legal and political structures among the human survivors. Nor do they possess any strong shared identity, common understanding or collective purpose other than that they are all human beings who wish to survive and flourish. Nevertheless, they all believe that principles of justice are important and they accept basic principles of human dignity, although they differ in their interpretation of these things. The question is this: according to what principles should the natural resources of Mini-Earth be distributed?

The survivors disagree about the correct answer to this question, which is not unsurprising given their different backgrounds. (Such differences would have come to the fore on Dworkin's desert island had he not made the simplifying assumption that everyone accepts the idea of an equal division.) Some favour a starting-gate type of distribution in which everyone is free to go off and acquire private property by some appropriate method. A subset of these people defends a proviso which states that acquisition should not worsen the situation of others. Another faction prefers a proviso which states that acquisition should leave enough so that everyone else can acquire an equally good share. Others prefer a pattern of distribution according to desert or need. Still others think that all of the resources ought to be held under common ownership for the foreseeable future. Finally, some maintain that since no one is antecedently entitled to any of the resources of Mini-Earth, the most appropriate thing to do is simply to divide the resources into equal shares. So what is to be done here?

The situation I have imagined is representative of what we might call *the global disagreement problem*: that disagreements between peoples are even more intractable than disagreements among one people and so there is little or no prospect of justifying a single uniform conception of distributive justice for the globe. Walzer, for instance, claims that there cannot be, at least not at present, one conception of distributive justice for every nation because the idea of distributive justice only makes sense within a 'bounded world' (or political community) with its own common meanings (Walzer, 1983, pp. 29–31).[1] Although I think that this is a relevant concern, I also think that the burden of proof does not rest entirely on the side of people who are optimistic about the possibility of consensus across political communities. It is correct to ask questions of the form 'What reason do we have for supposing that global consensus is possible?' but it is also appropriate to ask 'What reason do we have for supposing that global consensus is impossible?' My own view is that disagreements about justice at the global level are not entirely different from local disagreements about justice. They may be more pronounced and have greater numbers of people on each side of the debate, but it does not follow from this that they are somehow immune to rational analysis and common consensus. If there is a problem of plural social meanings at the international level, there is also such a problem at the national level (cf. Carens, 1995b).

Returning to my fiction, it is certainly possible that the different groups on Mini-Earth could start fighting among themselves and simply disperse around the planet seizing up land and distributing it as they see fit. But suppose instead that in the light of the alien onslaught they have no appetite for any further conflict and so they are willing to come together to discuss what should be done. Suppose also that they are willing for the sake of that discussion to pursue one particular conception of distributive justice to see where it takes them. Suppose they reach agreement for the time being on a conception which stipulates that the resources should be divided equally among them in accordance with the envy test. With this in mind the survivors elect a divider to achieve a division which satisfies the envy test. But how can the elected divider be sure to distribute resources in accordance with this requirement and in the most Pareto-efficient way?

I think that Dworkin's auction device can be put to useful labour here but not without addressing three practical difficulties. The first is epistemological. The survivors face the difficulty of gathering information about what they are bidding for and where the items are located. The danger is that if people lack adequate information, pre-auction ignorance could breed post-auction envy. If, for example, someone bids for an item which looks very much like a mango tree only to discover after the auction has finished that it produces only poisonous seeds or that it is located hundreds of miles away, then he is more likely to envy the resources of someone else. Nevertheless, suppose the previous inhabitants provided detailed and accurate records of all the resources on their planet. This Mini-Earth inventory or doomsday book could then be used by the survivors as an auction guide. If they use this information to decide what they will bid for, there is less chance that they will envy other people's resources at the end.

The second difficulty has to do with price speculation. The second difficulty has to do with price speculation. Suppose some of the survivors purchase banana trees and other similar items and then start to sell off future commodities, that is, future crops of bananas, independently of the auction. The result of this price speculation is that prices in the auction become greatly inflated. (Reflect for a moment on the current 'food crisis' which has seen prices more than double in some of the poorest parts of the world. The World Bank estimates that this crisis has forced 100 million additional people into absolute poverty with many parts of the world facing the very real possibility of famine. Among the many causes of these price rises are the actions of investors and speculators in domestic and international commodities markets.) It seems to me that Dworkinians have every reason to condemn this sort of practice. Indeed, there is a precedent for market adjustments in Dworkin's own discussion of the auction. He argues that the auctioneer is permitted to impose constraints on liberty under 'the principle of correction'. This principle justifies intervention to prevent pollution, for example. Hence the auctioneer may intervene to prohibit certain uses of resources post-action on the grounds that if the other people in the auction could have predicted the polluter's actions and organised themselves effectively they would have collectively outbid the polluter for the resources in question thereby preventing his or her actions (Dworkin, 1987a, pp. 31–2). Perhaps we could judge the activities of price speculators in a similar fashion. The auctioneer could impose a rule that anyone wishing to purchase land for farming may not sell off future harvests until the entire auction process has come to an end. This is justified on the paternalistic grounds that it secures what virtually everybody wants, which is affordable basic food commodities.

The third difficulty flows directly from the international dimension of the Mini-Earth scenario. The fact that the auctioneer is dealing with the survivors of different countries means that he must make a choice between two distinct methods of allocating clamshells. Call this *the auctioneer's quandary*. According to the first method, he hands out clamshells to people he regards as legitimate representatives of the different groups of survivors. This method bears similarities with Rawls international original position in which representatives of nations come together to specify the law of nations (Rawls, 1971, p. 378). The key difference is that on Mini-Earth each representative knows which particular nation he or she represents. How are the representatives chosen Perhaps the auctioneer gives the clamshells to any representatives who survived the alien onslaught. Or maybe the survivors have coalesced around new representatives who deserve to be recognised. At any rate once the representatives have been selected the auctioneer hands out clamshells so that they can bid for resources in the auction. At the end of the auction or series of auctions these resources are handed over to the representatives who will then divide them among the people they represent. Perhaps some of them will run a second auction. Others will do things differently. The only thing left for the auctioneer to decide is how many clamshells to give to each representative. One fairly obvious option will be to offer one clamshell for every individual represented.

In contrast to this, the second method allows each survivor to participate in the auction directly. Here the auctioneer gives an equal number of clamshells to every individual. In the case of children, clamshells are given to their parents or guardians. Once they have their share of clamshells, the survivors can decide whereabouts on the new plane they want to live and bid for land and resources accordingly. They might prefer to live closer to some people than others and so attempt to coordinate their bidding during the auction. They may even bid with a view to creating political communities on Mini-Earth along with other like-minded people. Or they might decide to live in isolation from other people and go it alone. But the key point is that each individual has the right to decide what to do with his or her clamshells within the rules set down by the auctioneer. The basic rationale for this approach is the familiar idea within cosmopolitan political philosophy that individuals rather than nations are the ultimate units of moral concern and the bearers of rights. In this case it is the right to equal bidding power.

One reason to prefer the second method is that it is more likely to satisfy the envy test as described by Dworkin. Even if every representative shares out the resources he manages to acquire more or less equally among the people he represents, some survivors may end up preferring the bundles of resources secured for other people. After all, a representative can only bid on the basis of what he believes either his people *will* desire or what they *ought to* desire. But whether the representative acts as a delegate or advocate there could be a gap between what he bids for and what people actually desire. If the people being represented do not end up with what they actually desire, then the chances are they will envy at least some other bundles. They may even envy other people's representatives, whom they believe are better representatives than their own. The second approach, by contrast, gives every individual the chance to purchase what he or she wants directly and this removes one major source of envy.

Perhaps a defender of the first approach could abandon the original envy test in favour of what we might call *an envy test for representatives*. According to this new test, no division of resources among representatives is equal if any representative would prefer another representative's bundle of resources and mouths to feed. But setting aside the original envy test in this way ignores the second principle of human dignity: that each person has a special responsibility for realising the success of her own life such as by exercising his judgement about what bundle of resources would be best for her. Now it might be argued that there is no genuine difference between the two methods. If one assumes that all representatives are motivated by a desire to give their people what they want, are not corrupt and are able to learn from their mistakes, then provided the auction is run a sufficient number of times they will be able to achieve an envy-free result. Nevertheless, this ignores the intrinsic importance of individuals choosing their own bundles of resources. On the first model, individuals exercise their personal responsibility only in the limited sense that they hand over the task of bidding for resources to their representatives. This division of resources is relevantly different from a process in which individuals act on their own behalf precisely because the latter allows them to play an active role in determining the set of bundles actually chosen. So, if one is a thoroughgoing individualist, then arguably one has reason to favour the second method over the first method which involves the alienation of personal responsibility. That being said, we may have paternalistic reasons for limiting how much special responsibility people may retain.

The auction method and problems of cultural diversity

Having addressed the three initial difficulties, I now consider two additional problems for the proposed auction which reflect profound cultural differences in the world today. I shall first outline both problems, and then try to show how they can be resolved.

The first problem is due to David Miller, who is one of the few contributors to the literature on global justice to have devoted any serious attention to Dworkin's equality of resources. Miller highlights the fact that before an equal distribution of resources can be judged, we need to know the rules that will govern how people may use their resources, including rules regarding what they will be permitted to grow on the relevant land and whether or not they will be at liberty to trade that harvest with others (Miller, 1999b, p. 192). Dworkin's preferred liberty/constraint system is broadly liberal in nature: 'the principle of abstraction' allows constraints on liberty for the sake of security or to address harmful externalities such as pollution but not for the observance of religious laws (Dworkin, 1987a, pp. 25–9). According to Miller, however, 'if we are thinking about the issue globally, it becomes problematic to define equality by applying Dworkin's favoured rules.' He continues,

> Suppose one country has land which, if used for the production of wine, would yield a rich harvest; but suppose also that the inhabitants of that country have for religious reasons prohibited the making and sale of wine. Should we count the country as resource-rich on the grounds that, if it adopted Dworkinian rules to govern property rights and market exchange, its inhabitants would together be in possession of a valuable asset? This would be controversial, because it seems to require that the value of resources should be measured by the market, and this is not a neutral yardstick as between, for instance, religious and secular cultures. The population of the country in question would argue that they should not be credited with 'resources' that only have a value if you already presuppose the legitimacy of certain ways of using them.

(Miller, 1999b, pp. 192–3)

How does this objection apply to the auction? According to Dworkin, the auction is fair because it forces individuals to pay the opportunity costs of their own consumption choices (Dworkin, 1987a, p. 31). Nevertheless, Miller's objection might be this. Even though religious people wish to use land for purposes other than making wine, they have to bid against people who *do* wish to use the available land for that purpose. So, if the liberty/constraint system being used is liberal, religious believers will have to pay a higher price for the land than if an alternative religious system had been used. The liberal liberty/constraint system imposes an externality on their way of life, and this Miller finds discriminatory. Where people have to pay more for their land because of a system of rules that favours some conceptions of the good over others 'this makes it inappropriate as a way of defining equality of resources at global level in circumstances where not all cultures embrace these liberal ideals' (Miller, 2007, p. 62).

Before outlining the second problem, I want first to address Miller's claim that when we think about the issue globally 'it *becomes* problematic to define equality by applying Dworkin's favoured rules'. This is ambiguous between the claim that defining equality of resources using Dworkin's approach *only* becomes problematic at the global level and the claim that it becomes *more* problematic to do so at the global level. Either way, Miller seems to think that something new comes to light within this domain. But is this true? Surely much depends on the kind of society one has in mind. If the citizens of a state have a common understanding of the purpose of political community and shared beliefs about what liberty/constraint regime best realises that purpose, then presumably the problems of specifying equality of resources will not be as severe as the problems of specifying equality of resources at the international level where differences are much greater. In contrast to this, if citizens lack such common understanding and shared beliefs about liberty, this is likely to present problems similar to those at the international level. It seems to me that the problems of specifying equality of resources across people from different countries whose majority populations have contrary beliefs about liberty are not dramatically different from the problems of specifying equality of resources across people who hold divergent beliefs within the same country. (Of course, equality of resources is not a principle of distributive justice that Miller would actually endorse even in the national context).

A second problem has to do with varying attitudes concerning what the relevant lots should be. One such problem has to do with whether or not it is appropriate for certain things to pass into private as opposed to common ownership. Dworkin stipulates that his shipwreck survivors 'do not yet realize [...] that it might be wise to keep some resources as owned in common by any state they might create' (Dworkin, 1981b, p. 285). But what happens if we remove this simplification in the case of Mini-Earth? Perhaps some people would like to be treated as members of a nation at least when it comes to bidding for certain geographical areas such as deserts, forests, coastal areas or large natural objects such as rivers, lakes and mountains. The French, for example, might wish to purchase a mountain on Mini-Earth which reminds them of Alpe-d'Huez. Now the auctioneer could ask representatives to stand as place holders for larger numbers of people when it comes to clearing the market for certain kinds of lots. But he would then need a theory to tell him which things should and which things should not be sold in this way. Moreover, Dworkin suggests that all the items are to be listed as a lot to be sold 'unless someone notifies the auctioneer [...] of his or her desire to bid for some part of an item, including part, for example, of some piece of land, in which case that part becomes itself a distinct lot' (p. 286). This means that the attempt to put an entire mountain up for auction could be blocked by any individual who wishes to own a part of it. The problem here is that by allowing the auctioneer to break up the lots into small parts – as per the principle of abstraction (Dworkin, 1987a, p. 27) – the theory favours those who wish to bid for small pieces of land over those who would prefer to see large items sold to groups in accordance with national identity.

A related problem is that different cultures may have different ways of chopping up the world from an ontological point of view. Some groups of people could see conceptual significance or imbued value within certain chunks of the world that others simply do not comprehend or value. So, for example, Dworkin makes reference to someone being elected to distribute 'the nondivisible resources, like milking cows' (1981b, p. 285). But what if some of the shipwreck survivors simply do not recognise 'the milking cow' as a non-divisible resource because they do not drink cow's milk but instead regard it as hunks of meat on bones? Whether or not these can be considered special problems of the global sphere depends on which individual countries one is drawing a comparison with. Perhaps some countries will be sufficiently diverse to make these problems of domestic justice as well. Even so, my main interest at this stage is with global justice.

Do these two problems represent insurmountable obstacles to applying the auction strategy to the global sphere? I do not believe so and I shall now try to explain why. The first problem is that to impose a liberal liberty/constrain system forces people with religious beliefs to pay inflated prices for the available resources and thereby favours one system of rules over another. Now it might be argued that in the absence of a formal legal system, the question of how the survivors may use their resources after the auction simply does not arise. If people are not in a position to enforce any rules, how can this be regarded as discriminatory against some people and not others? But I do not intend to rely on that response here. We can suppose that even though there is no effective law enforcement as yet, compliance with the results of the auction will be reasonably good because the survivors appointed the auctioneer and they have a general desire to respect property rights. If Miller is right, then we require a liberty/constraint system which is neutral in the deep sense that it does not presuppose the superiority of one set of rules over another. Perhaps he would say that the reason why defining equality of resources poses particular problems at the global level is because we cannot rely on a democratic solution to the problem of selecting one set of rules for everybody.

Fortunately, I think there is another way to deal with the problem. Suppose the auctioneer puts up for auction lots which are constituted out of permits or control rights covering particular resources or plots of land – for example, the right to use, to exclude, to charge economic rent, to transfer and to dispose of a particular resource or plot of land. This system would then allow people to bid for lots safe in the knowledge that they will be able to use particular things and in particular ways. Obviously in many instances both liberals and religious people will want to bid for the same resources or plots of land, with different sets of control rights attached to them. So each person is given the right to notify the auctioneer of the kind of auction lot he or she would like to bid for. Some people, for example, notify the auctioneer of their desire to bid for lots that will enable them to use fertile land in ways that a liberal system would allow. Others notify the auctioneer of their wish to bid for lots that will enable them to use fertile land in ways a religious system would prescribe. But suppose the auctioneer constructs, as far as possible, a number of separate lots catering to these different wishes, where no two lots contain permits for the same particular resource or plot of land. Now one might naturally expect liberals to only bid for lots containing liberal control rights and religious people to only bid for lots containing the relevant religious control rights. However, if the prices of certain kinds of lot become either very high or very low, we might start seeing the liberals bidding for the religious lots and perhaps religionists bidding for the liberal lots secure in the knowledge that they will not use them in sinful ways.[2]

One important question is whether or not such a system could achieve an envy-free result. Much depends on whether or not the auctioneer will be able to ensure that there are enough lots up for auction of different kinds to adequately satisfy all the survivors. Recall that each of the survivors remains free to change his or her bids and to propose a different set of lots. I expect that there will be much trial and error here and that the combined process of bidding and proposing may take some time. Nevertheless, I think that it is not unreasonable to suppose that it could come to an end at some point with everyone declaring themselves satisfied in the sense that they do not envy anyone else's lots and they cannot feasibly expect to do any better by further runs of the auction.

More significantly, I suggest that this proposal can deliver the deep neutrality we are searching for here. If certain people want a set of liberties and constraints to be available to them which are impossible except under their preferred religious laws, they must pay the social cost of having such liberties and constraints as fixed by what other people are willing to pay or not pay for the relevant auction lots. Provided that the auctioneer is able to construct enough lots of each kind and everyone must bid for the available lots with the same number of clamshells nobody will be able to complain that the auctioneer used a non-neutral yardstick as between religious and secular values. A further benefit is that once the auction process comes to an end, there is no suggestion that the resources themselves must be physically redistributed around Mini-Earth. So, for example, if someone purchases a lot which includes the right to command economic rent from a specified resource or piece of land, he need not travel to where the land is or pay to have that particular resource transported to where he is. He can simply collect the rent owed to him, although he may have to pay someone to do that on his behalf.

Turning now to the second problem, this had to do with differing attitudes towards the kinds of objects that should be put into the auction and how they should be owned. One possible solution is for the auctioneer to allow a rudimentary system of pre-auction contracts on Mini-Earth such that it is possible for individuals to come together and agree to purchase all of the lots which comprise a larger item such as a mountain which they intend to own in common. For example, each individual member of the French nation could agree in advance to use his or her personal allocation of clamshells to acquire lots relating to the Mini-Earth Alpe-d'Huez on the understanding that the mountain will be transferred by them into their common ownership once the auction is finished. Of course, once it becomes clear what the French are up to, others will be free to enter into a bidding competition with them. Some may genuinely wish to become owners. Others just want to push up prices so that the French are forced to expend all their clamshells. But we can suppose that after a number of runs of the auction the French will simply call the bluff of the price-inflators and prices will reach equilibrium.

However, suppose that only small numbers of the French population survived the alien attack. As a small minority on Mini-Earth they have scarcely any chance of successfully bidding for the lots covering the whole of the Alpe-d'Huez facsimile. Naturally they could bid for some of the lots covering a small proportion of the mountain, but what they really want is the ownership of the whole thing to control as they see fit. Indeed, other groups of people such as the British may decide to enter into pre-auction contracts with one another to bid for this mountain as well. If they refuse to allow the French to enter into this pre-auction contract with them, and use their economic power to freeze-out the French, this could generate post-auction envy. That is, we can no longer be certain that the envy test will be satisfied because we cannot ensure that no person denied entry into one of the pre-auction contracts will prefer the bundles of any of those people who are able to gain entry.[3] This is one instance of what Scheffler calls 'the distributive objection' to associative obligations (Scheffler, 2001, p. 56).

On closer examination, however, it is not entirely clear the sense in which a French person will envy a British person. If a group of people who share a common culture, language, set of values and concomitant way of life choose to club together with the ambition of purchasing a mountain to be held in common among them, the relevant question is not simply whether other persons would envy the mountain but whether they would envy the way of life which develops over time on that mountain. In other words, we should regard envy as a matter of looking at someone else's bundle of resources and national life and preferring the totality of what he or she has got. Once we have understood envy in this way, it is much harder to see how someone committed to the French way of life could envy those who live on and use the mountain very differently.

But perhaps the objection comes to something else. It is not that the French would envy the particular way of life that ensues on the Alpe-d'Huez lookalike. Rather, it is that they would envy any group of people who have the opportunity to build a way of life in this way. It might be objected that allowing numbers to count in the ownership of rivers, lakes, mountains and so on is antithetical to global equality of opportunity because it puts at risk the long-term survival of partic-ular nations. Furthermore, one of the features of the thought experi-ment is that it relocates the human population to a new planet, but it might be thought that this is a weakness rather than a strength, for it does not make room for the importance to certain groups of locations that are of special significance to them by virtue of their history – a battle was fought on *this* hill, or a prophet was born or died on *this* spot, for instance. In other words, my thought experiment effectively casts out certain attitudes about national interests or group claims based on culture or religion by creating a world that is not *our* world.

Nevertheless, the account of global justice defended here is individualistic in the sense that it attaches to persons one by one. So although persons of different nations should enjoy the same bidding power, this does not mean that nations have a right to equal bidding power. After all, not all persons will want to give the same weight to such interests and claims, and finding oneself in the midst of a group that attaches absolute weight may be a great misfortune from an individual perspective. So I offer the example of a new planet to make it clear that individuals would not be beholden to previous constraints relating to national membership, geographical location, political borders and sites of cultural significance if they did not wish to be. That is not to say, however, that the continued existence of families, villages, tribes, nations, countries and sites of cultural significance cannot become units of concern. On the contrary, individuals may acquire resources with the intention of establishing such entities or creating new historical sites. Rather, it is to say that such things may only become matters of concern in so far as they are revered by individuals. Justice as equal concern demands only that persons should be able to make the best sort of life they can with their fair share of resources. It does not demand the long-term survival of particular nations viewed as inherently valuable. For this reason the French may have to accept the loss of their beloved Alpe-d'Huez on Earth without the compensation of being able to have exclusive property rights over another similar mountain on Mini-Earth.

To further motivate this response, it seems to me right to place deeply held national affinities and attachments to particular historical sites or ancient artefacts on the personality side of the personality/circumstances distinction. To use Dworkin's way of thinking, we might say that people ordinarily identify with these affinities or attachments and do not regret having them. So it may be bizarre to compensate persons for not being able to purchase a mountain that happens to remind them of a lost homeland. In other words, the idea that having a small population is grounds for special treatment (as a form of brute luck) is incompatible with regarding national belonging as a matter of personal pride, where this means adhering to the nation because one thinks it is great no matter its size.[4] Of course, it might be countered that identifying with one's nation, and feeling a sense of collective responsibility for its success or failure, is one thing when it relates to matters that are within its control such as doing well in the Olympic games or waging of wars, whereas regretting the fact that an alien onslaught has left one's nation in a minority and fighting for its survival is quite another thing, and does amount to compensable brute luck. However, I believe that there are good independent reasons for placing national affinities or attachments on the personality side of the relevant distinction despite this. One is that doing so seems to capture an important truism about such commitments, namely, that they are generally regarded not merely as 'costs' but as 'sacrifices' that must be borne. To offer special dispensation to the French may wipe out the sacrifice that is part of what it means to be a true nationalist and thereby destroy the meaning of the action. If the French want to buy the mountain, then they can endeavour to work hard, bear lots of children, attract new members and acquire the land inch by inch. Through this action the ownership will become redolent of national pride and sacrifice. That each individual should receive a fair share of resources with which to pursue valuable national projects of his or her own choosing is already factored into the story. To give individual members of the French nation more resources merely because they are now few in number would be double-counting and unfair. That being said, if individuals would, on average, choose to purchase insurance against the loss of access to artefacts or sites of national importance under conditions of *ex ante* equality, then justice is again called into action. I would also distinguish this example from cases in which actual nations have taken without permission or obtained with ambiguous permission the national treasures of another country. Here principles of national responsibility may dictate the return of the artefacts (see Miller, 2007, ch. 6).

I propose that with the foregoing amendments it is possible to make sense of global equality of resources even against a background of cultural differences and without significant departures from the two principles of ethical individualism. The next stage in the argument must be to develop an account of global equality of resources over time. But before doing so I want first to say something about the application of the theory as it stands. How useful is the auction thought experiment for thinking about what equality of resources would be like at the global level? To whom or what is it supposed to apply and how?

Putting the auction to work

Dworkin mentions three ways in which the auction thought experiment could be useful in the context of debates over domestic distributive justice. The first is that it could be used to develop a coherent and complete idea of equality of resources. The second is that it might be used as a moral standard for judging existing institutions and distributive arrangements in the real world. The third is that it could be used as a guide for the design of economic institutions in the future (Dworkin, 1981b, pp. 290–1). How well do these reasons carry over to the global version I have imagined?

With regards to the first reason, I shall assume that even though there were technical challenges in coming up with a suitable version of the auction for the global scenario I imagined, it was possible to specify what might count as an equal share in that context. The fiction, in other words, enables us to make sense of global equality of resources. At this stage I am more interested in the second and third reasons.

For what things might global equality of resources provide an appropriate standard of justice? One obvious thing is exploitation of, and trade in, the Earth's natural resources, including gas, oil, coal, timber, iron ore, copper, zinc, tin, uranium, coltan, gold, diamonds and so on. The question is, to what extent can existing exploitation and trade be interpreted as falling within the set of possible distributions of natural resources that might have been produced by equal shares and ensuing markets? To put the same question more forcefully, to what extent can persons living in countries who are blessed with a super-abundance of natural resources – such as a great many of the inhabitants of Brunei who enjoy the highest per capita incomes in Asia – reasonably expect to get rich off the back of their gas and oil reserves without redistributing at least some of this wealth to less-fortunate countries? It is a further question, but one that I do not have space to discuss here, which of the many alternatives is the best proposal for a system of taxation to generate revenues from exploitation and trade of natural resources ready to be transferred back to resource-poor individuals (see Barry, 1982, p. 242; Tobin, 1982; Pogge, 1994; 2002a, ch. 8).[5]

However, how can global equality of resources be said to provide a standard of distributive justice for countries which are in fact blessed with above average shares of natural resources but nevertheless suffer the resource curse? It was the economists Richard Auty (1993) and Jeffrey Sachs (1995) who first documented the negative correlation between resource abundance and economic growth in Africa. Botswana is a possible exception to a resource curse which blights much of sub-Saharan Africa. But what causes this? Leif Wenar blames a failure by national and international institutions to properly enforce existing private property rights – rights that are widely affirmed in local and international law but violated when dictators and civil warriors sell off a territory's resources (Wenar, 2007b). The weakness of local property rights is, of course, aided and abetted by the actions of governments,

corporations and private individuals around the world who are apt to recognise, negotiate and trade with local rulers who directly or indirectly have
insufficient democratic mandate to sell the natural resources in their grasp
(Pogge, 2002a, pp. 162–6).

At this stage I rely on the compound nature of global equal concern
and respect. In these instances we ought to show equal concern by
bringing pressure to bear on governments, international organisations
and transnational corporations to recognise and protect the private
property rights of local persons against corrupt rulers and local warlords
who seek to control resources for their own personal ends. We should
also show equal concern directly by not purchasing tainted resources or
shares in companies involved in this sort of trade. Global equality of
resources will then provide a standard to measure the share of resources
that rightly belongs to individuals in the areas affected. If these areas are
blessed with an above average wealth of natural resources, then this
share will be somewhat less than full ownership of what is there. Even
with this caveat, however, this share is still likely to be significantly
greater than what these persons currently have at their disposal given
the activities of corrupt rulers and local warlords.

In light of the fact that the resource curse afflicts countries with
abundant natural resources, what does the rest of the world owe to
people in the event that enforcing local private property rights proves
impossible to achieve without military intervention and ending the
international resource privilege takes time to achieve given powerful
vested interests? What transitional measures are appropriate? I propose that it is still possible to capture the plight of local individuals
within the framework of global equality of resources in the following
nuanced way. All we need to do is ask whether or not we would have
chosen under conditions of *ex ante* equality to purchase insurance
against being born into a country faced with the resource curse. If
one thinks, as Dworkin does, that it is appropriate to ask whether or
not we would wish to purchase insurance against the risk of being
born to poor parents, then surely it is also fitting to ask whether or
not we would wish to purchase insurance against being born inside a
country ravaged by weak property rights, bad government, corruption, endless civil wars and ruthless warlords. In other words, the provision of foreign aid based on hypothetical insurance might be an
appropriate technique for showing global equal concern as a transitional measure in these sorts of cases.

Putting the resource curse to one side and focusing on rich countries
that are blessed with abundant natural resources, I also think that global
equality of resources can provide a standard of justice for current levels

of official development assistance. The question is, can the level of ODA currently provided by resource-rich countries such as Australia, Brunei, Canada, Norway, Russia, Dubai, Kuwait and Saudi Arabia be viewed as approximating the amount of money they are morally obliged to pay to less-fortunate countries by virtue of being in possession of a larger share of natural resources than they would have been able to purchase during an auction for the planet's natural resources held under conditions of *ex ante* equality? If we can make sense of and even give a rough answer to this question, then I believe we have an appropriate standard with which to judge current levels of development assistance around the world. Historically the Arab states of the Persian Gulf have been the most generous donors in the sense of contributing the highest percentages of GNI in development assistance. On the present view, this is entirely fitting given that they are also blessed with some of the world's most valuable oil fields. The donations of oil-rich Russia may not compare so favourably.

By focusing on the exploitation of, and trade in, natural resources I do not mean to downplay the moral significance of other forms of exploitation and trade. As suggested at the start of Chapter 3, intellectual property is another obvious area where questions of justice arise. Both international agreements on the trade of intellectual property rights and the practice of international patent law can exacerbate problems of hunger and disease around the world, especially in the areas of new technologies, agriculture and pharmaceuticals (see Pogge, 2002c, pp. 117, 218, n. 23).

But turning now to the third possible use identified above, the question is whether or not a conception of global equality resources could act as a practical guide for the design of new institutions. One reason for thinking that it could has to do with the global commons. Thomas Franck's work on the role of distributive justice in international law is notable for many things one of them being his assertion that internationally, distributive justice is never off the agenda, 'whether the subject is manganese nodules on the ocean floor, geostationary orbits in outer space, or penguins and the Antarctic ice-cap' (Franck, 1995, p. 436). Obviously this raises the possibility of an auction for the use of these nodules, orbits and ice-caps. A related reason is based on an analogy with international carbon-offset markets. Faced with carbon-caps set by the 1997 Kyoto Protocol, companies from rich industrialised countries are permitted to purchase emissions quotas from poorer parts of the world where emissions fall below national limits. Under the present system of 'grandfathering' companies are simply given their initial permits on the basis of their historical emissions. However, many experts now support an alternative proposal to run periodic auctions for carbon permits as a way of generating additional revenue. That extra revenue could then be paid out to people in less-developed countries who are suffering the affects of climate change or else deployed to fund international mitigation and adaptation efforts (Cramton and Kerr, 2002). Perhaps something like this auction could be used to regulate the practices of governments and corporations engaged in the exploitation of, or trade in, natural resources across the board.

However, it is worth noting that if the auction method is workable in the case of carbon quotas it is only because the society of peoples has already accepted certain standards of equality with respect to limits on greenhouse gas emissions in different countries. The auction and post-auction trade simply allows companies to determine the exact shape of that equality, with some companies preferring hard cash to carbon permits and *vice versa*. But the reasons which recommend the auction in this case may be absent if we reflect on the possibility of a more general auction for the world's natural resources. Since countries have not yet reached agreement on the principle of equality of resources regarding the planet's total compliment of gas, oil, precious stones, phosphates, arable land and so on, and since some countries currently have far more bargaining power than others when it comes to the sale and purchase of such items on the international commodities markets, it is questionable whether an auction could work under present conditions. What would be required as a necessary preliminary step is for countries to agree upon limits to the exploitation of, and trade in, natural resources in and between countries.

This last point raises a question that has been waiting in the wings throughout this chapter. Why should we think that global equality of resources is recommended for us here on Earth merely because it is something that my fictional persons are willing to pursue on Mini-Earth? It seems to me that the time has already come that such an account of global distributive justice can do work for us here. The account ought to have universal appeal precisely because it lights on a distributive goal that can be endorsed by everyone around the world. Every person born has an interest, no matter what other interest they have, to have an equal share of the Earth's natural resources. In this way global equal concern is shown by adopting goals that are compatible with each person's own goals.

Emerging global inequalities

Let us now suppose that the natural resources on Mini-Earth have been redistributed in accordance with equality of resources. What happens next? As the individuals on Mini-Earth begin to consume or exploit their natural resources, engage in diverse kinds of industry and form associations and even political communities with one another, inequalities will begin to emerge. The question then becomes whether or not it would be appropriate to create institutions which have the power to redistribute resources or to prohibit these inequality-generating activities in the first place.

A number of theorists have argued against global redistribution of income and wealth (see Rawls, 1999, pp. 59, 117–19; Miller, 1999b, pp. 193–4; 2007, ch. 3; Bertram, 2005, pp. 75–92). They affirm that the collective choices of peoples concerning their own consumption, production, trade and population size must be allowed to stand, and that to regard the resulting inequalities as unjust is to fail to show due toleration or respect for national identity and sovereignty. There are, however, two problems with this line of reasoning. The first problem has to do with background justice. In actuality the collective choices of different peoples are taken against the background of a system of international arrangements, rules and practices which are either unjust or of uncertain justice. Pogge, for example, argues that to hold poor countries responsible for global inequalities is to commit the fallacy of 'explanatory nationalism', that is, to falsely attribute all the causes of poverty to national factors (such as corrupt leaders or the culture of the country) thereby ignoring the role of the unjust global institutional order in creating poverty (Pogge, 2002a, pp. 140–1).

The second problem relates to the distinction between collective and individual choice. Caney, for example, argues that it is unjust to hold individuals responsible for decisions taken on their behalf by the leaders of the political communities into which they are born and cannot easily exit (Caney, 2005, pp. 129–30). This is to ignore a basic tenet of ethical individualism: that each and every individual should enjoy a special responsibility for the success or failure of his or her own life. Arguably, this is *a fortiori* unjust in undemocratic hierarchical societies where particular groups are not merely hampered by their own countrymen but are persecuted by the political system. In such cases individuals who suffer relative deprivation 'can in no sense be said to have brought it upon themselves' (p. 130).

I think that these are important points. But I also think that they verge on committing two additional fallacies. One is the fallacy of explanatory institutionalism: to falsely attribute all the causes of global inequality to an unjust global order thereby ignoring responsibility-attracting choices made by local populations. The other is the fallacy of explanatory collectivism: to falsely attribute all the causes of global inequality to local rulers thereby ignoring responsibility-attracting choices made by individuals. It is important to recognise that there are a number of different causal factors in play and which no adequate theory of global distributive justice can afford to ignore. In what follows I attempt to introduce the required degree of complexity into the analysis of global inequality by appealing to the now familiar Dworkinian distinctions between ambition and endowment, brute and option luck, and by drawing on the transformative power of insurance.

Ambition and endowment at the global level

Whatever else one might want to say about the role of the global economic order in creating and maintaining global inequalities it is clear that different levels of ambition and endowment within a country can also affect its relative wealth. Take the remarkable case of Nauru, the world's smallest island nation and least populous member of the UN. Nauru is a rock island in the Micronesian South Pacific which was at one time blessed with large deposits of phosphates built up from thousands of years of fossilised bird droppings. Exploitation of these deposits began in the early twentieth century and by the 1970s Nauruans were amongst the richest people in the world. The government employed the majority of the population and provided free medical care and schooling. The problem is that most adults opted to fritter away their wealth. Many Nauruans purchased expensive cars to drive the short circuit around the island and the average lifestyle involved high consumption of alcohol and unhealthy foods combined with little exercise. Few parents bothered to send their children to secondary school. When Nauru's phosphate reserves dried up it left the island with little to offer. Lack of ambition on the part of its citizens and wasteful investments and incompetence by its government left most of the islanders poverty-stricken, uneducated and unhealthy. In the 1990s Nauru decided to become a tax haven and offered passports to foreign nationals. This improved its fortunes for a time as it became an international destination for money laundering by the Russian mafia. So much so that many banks and financial institutions started to refuse to handle transactions involving Nauru. More recently, Nauru has sought to make its money by becoming a detention camp for individuals seeking asylum in Australia. Time will tell whether or not this new venture proves to be any more worthwhile.

The case of Nauru demonstrates rather vividly how the fortunes of an entire nation can ebb and flow just as easily as those of an individual within a society.[6] If the relative prosperity of a nation reflects *only* the ambition of its people, collectively and individually, it is difficult to regard inequalities as unjust. Global equality of resources demands only that an equal share of natural resources should be available to individuals around the world, not that equality should be maintained in the face of differential ambition. There are, however, three significant factors which complicate any simple account of global inequality.

The first is that there are different kinds of ambition and not every kind can legitimise global inequality. Some countries are blessed with a high proportion of entrepreneurs who possess a burning ambition to improve their lives through successful business ventures. They will take up the opportunities presented to them by their leaders and make opportunities for themselves at home and abroad. We might put this kind of willingness to work and increase wealth under the general heading of *benign ambition*. The willingness to create and maintain wealth irrespective of the harm that doing so might cause other persons seems to have a different moral status. Think of all those persons who were involved in the slave trade or made money from colonial territory, or companies that are still ready to exploit child labour in developing countries, and corrupt leaders and local officials who put commodities donated by aid agencies onto the black market or who divert ODA away from its intended purposes and into the hands of local militias or warlords. I shall group these activities together under the separate heading of *malign ambition*. I suspect that most people would say that a just distribution should be sensitive to benign ambition but not sensitive to malign ambition. The problem is to determine in a tolerably accurate fashion what proportion of a nation's GNI is due to benign ambition and how much is borne of malign ambition.

The second complication stems from the interaction between ambition and endowment. Consider a country rich in valuable oil deposits but whose own people are unable to extract the oil in profitable ways because they lack the requisite technological skills and knowledge. They are then faced with the choice between leaving the deposits where they are, trying to extract them as best they can or inviting in foreign companies. Whatever they decide to do, it is likely that they will be at a disadvantage as compared to countries blessed with greater development capacity. Nevertheless, it is important to understand that skills and knowledge are not static but develop over time. Suppose the country concerned lacks the requisite skills and knowledge because it has in the past supported a hierarchal educational system in which only the very rich can afford to send their children to school. Many other countries, by contrast, adopted a liberal regime of state funding of education and were able to attract additional talent to their shores because of the lifestyle on offer. Why should the liberal country in this scenario not be allowed to prosper on the basis of its wise investment in people?

The third complicating factor has to do with interplay between the individual and collective levels. Take a country which is poor not because of any lack of natural resources or development talent but because of the actions of corrupt leaders and local warlords. Suppose they have been squabbling over its rich diamond mines ever since the country gained independence from its colonial rulers. On the one hand, it is does not seem fair to hold its citizens individually responsible for the situation in which they find themselves. But on the other hand, it also does not seem fair to fully waive responsibility for any lack of ambition at the individual level that may have contributed to or exacerbated the problems experienced at the collective level. Perhaps ordinary people did not show reasonable ambition in trying to retain possession of their land or in identifying corrupt leaders or in getting rid of oppressive warlords. But what is reasonable ambition? How can we possibly know what level of ambition the people of this country would have demonstrated if they had not been the victims of a colonial past, for example?

Option luck and brute luck at the global level

Another significant source of inequality in the world today is luck. We have already seen that Dworkin subdivides the concept of luck into brute and option luck. But can this distinction – or something like it – be applied to the global level? Suppose for the sake of argument that at some time in the near future Venice is entirely destroyed as a result of a general rise in sea levels that was entirely foreseeable. Rich Venetians had the wealth to move away but decided to stay and take their chances. Is this a matter of brute luck or option luck? According to Rakowski, 'any losses resulting from whatever risk was a necessary concomitant to the ownership of property essential to live a moderately satisfying life in a given society would, as instances of brute luck, be fully compensable' (Rakowski, 1991, p. 80). This characterisation, however, seems to imply that if the ownership of property in Venice is essential to living a moderately satisfying life in *that* society, then any losses are a matter of compensable brute luck. But why should the population of Venice have redistributive claims against the rest of the world (including people who do not live so precariously) merely because to live in that society is to live on a small man-made island off the Northeast coast of Italy? Why not make the comparison with wider Italian society or even European society? For this reason it might be better to say that a gamble becomes brute luck only when people could not live a reasonably comfortable life without taking that gamble where a reasonably comfortable life is defined by universal standards and therefore does not favour some cultures over others.

Sometimes the difference between option and brute luck is further complicated by the interplay between the individual and the collective level. Suppose all of the farmers in a country simultaneously decide to abandon existing kinds of agriculture in favour of the production of palm oil. It might seem fair to say that whether they gain or lose from this deliberate and calculated gamble in comparison to farmers in other countries is a matter of option luck and not objectionable from an egalitarian point of view. The problem is that in reality the gambles undertaken by individual farmers are often influenced by collective decisions made by their governments. When the Nixon government negotiated large contracts for grain sales to the Soviet Union in the 1970s, for example, US farmers were urged to increase grain production to meet these obligations. When the political wind changed and grain sales to the Soviet Union were blocked the price of grain dropped and the Federal government was forced to spend billions to support farmers. More recently, the US Federal government has used an array of financial incentives to persuade farmers to switch from the production of traditional crops such as corn, soybean and cereal grain to the production of bio-fuels in an attempt to address concerns related to the environment and energy shortages. This sort of interaction can make it difficult to identify genuine option luck on the part of individuals living with a country.

Insurance at the global level

As discussed in Chapter 3, Dworkin believes that insurance can provide a useful link between brute and option luck, though he insists that brute luck is transformed into option luck only if everyone had an equal risk of suffering certain catastrophes, everyone knew roughly what the odds were and had ample opportunity to purchase insurance. To this we might add the condition that the insurance must be modestly and reasonably priced. But how easily does this account transfer to the current global situation? Consider a small family living in Bangladesh producing just enough cash crops for their day-to-day needs with a small surplus of $2 a month. These farmers are vulnerable to sudden fluctuations in the price of their crops. They will face starvation if markets shift against them. This might be regarded as a matter of option luck were it not for the fact that trade protectionism and price fixing across the globe often inhibits fair competition. In addition to this, suppose they are unable to access financial products such as crop insurance because most commercial insurance companies consider them to be a bad bet. They simply cannot afford the high premiums that the insurers wish to charge them. The high insurance premiums reflect the fact that the majority of developing countries lie in tropical and sub-tropical regions including sub-tropical deserts, semi-arid steppe lands and small island states, and these are predicted to be most seriously affected by the environmental impacts of climate change, where this includes changes in rainfall patterns, increased frequency and severity of floods, droughts, storms, heat waves, desertification, changes in growing seasons, regions, water quality and quantity, and rising sea levels. These environmental impacts are further compounded by the fact that low-income peoples tend to have less-robust buildings and infrastructure, fewer emergency services, are highly dependent on climate-sensitive natural resources and are less able to adapt to permanent climatic changes (IPCC, 1995, p. 94; 2001, pp. 41–2).

Another complicating factor is the way in which the same disasters will have different consequences depending on what precautions local governments have taken in responding to the dangers. Take the case of Hurricane Katrina, which caused destruction along the US Gulf coast in August 2005. No doubt more could have been done to mitigate the affects of hurricane storms and increased water levels in and around New Orleans. Indeed, it has been argued that the leaders of this community were too stingy, myopic or even racist to pay for flood defences which they could have afforded. So it hardly seems fair to hold individual residents of New Orleans responsible for decisions made by their local leaders. On the other hand, perhaps there is something to be said for the view that the local population could, and should, have done more to put pressure on their political representatives to raise taxes and build better flood defences. Moreover, some residents could have taken the decision to leave if they believed that the defences were not good enough. In fact many residents made the decision to ignore the warnings preferring instead to wait out the storm. However, this argument may not be appropriate for many thousands of poor black voters with limited education and political influence and no money to up sticks and move. Given these complexities, how should we draw the distinction between option luck for which individuals should be held responsible and brute luck for which other people, whether nationally or internationally, should take responsibility?

Global hypothetical insurance markets

Hitherto Dworkin has employed hypothetical insurance markets to tease out the demands of equality of resources in a wide variety of cases ranging from the risk of physical disability, lack of talent and redundancy to the risk of ill-health and being born to poor parents (Dworkin, 1981b; 2000, chs. 8 and 9). It should be obvious what is coming next. Perhaps this device might also be used to address the numerous unresolved problems outlined above. More specifically, I propose the use of hypothetical insurance to conceptualise and evaluate risks ranging from being born into a country which lacks proximity to natural resources or that has abundant natural resources but is afflicted by different forms of the resources curse – including lack of development capacity, corrupt leaders, civil war and weak private property rights – to the risk of being born somewhere ravaged by disease pandemics, bad climate, crop failures and various sorts of natural disasters.

Rather than trying to explain how hypothetical insurance would operate in every possible case I instead focus on two main illustrations. The first is a hypothetical insurance market for development talent. Consider a country with plentiful gas, oil and coal deposits but also a shortfall in the skills and knowledge required to extract these things. According to Miller, this type of example shows that Dworkin's auction is not suitable as a measure of global equality of resources. Perhaps the country could ask foreign companies to come in and extract its resources. But it would also have to pay a premium. Can this really be what equality means (Miller, 1999b, p. 193)? Although this objection scores points against the auction taken in isolation, it is important to keep in mind that the auction is not intended to realise equality of resources alone. On the contrary, Dworkin makes it clear that the auction could establish an ideal only if there were no differences among people in respect of their personal resources. Since this is not the case – because some people 'may be more skilful than others at producing what others want and will trade to get' (Dworkin, 1981b, p. 292) – the auction must be supplemented. He introduces a hypothetical insurance market for talent as a way of achieving overall equality of resources. Correspondingly, suppose that by virtue of stipulated uncertainty about what skills and knowledge are required to exploit natural resources the Mini-Earth survivors have an equal antecedent chance of lacking the skills and knowledge required to make use of their equal share of post-auction resources up to different levels of financial return but also the same ample opportunity to purchase insurance against that risk. Depending on what level and type of insurance they decide to purchase, this could be used as a standard for development assistance in the real world. With secure access to this higher level of development assistance, poor countries will be in a much better position to decide whether or not to invite multinational mining companies to come in and extract resources on their behalf and on what terms.

I also believe that there is value in extending the hypothetical insurance scheme to the case of natural disasters. Suppose that the survivors have knowledge of the kinds of natural disasters that strike Mini-Earth but are uncertain about the probabilities involved. Because of this, each survivor supposes that he or she has the same chance as anyone else of facing some sort of natural disaster of different magnitudes whichever region he or she decides to purchase land in. Following Dworkin, I do not assume that the survivors enter into forward contingent claims contracts whereby they come to own resources and plots of land only if certain states of nature occur including physical conditions of the environment such as rain or shine (Dworkin, 1981b, p. 287, n. 2). Rather, I propose that there are insurance companies on Mini-Earth which provide policies against loss of life and limb, damage to property and loss of livelihood caused by natural disasters. Premiums will vary with the level of coverage chosen but are the same for every survivor at any particular coverage level. They can be paid out of the policy holder's initial stock of impersonal resources or from future earnings. So we ask, how much of such insurance would the survivors, on average, choose to purchase, covering what particular risks and at what cost? If this question is amenable to rational deliberation, the average level and kind of hypothetical insurance purchased could be used as a suitable benchmark for a global scheme of relief for natural disasters. Perhaps most people would purchase at least life insurance but also insurance for damage to property up to a certain level. Maybe the most popular policies − because of their cheaper premiums − will require policy holders to build and maintain flood defences as a condition of receiving coverage.

Whatever the particular details of the decisions made, however, the thought experiment provides a set of idealised conditions for transforming brute luck into option luck in contrast to the unjust background conditions found in the real world. Sticking with the example of natural disasters, conditions in the real world are unjust for the following reasons. First, some people have an unequal antecedent risk of natural disasters and so face higher insurance premiums as a result. Second, due to lack of development and infrastructure within their own countries some people are likely to suffer greater impacts from the same natural disasters than others, where this is measured in terms of loss of life, damage to property and forfeiture of wealth. This will also push premiums up. Finally, wealth is distributed unequally around the world as a result of unequal access to natural resources, wealth-creating talent, and an unjust institutional order of foreign trade, investment and lending. This means that some people simply cannot afford to purchase ample insurance or move to an area where insurance is unnecessary. That the scenario described above achieves equality in these respects confers ethical legitimacy on the level and type of insurance that the survivors, on average, would purchase.

The problem of cultural differences in attitudes to insurance

I now wish to address the issue of whether or not the hypothetical insurance model can claim to show equal respect for different conceptions of the good, including comprehensive religious doctrines, in the sense that it does not favour any particular conception of the good of another. One potentially troubling aspect of the hypothetical insurance approach is its method of extracting actual policies from an average of counterfactual choices. This opens up the possibility that it might overlook important cultural differences between peoples. Consider once again the case of natural disasters. Can it be right to assume that natural disasters are things which virtually everybody would wish to purchase insurance against? What if, given a free choice, some people would not wish to buy any insurance whatsoever? Does this mean that what happens to them is a matter of counterfactual option luck and therefore they have no redistributive claims against the rest of the world? But what if the primary reason for their choice not to buy insurance is based on their commitment to a religious doctrine?

First things first, what reasons do we have for supposing that there are profound global differences in people's attitudes to the appropriateness of purchasing insurance against natural disasters? At first glance, the world's major religious faiths do not see natural disasters in entirely dissimilar ways. Some members of the Christian faith explain natural disasters as acts of God in the literal sense of God seeking to punish the sins of man. Many Hindus also view suffering caused by natural disasters as punishment for misdeeds committed in this lifetime or in past lives. In Islam, the Qur'an refers in various places to Allah using natural disasters as a test of faith or to inflict punishment on a population. Likewise, some followers of Judaism regard natural disasters as caused by a weakening in devotion to God. On the other hand, there is in virtually every religion that has at all stood the test of time an expectation that people should not repose all responsibility for the success or failure of their own lives in the hands of God. They must also learn to help themselves. For this reason it might be argued that there are no religious grounds for thinking that purchasing insurance policies against natural disasters is disrespectful to God. By taking out an insurance policy the policy holder is not seeking to avoid the punishment of God for his sins or failing to show due humility for God's supreme power or replacing his trust in God with trust in man.

However, a significant division between the world's major religions does come to the fore when one reflects on the question of commercial insurance. Christians and Hindus see no wrong in commercial insurance. Indeed, many churches make use of commercial insurers to purchase policies covering buildings and contents. Islamic law, by contrast, contains a very powerful injunction against commercial insurance. It prohibits any business which trades in risk or uncertainty. Muslims believe that anything people trade in must be of concrete value. Hence casinos are banned because they make money by calculating probabilities and selling chances. A commercial insurance company is analogous to a casino because it offers protection against uncertain outcomes for the price of the policy. Given this major difference, how can we possibly regard the insurance approach as appropriate for everyone around the world Christians and Muslims alike?

One possible response to the problem is to emphasise the hypothetical nature of the insurance scheme. From the mere fact Muslims object to actual commercial insurance it does not necessarily follow that they would object to thinking about what justice requires in terms of hypothetical commercial insurance. But this consideration, in itself, cannot demonstrate that *no* Muslims would object to hypothetical commercial insurance. So I do not intend to rely on it here. A second possible reply is to insist that justice as global equal concern and respect is not supposed to be neutral between secular values and religious values when the latter embody unjust beliefs about the restriction of individual liberty and free markets. If it is unjust to ban competitive insurance markets on religious grounds, then Muslims cannot rightly complain about the insurance method. But this response relies once again on the controversial liberal assumption that religious law is not an appropriate basis for restricting liberty. If the aim is to achieve a deeper form of neutrality, then principles of global equality of resources must in some sense reflect the choices that non-liberal peoples would have made about insurance, where this includes the fundamental choice not to purchase commercial insurance.

Now at this stage some people might be tempted to grasp the nettle and judge that if Muslims would 'choose' not to purchase commercial insurance, then this is a religious sacrifice the cost of which is rightly theirs to pay. Although I think that there is a case to be made for religious sacrifice, I am not persuaded by that case in this particular context. What we need, I think, is a more sophisticated account of the kinds of insurance opportunities that could be available in our imaginary scenario. In view of this, suppose that instead of only commercial insurance companies operating on Mini-Earth, there is at least one insurance agency offering *Takaful* or Islamic insurance. Takaful is a form of social or not-for-profit insurance in which members guarantee each other a certain level of assistance in the event of misfortune. Takaful insurers are said to observe Islamic law by virtue of the fact that they offer mutual protection to members of the Islamic faith who find themselves in distress rather than making profit through the commodification of risk. With this amendment we have a richer set of insurance opportunities that cater to peoples with very different attitudes to insurance. So there may be a chance after all of turning brute luck into option luck in a way that everyone can endorse.

Reforming foreign aid in the light of global equality of resources

Having looked at emerging inequalities over time, I now return to possible sites of global equality of resources. My suggestion is that foreign aid is as just as we can reasonably expect it to be only if it brings individuals around the world much closer to the levels of prosperity they would have enjoyed given an egalitarian auction of the planet's natural resources and an ample opportunity to purchase insurance against a range of risks under conditions of *ex ante* equality. So, for example, ODA should address shortfalls on the side of access to natural resources and where a country has plenty of natural resources but low development capacity it should mimic the insurance that individuals would have purchased on average against being born into such a country. Living up to this standard would, I think, require levels of redistribution well above the 0.16 per cent and 0.36 of GNI given by the United States and the United Kingdom respectively, and conceivably above the conventional 0.7 per cent target. That is not to say that the 0.7 target is not useful in terms of addressing severe poverty, and as something that can be 'sold' to rich, developed countries as realisable (see Sachs, 2005). Rather, the point is that interpreting foreign aid in the light of the imaginary auction and hypothetical insurance markets provides scope for moving beyond what is widely accepted to what is even more just.

I also believe that global equality of resources can provide an appropriate standard against which to judge present levels of humanitarian aid. On this interpretation, an important point and purpose of humanitarian aid is to indemnify people around world against a range of risks including natural disasters, food shortages and health epidemics. The level of assistance that people living in blighted countries could expect to receive depends on the average level of insurance coverage purchased under conditions of *ex ante* equality. To interpret the provision of humanitarian aid in accordance with this ideal would be to regard people living in the flood planes of Bangladesh, for example, as having a right to the kind of insurance coverage that we can reasonably infer they would have purchased counterfactually. Arguably this means coverage which is reliable, reasonably comprehensive and not subject to political influence. One of the benefits of this approach is that local populations will be in a much stronger position to plan in advance of emergencies, which is a far more efficient use of resources. Of course, in better times they too will be called upon to assist others and this represents the premiums they would have had to pay for their own insurance coverage. Arguably this was the case when Guatemala, Guyana, Cuba, Honduras, India and Indonesia offered aid to the United States in the aftermath of Hurricane Katrina.[7]

Having given a brief overview of how global equality of resources could provide standards for judging existing foreign aid, I shall now say a bit more about the relevant duty bearers and the content of these duties. Though global equality of resources recognises states, international organisations such as the EU and UN, corporations and NGOs as secondary duty bearers, individuals remain the primary duty bearers of global equality of resources. (Of course, this may not be the case as far as other aspects of global equal concern and respect are concerned.) So I take it as read that individuals have a responsibility to support just foreign aid. For people living in some countries, where governments already provide just foreign aid, this may simply mean paying one's taxes or making sure that one is in a position to pay taxes. But for most people it will mean voting for political parties which favour such transfers and in the meantime finding alternative ways to make donations such as through NGOs. Otherwise, individuals have a duty to support the creation of mechanisms for identifying the money that the average person would have devoted to insurance as well as mechanisms for ensuring that the money is transferred from individuals who would have been policy holders to individuals who would have been the beneficiaries of such policies.

In order to provide a more precise standard for judging just individual contributions at any particular time, however, we require an account of what level of giving is appropriate. In his *Practical Ethics*, Peter Singer famously challenges wealthy people to keep giving money to poorer people up until the point that they give away something of 'comparable moral importance' (Singer, 1972, p. 231).[8] I favour a less demanding, more nuanced account of what we owe to the world's poor based on the idea of hypothetical insurance. Even so, we still require a guide for making intelligent estimates about the particular kinds and levels of insurance that are likely to result from counterfactual decisions. To this end, it might be useful to look at some existing insurance enterprises. Although we must keep in mind the fact that actual insurance markets are imperfect by the yardstick of *ex ante* equality, they might provide guidance for discovering the variety and shape of insurance policies and some ballpark figures on premiums. Take the case of the Micro Insurance Agency which began working with the World Bank in 2005 to develop weather-indexed crop insurance for smallholder farmers in Malawi. At the time most uninsured farmers could not get agricultural funding from local banks because of the high risk of crop failure due to flooding and drought. But some banks were willing to lend if the weather risk could be indemnified against. The Micro Insurance Agency works to provide affordable insurance to unlock the funding. It collects average premiums of approximately \$2 per month from the people it covers. Using this enterprise as an approximate guide, it might be thought that the minimum worldwide individual contribution called for by global equality of resources in respect of insurance against crop failure is somewhere in the region of \$2 per month.

An additional function of global equality of resources could be to guide the formation of new institutions. Thus far the principal instruments for international redistribution have been ODA and humanitarian aid. But interpreting these practices under an ideal of equal concern may support a transformation of the current patchwork of bilateral and multilateral aid agreements and NGOs into something like a Global Insurance Fund (GIF) administered by a global financial institution such as the World Bank. One of the main points in favour of the use of insurance is that people would be able to access funds relatively quickly in the event of a crop failure or natural disaster and as a matter of entitlement. Ideally the GIF would indemnify individuals across the globe against a range of risks, but sticking with the present example it could be used to provide monetary assistance to people living in parts of the world hit by drought or other natural disasters. Of course, it is a further issue how to secure contributions to the GIF. But I think that it is possible to imagine a situation in which countries with a long track record of providing foreign aid would commit themselves to the setting up of a GIF. They would then authorise a governing body to make decisions about levels of coverage, to keep track of where the funds go and to ensure that countries fulfil their financial commitments to the GIF and where necessary impose economic sanctions against countries who fail to pay their premiums.

Clearly there could be more or less centralised versions of the GIF. On the most centralised version, the relevant global institution will itself act as the insurance broker. A slightly less centralised version would be for the GIF to transfer funds to national governments to augment the money they already have available to purchase insurance policies from international insurance companies. In 2006, for example, the WFP brokered a deal with the Axa Re insurance company to provide drought insurance to 62,000 families living in rural Ethiopia using money provided by the US government, the Ethiopian administration and other donors. The insurers agreed that below a certain minimum of rainfall, they would pay $7 million within a matter of days, to be spent on food aid or payments to farmers. The insurance premium paid for this cover was $930,000. In the end, levels of rainfall stayed above the minimum and so the insurance company made a tidy profit, but that year at least these farmers did have insurance. Finally, the body in charge of the GIF could give funds directly to charitable organisations working at the local level to develop micro-insurance schemes. So, for example, the Consultative Group to Assist the Poor (CGAP) was founded in 1995 in partnership with the World Bank and provides the financial industry, governments and investors with information and solutions on how to expand access to financial services for the global poor. The CGAP Working Group on Micro-Insurance works specifically to promote the development of insurance services for low-income persons. The Impact subgroup includes the Micro Insurance Academy (MIA), a Delhi-based charitable trust that has been working since 2007 to provide information, training and advisory services on setting up community-based micro-insurance schemes in India, including crop and health insurance.

One reason to favour the third, bottom-up approach is that it puts individuals or families in control of their own destinies with the help of their local community. CGAP has already gathered some empirical evidence to suggest that people who have participated in micro-finance programmes were able to improve their well-being at both the individual and household level much more than those who did not have access to these services (CGAP, 2008). But perhaps more important is the fact that charities like MIA are able to work with poor communities as equal partners, helping them to assume the majority of insurance functions at the grassroots level. In this way the GIF is able to show not only equal concern but also equal respect for the special responsibility of the people it seeks to indemnify. On the other hand, there may be a case for a degree of central control over global insurance coverage on paternalistic grounds. Indeed, there may be cases where insurance is best provided remotely as with isolated tribes that would not benefit from closer contact with the outside world. Consider an insurance policy which protects a remote rainforest tribe against the threat of forest fires.

How could it be possible for the GIF to show equal respect for all people given the religious diversity in attitudes to insurance discussed above? This is an important question but it can be answered by pointing out that not all models of the GIF seek involvement from commercial insurance companies. Respect for religious diversity provides at least one reason to favour models that do not. These models may lack the benefit of competition in driving down costs, but they are suitable for a wider class of people. Even so, it might be pointed out that the GIF is itself still funded by, and provides insurance to, a range of different faith groups including both Muslims and non-Muslims. Since it cannot be construed as offering a scheme of mutual cooperation between people *of the same faith*, some Muslims might take exception to the GIF fund. They might insist that the Muslim community is like the human body – when one of its parts is afflicted with pain, then the rest of the body will be affected – and so there can only be mutual insurance among parts of the same whole.[9] The breaking up of the GIF may be lamented for a number of reasons, not least the material, if not spiritual, well-being of those who wish to opt out. But in this event the best we can hope for is a twin-track GIF including Islamic and non-Islamic programmes. On this split model, people from Islamic nations pay into and receive assistance only from other Muslims. It is likely that rich Gulf States would then become the main premium payers and benefactors of poorer Islamic states. Indeed, we can already see a model for this type of division of redistributive labour in the 2008 Dakar meeting of the Organization of the Islamic Conference (OIC). Here member states reached an agreement on ways to reduce the imbalance in wealth between rich and poor countries in the Islamic world by creating a $2.6 billion anti-poverty fund.

With these comments in place I am now finally in a position to sub-stantiate a claim I made in Chapter 6 about duties of justice, to wit, that individuals can be among the primary duty bearers in relation to justice as global equal concern and respect. Some of an individual's duties relating to global equality of resources are: the duty not to purchase natural resources from agents whose claim is of uncertain status, such as by mak-ing use of diamond certification schemes; the duty to support forms of taxation that could be interpreted as upholding global equality of resources, such as an international charge on transactions involving nat-ural resources; the duty to answer appeals made by aid agencies to donate amounts of money that could be reasonably interpreted to mimic hypo-thetical insurance premiums and corresponding payouts, such as money collected to pay for the rebuilding of a hospital after a hurricane; the duty to support just ODA by paying one's taxes and by conscientiously voting for political parties who are willing to sign up to just and unambiguous agreements on foreign aid and where necessary voting against parties who are not committed to fulfilling the just pledges of preceding governments. Other duties fall on NGOs, local officials and individuals to make good use of foreign aid and thereby to show equal concern and respect to donors and to genuine claimants. Moreover, the list should also include duties not to support a world order that recognises the unjust property claims of local warlords.[10]

In this chapter I have sought to provide a more complete interpreta-tion of the demands of global equal concern and respect as they pertain to international exploitation of, and trade in, natural resources and for-eign aid, not merely in terms of reforming existing rules, practices and individual actions but also in terms of the design of new institutional structures. I have suggested that a revised Dworkinian auction provides one way of thinking about what equality of natural resources would be like on a global scale and that various other sources of global inequality can be modelled using the idea of hypothetical insurance. We have seen that, cultural differences do raise difficulties in articulating, applying and implementing equality of resources at the global level. That such cultural differences exist is important for both the theory and the practice of global equality of resources. But I have tried to show how it is possible to surmount these problems by making appropriate modifications – sometimes achieving deep neutrality, at other times sticking to principles of ethical individualism.

8
Conclusion

This book has explored Dworkin's theory of equality as it applies to both domestic and global domains. In this chapter I shall review the arguments of the previous chapters and offer some general remarks about what I think they all add up to.

The aim of Part I was to critically examine the core elements of Dworkin's theory of equality. Chapter 2 scrutinised his thesis that equality of welfare is a defective conception of justice as equal concern in the genre of distributive justice because it cannot be specified without drawing on a prior conception of fair shares and because it leads to counter-intuitive consequences in the case of expensive tastes. His critics insist that the radical criticism is impotent against objective theories and that the objection from expensive tastes defeats equality of welfare but not equality of opportunity for welfare. Cohen, for example, maintains that although Dworkin was on the right path to the truth about egalitarian justice, he did not 'quite get there'. For Cohen, the truth of the matter depends on a distinction between what does and what does not lie within a person's voluntary control, where this distinction cuts across many different dimensions of advantage including both resources and welfare. For his part, Dworkin rejects Cohen's framing of the purported distinction arguing instead that it would strike us as bizarre for persons to claim compensation from the rest of society for their unchosen tastes, preferences and ambitions because such items are ordinarily supported by underlying aspects of our personalities such as our beliefs, convictions and judgements of value of different sorts. Cohen attempts to drive a further wedge between personality and circumstances with the idea of bad price luck. But once again Dworkin refutes the suggestion that there is a form of compensable bad luck lurking in the corner here. On the contrary, the tastes and preferences of others form the background against which the value of resources is to be determined. The Dworkin–Cohen debate has produced some of the most intricate as well as interesting disagreements in the egalitarian literature. In the end I came down on the side of Dworkin arguing that Cohen has not done enough to demonstrate that a failure to compensate persons for their expensive tastes is unjust in the largest sense, depending on the challenge model of ethical life.

Chapter 3 addressed Dworkin's preferred conception of justice as equal concern, equality of resources. Although his detractors have sought out weaknesses at every level, I argued that many of these criticisms miss their mark and those that do hit the target are far from fatal to the project. In the case of Anderson's objections, for example, Dworkin has been at pains to distinguish his own view from the luck egalitarian family of views as defined by Anderson. He points out that equality of resources does not aim to fully compensate brute bad luck but to transform brute luck into option luck through the provision of ample opportunity to buy insurance under conditions of *ex ante* equality. Any insurance policy that people would wish to purchase under idealised conditions must reflect the opportunity cost of that insurance, so they are unlikely to purchase an insurance policy which pays out full compensation. This is a telling response. But it is also one that raises the question of what it means for a theory to be egalitarian. In answering that question I tried to show that despite Dworkin's talk of a safety-net, that is, a minimum amount of insurance that we can safely assume people would choose to purchase on average, equality of resources is an avowedly egalitarian doctrine precisely because it relies so heavily on the idea of *ex ante* equality.

Chapter 4 scrutinised Dworkin's claim that virtually every normative theory of social arrangement from Kant onwards can be presented as occupying a certain kind of egalitarian plateau. The idea of an egalitarian plateau has been hailed by some as a profound move, one that tells us something very important about the unity as well as diversity of contemporary political thought. But even if we accept the truth of the egalitarian plateau thesis, the question I considered is whether this makes any real difference to political argument. Ultimately I argued that the egalitarian plateau can make a great deal of difference provided that abstract egalitarian rights are interpreted as having a much wider scope than Dworkin himself envisages.

Having tested the foundations of Dworkin's theory of equality, Part II of the book attempted to develop a Dworkinian theory of global distributive justice. To this end Chapter 5 put under the microscope Dworkin's assumption that there is something special about a true political community which means that a government owes equal concern to its citizens and fellow citizens owe equal concern to each other, but not to other people. In this respect Dworkin's theory of equality is not uncharacteristic of the statist tradition within international political theory. Even so, I argued that this assumption is open to question on two main grounds. First, I considered whether or not it might be possible to make a case for the existence of a global political community with the sorts of characteristics highlighted by Dworkin in the domestic realm, namely, dominion, democracy, integrity and fraternity. Though there is something to be said for this argument, in the end it proved too treacherous to make a convincing case for a global political community given Dworkin's description of what true political community is. Secondly, I turned to consider whether or not there might be other sites of global egalitarian justice. I argued that various kinds of things, including foreign aid, have features which make them interpretable as sites of global justice, not least that they have a profound and pervasive impact on other people's life chances around the globe.

Towards the end of Chapter 5, I distinguished two general questions we should ask about foreign aid. The first asks what level of foreign aid is required in order for our actions to count as treating all human beings with equal concern and respect according to a gold standard of what that means. The second asks what level of foreign aid is required to display a good faith attempt to treat all human beings with equal concern and respect according to a minimally adequate conception of what that means. I am now in a position to explain how I answered these two questions. Chapter 6 suggested that the gold standard of equal concern is constituted in part by the highly abstract idea of interpretive global luck egalitarianism, while Chapter 7 tried to argue that the minimum level of aid that is required to display a good faith attempt to treat all human beings with equal concern and respect is captured by global equality of resources.

Reflecting on these arguments, however, the reader might be unsure as to what *kind* of standard global equality of resources sets if not the gold standard of global justice. Unfortunately we are not especially well served by the English language with respect to capturing the concept of a minimum standard of rightful behaviour, on the part of individual and collective agents, in matters of global distribution. If we call this a standard of *international legitimacy*, we evoke the idea of legitimacy as respect for state sovereignty rather than the idea of standards of just distribution which transcend state borders. If we call this instead a standard of *human rights*, we are in danger of being dragged into a hoary dispute over the existence of socio-economic human rights. So I propose instead that we simply call this *doing the right thing by foreigners*.

Another important challenge might be that global equality of resources would be too demanding in the best of times but utterly disastrous in times of recession such as during the earlier 1980s, early 90s and now in the late 2000s. Even so, the account developed here accepts the fact that in straightened financial circumstances individuals and national governments will need to balance the duty to make payments to distant others against the necessities of safeguarding their own basic prosperity in the face of a global downturn. What I do wish to reject, however, is the notion that global equal concern and respect is somehow intrinsically too demanding. That we should risk bankrupting ourselves in order to close the global income gap is antithetical to what it means to show equal concern and respect to all human beings. Rather, interpretive global luck egalitarianism or, more specifically, global equality of resources demands only that we make payments to people around the world at a minimum level we can safely assume would have resulted from an imaginary global auction and hypothetical insurance markets. I suspect that this minimum level is likely to be in excess of the widely accepted 0.7 per cent target for development assistance. Even so, provided any increase in the percentage of GNI devoted to foreign aid is made in a measured and sustainable within a reasonable time frame, I conjecture that it need not be crippling to economic growth in the developed world.

The position adopted in this book calls for a reduction of global inequality, and so, I reject the idea that somehow local populations are always fully responsible for the situations in which they find themselves. But by the same token I reject the opposite idea that they bear no responsibility. One of the aims of global equality of resources is to provide a standard of justice that offers an appropriate interpretation of the highly abstract requirements of global luck egalitarianism. In addition to this, I tried to show how it is possible to modify Dworkin's equality of resources in order to take account of global cultural diversity. Without these modifications the account would seem to favour some political cultures over others and in ways that we have reason to regret.

Although much of Part II focused on foreign aid and on the exploitation of, and trade in, natural resources, I do not claim that these exhaust the sites of global justice. Far from it. It is important not to overlook injustices associated with colonialism, slavery, human exploitation, border controls, climate change, trade protectionism, structural adjustment policies, fiscal privileges granted to corrupt rulers and tyrants, and much more besides. For these reasons I argued in favour of a compound approach to global justice which is sensitive to different sites of injustice and has room for different principles of justice at lower levels of specificity. It seems to me that such an approach provides as plausible an interpretation of global justice as any of the other leading alternatives taken in isolation, and is in many respects more plausible for what it adds.

If the arguments of this book are correct, then global equal concern and respect is one of the appropriate standards for judging the exploitation of, and trade in, natural resources. In addition to developing principles of global justice appropriate to these areas, in Chapters 6 and 7 I also tried to develop a complete account of who the relevant duty bearers are and what it is that they are suppose to do, and not only in terms of reforming existing rules, practices and individual actions but also in the design of new global institutions.

I end now with some final observations about my project. In the introduction of this book I pointed out that few books and articles written on the subject of global distributive justice begin without listing at least some brute facts about global inequality. What is much less common, however, is for theorists to address the fact that there has actually been a modest decline in global inequality since 1980 (Dollar, 2007, p. 84).[1] This fact itself raises an interesting question about whether domestic inequality would still matter in the context of a more significant reduction of global inequality. My own view is that reductions in global inequality do not obviate the imperative for reductions in domestic global inequality, especially given the fact that the decline in global inequality since 1980 has been matched by an increase in domestic inequality in highly populated countries such as China, India and the United States (p. 87).

Perhaps Dworkin would insist that my project has been misconceived from the start. Since there is no reason to suppose that showing equal concern and respect is a global duty, there is no point in thinking seriously about either an auction for the world's natural resources or hypothetical insurance markets at the global level. Or he might patiently try to explain that in much the same way that Rawls' law of peoples diverges from justice as fairness for reasons of due toleration, so a Dworkinian account of global justice must depart from equality of resources. Nevertheless, what I have attempted to do in this book is challenge this particular way of thinking. I have argued that the constructive interpretation of the sites and principles of global distributive justice need not differ radically from the constructive interpretation of the sites and principles of domestic distributive justice. Just as the principles of domestic justice try to give expression to the abstract idea of making the distribution sensitive to choice but not sensitive to brute luck, so the principles of global justice try to give expression to the abstract idea of making the distribution sensitive to local choice but not sensitive to arbitrary deprivation. Both sets of principles draw on deeper principles of human dignity and both sets of principles stand in need of further interpretation at the level of practice.

In short, for those readers who have been influenced by Dworkin's theory of equality at the domestic level, I have tried to offer a coherent and in some respects attractive picture of how this theory might play out at the global level in spite of Dworkin. Even if I have been unable to convince the reader of the truth of these admittedly contentious propositions, I hope that I have at least pointed out some possible merits of bringing Dworkin's method of constructive interpretation to bear on these debates. The value can be seen in the following stark contrast. Either we accept the method of *a priori* political philosophy which embarks on the enterprise of understanding global justice without first examining the things to which the principles of justice are supposed to apply or we pursue the simple constructivist method of building an account of global justice from what actually exists and how institutions and practices are conventionally understood by persons engaged in them. In Part II of this book I have tried to show that Dworkin's method of constructive interpretation enables us to pose a third kind of methodological question, 'What is the real purpose and value of our rules, practices and individual actions?'

Notes

1 Introduction

1. Berlin, of course, held that there is not one but a number of fundamental political values (including equality and liberty), which can, and often do, conflict to give contrary directives in matters of political morality. Although this leaves the difficult task of trying to establish which values are to be promoted or sacrificed at any given time, it is better to be a pluralist fox – to be tolerant, liberal and reasonable – than to be a monist hedgehog – the creed of the authoritarian politician. See Berlin (1978), p. 22.
2. For critical assessment of these claims, see Williams (2001) and Otsuka (2002) respectively.
3. In contrast to Rawls' veil of ignorance, Dworkin's hypothetical insurance argument is designed to allow people 'enough self-knowledge, as individuals, to keep relatively intact their sense of their own personality, and especially their theory of what is valuable in life' (Dworkin, 1981b, p. 345).
4. Of course, to accept Dworkin's interpretation of the practice of interpretation is to turn down a competing interpretation which claims that when an interpreter asserts that something 'really is' just or that his is 'the correct' interpretation by this utterance he means that his interpretation corresponds to facts which exist 'out there' in the universe.

2 Equality of Welfare

1. See also Griffin (1986), p. 47 and Schaller (1997), pp. 262–6.
2. Dworkin insists that the radical criticism enfeebles not only single conceptions of welfare but also any composite conception of welfare which might otherwise seem attractive. See Dworkin (1981a), p. 228. The thought appears to be that if no single conception of welfare can be specified without drawing on some prior conception of fair shares, there is no hope that a compound conception involving combinations and trade-offs could be so specified.
3. Some contributors question the plausibility of Cohen's description of Paul's state of mind. If nothing other than photography could or does please Paul so he is miserable without it, then, as Rakowski puts it, 'Paul is an exceedingly rare person' (Rakowski, 1991, p. 57).
4. Rawls, for example, affirms that the reason why expensive tastes do not raise a case for compensation is not because of a metaphysical assumption about free will or even an empirical generalisation about human agency. Rather, the reason is that justice as fairness is a political conception based on ideas found in the public political culture of a liberal society, vis-à-vis, that citizens are regarded as having a capacity to form, revise and pursue their own conceptions of the good and therefore as being responsible for expensive tastes. See Rawls (1982), pp. 168–9 and (1996), pp. 186–90.

5. Cohen tries to deal with Scanlon's example of religious guilt with the following amendment to the original distinction between voluntary and involuntary disadvantage. 'Instead of saying, "compensate for disadvantages which are not traceable to the subject's choice," say, "compensate for disadvantages which are not traceable to the subject's choice *and* which the subject would choose not to suffer from"' (Cohen, 1989, p. 937). This means that if the religionist would not choose not to suffer from guilt, then he is not owed compensation. But it is debatable whether this revision is, as Cohen claims, 'a natural development of the original view'. Whereas the original view took as its touchstone the genesis of choice – a metaphysical fact – the revision seems to bring into play how the agent views his disadvantage, namely, whether he would choose not to suffer from guilt. Indeed, Cohen suggests that when someone says, "I would not give it up if I could" he is not making a prediction about what he would do (p. 937, n. 68). But then what is he doing? In so far as the most plausible explanation as to why a religionist would not choose not to suffer from guilt is because he identifies with this aspect of his personality this brings Dworkin's moral psychological back into the picture. At the very least the onus of proof lies with Cohen to explain why someone would make this counterfactual choice.
6. For further discussion of whether or not religious costs should be considered on a par with expensive tastes, see Jones (1994), Cohen (1999), Parekh (2000), Barry (2001) and Miller (2002c).
7. If the mental handicap is serious enough, then insurance companies will offer policies and people will want to buy them. A person is then entitled to assistance for a psychological craving or obsession as a form of deficiency in personal resources as opposed to a lack of enjoyment or preference satisfaction. See Dworkin (2000), pp. 297, 490–1, n. 11.
8. Of course, not everyone is like this. Consider Harry Frankfurt's case of the willing drug addict who is unusual in that he fully identifies with and does not regret the cravings that govern his every waking moment. This willingness, claims Frankfurt, may be sufficient to justify holding the addict morally responsible for his actions. See Frankfurt (1971).
9. I have in mind David Cameron, leader of the UK Conservative Party.
10. Compare Scheffler (2005), p. 15 and Goodin (1995), ch. 1.
11. cf. Daniels (1990), pp. 288–90. See also footnote 7.

3 Equality of Resources

1. Cohen's example of involuntary eye transplants demonstrates this point very nicely. See Cohen (1995), p. 70.
2. For more on the question of intellectual property rights, see Gosseries (2008).
3. Unfortunately I do not have space in this book to examine Michael Otsuka's alternative to the auction, which is a starting gate theory combined with an egalitarian proviso. See Otsuka (1998) and (2003). Of course, two of the main differences between Dworkin's auction and Otsuka's proposal are that the latter puts self-ownership at the heart of the theory and defines the egalitarian proviso in terms of equality of opportunity for welfare.

4. See Chapter 2 above.
5. See Lippert-Rasmussen (2001), Fleurbaey (2001), Otsuka (2002) and Sandbu (2004).
6. Dworkin also acknowledges that a moderate version of *ex post* equality would also resists spending the entire social product on full compensation for the severely disadvantaged. But he argues that 'reasonable' *ex post* equality 'is an undisciplined standard that leaves great room for hypocrisy and self-deceit and so offers very little protection for the poor, even in a society that embraces it enthusiastically' (Dworkin, 2006, p. 111).
7. Two smaller points. Macleod alleges that because the hypothetical insurance firms themselves are able to judge with a tolerable degree of accuracy a person's talent-based earning potential this 'obviates the need to rely upon the hypothetical insurance in the first place' (Macleod, 1998, pp. 145–6). Now the hypothetical insurance firms may be able to judge talent-based earning potential, but what they cannot do is judge what proportion of each person's talent is itself determined by ambition or circumstances. Macleod also accuses Dworkin of having 'inadvertently' drawn attention to the inability of the insurance scheme to track ambition-sensitivity by failing to make mention of that particular requirement in the description of the scheme (pp. 147–8). Putting to one side my claim about the inaccuracy of the tracking interpretation of Dworkin, this criticism ignores the fairly obvious point that people's decisions whether or not to purchase insurance and at what level are themselves expressions of ambition.
8. I do not intend to discuss here the further, technical claim made by Fleurbaey that the insurance device produces 'exactly the allocation which maximizes the sum of individual utilities in an essentially utilitarian fashion' (Fleurbaey, 2002, p. 94). For Dworkin's reply, see his (2002), pp. 129–36.
9. At first glance, it is somewhat less clear how equality of resources would cope with people who lack the minimum cognitive faculties necessary to think intelligently about risk and insurance. The insurance technique that would otherwise provide a suitable mechanism for dealing with other sorts of capabilities is not appropriate here, for it seems we cannot fairly ask the question about whether or not someone lacking in these faculties would purchase insurance. Nevertheless, I think that there is another technique we can employ. Perhaps in these cases we should ask what insurance a well-motivated guardian would choose to purchase on behalf of someone who lacks the requisite mental wherewithal to make such decisions alone. cf. Dworkin (2000), p. 339.
10. Scheffler's own analysis of Rawls makes for an interesting comparison at this stage. Scheffler points out that even though Rawls says that 'no one deserves his place in the distribution of native endowments, any more than one deserves one's initial starting place in society', he also distances justice as fairness from the principle of redress. Rawls endorses the difference principle rather than the principle of redress because full redress is likely to mean lowering the average standard of living and perhaps even the abolition of the family. Given these facts, Scheffler argues that it makes questionable sense to interpret Rawls as a luck egalitarian. Scheffler (2003), pp. 8–12. I think that Scheffler would do well to interpret Dworkin's theory of equality in a similar fashion.

11. For critical comment on this assumption, see Markovits (2003), Cohen Christofidis (2004) and Vincent (2006).
12. For more on Anderson's general criticisms of luck egalitarianism, and responses to those criticisms, see Arneson (2000b), Kaufman (2004), Brown (2005), Barry (2006), Segall (2007) and Voigt (2007).
13. For a more detailed account of his views on paternalism, see Dworkin (1993).

4   The Egalitarian Plateau

1. Indeed, Dworkin suggests that different political theories (as in, different interpretations of the abstract right to equal concern and respect) will differ not only in terms of the concrete rights and collective goals they each posit but also in terms of the purpose and relative strength they attach to concrete rights and collective goals. See Dworkin (1977), p. 95.
2. See, for example, Spiegelberg (1944), W. von Leyden (1963), Wilson (1966), pp. 15–23, Benn (1967), Oppenheim (1970) and Rees (1971), pp. 11–27. cf. Williams (1962).
3. See also Chapter 3, footnote 10.

5   Political Community and Beyond

1. Of course, other scholars are far more wary about identifying universal principles of distributive justice in the international legal sphere given what they see as deeper, possibly entrenched pluralism. See Tasioulas (2002).
2. Theorists who are attracted to this method characteristically accept what Andrea Sangiovanni has dubbed the *'Practice-dependence Thesis*: The content, scope, and justification of a conception of justice depends on the structure and form of the practices that the conception is intended to govern' (Sangiovanni, 2008, p. 2).
3. What, then, of a society that uses its 'legal' system for evil purposes, as with the Nazi state? Are we compelled to say that it is a community of integrity simply because its officials act with consistency and a single vision of justice? Faced with this example, Dworkin insists that it makes perfect sense for an interpreter to take a deeply sceptical attitude towards the Nazi system of 'law' and 'integrity' by appealing to his or her own moral and political convictions about what a normal flourishing legal system looks like and what counts as genuine integrity. See Dworkin (1986), p. 104. For a critical discussion of Dworkin on this point, see Guest (1991), ch. 4 and Green (2004). Dworkin's reply to Green can be found in his (2004a).
4. There are striking similarities here with Walzer, who also argues that membership of a political community matters as far as justice is concerned 'because of what the members of a political community owe to one another and to no one else, or to no one else in the same degree' (Walzer, 1983, p. 64).
5. For a distinction between kinds of necessary conditions, see Abizadeh (2007), p. 324.
6. For a more optimistic view of global democracy, see Gould (2004).
7. A similar problem afflicts the concept of solidarity which is a close cousin of fraternity. Traditionally solidarity is thought to be a matter of loyalty, shared goals, mutual concern and trust between members of a single cohesive group

or society. Built into this conception of solidarity, then, is some version of the distinction between 'them' and 'us'. To have solidarity is to have loyalty to some and not others; goals that are shared with some people but not all; concern for those within the sphere of solidarity as distinct from those outside; trust for some and not others. In so far as this is the case, there is the problem of identifying the relevant 'them' in the case of a truly global solidarity movement. For an interesting attempt to move beyond this traditional conception of solidarity to the idea of overlapping solidarities worldwide, see Gould (2007a).

8. There are some obvious parallels here with the status quo objection levelled against Rawls; that is, against his view that questions of just or unjust socio-economic inequalities only arise within a scheme for reciprocal advantage. See Buchanan (1990), Gibbard (1991), Barry (1995) and James (2005).

9. That we are asked to imagine an already just society helps to demarcate this thought experiment from something like the New York City blackout of 1977 when looting, violence and arson occurred in the absence of law and order against a background or racial discrimination and crippling poverty.

10. There is a growing literature on border controls and immigration that sadly I do not have room to delve into here. Thomas Nagel, for example, argues that because rights to equal concern and respect only make sense in the context of a collective enterprise of coercively imposed legal and political institutions immigration policies may be enforced against the nationals of other states without justification. See Nagel (2005), pp. 129–30. For a response to this argument, see Julius (2006), pp. 184–5. Other writers have argued that people born within poor countries have a right to request entry into richer countries based on the fact that their being born within poor countries is a matter of birth or natural contingency. See Carens (1992), (1995a) and Bader (1997). Yet others defend open borders based on principles of freedom and humanity, see Kukathas (2005). For opposing perspectives on both, see Miller (2005b) and (2007), ch. 8.

11. For a detailed exposition and defence of the view that distributive justice must be essentially domestic since a contractarian-based theory of justice cannot account for global distributive justice, see Heyd (2007).

12. Somewhat similar points are made by O'Neill (2004), p. 255 and Miller (2007), p. 247. For an account of the extent of the problem of aid diversion, see Wenar (2006), pp. 3–4.

13. There is an extensive and engaging literature on this debate which deserves more attention than I can offer here. See Walzer (1977), Tamir (1991), Pogge (1992a; 1992b), Teson (1998), Buchanan (1999), Shue (2004) and Caney (2005), ch. 7.

6 Global Luck Egalitarianism

1. The general idea that persons should not be held responsible for the doings of nature is arguably supported by other international legal practices and customary norms. The International Criminal Court, for example, provides arbitration for business disputes of an international character. Not only does it recognise *force majeure* clauses but it has drafted model versions of the clause which it recommends to businesses for use in international contracts.

Force majeure is a standard clause which dissolves liability or obligation if an extraordinary event or circumstance beyond the control of the parties prevents one or both from fulfilling their obligations under the contract. Among the conventional examples of extraordinary events are war, strike, riot, crime and acts of God such as flooding or earthquake. Of course, *force majeure* does not typically excuse negligence or malfeasance as when non-fulfilment of contractual obligations is caused by inevitable or everyday acts of nature such as when rain stops an outdoor event.

2. Some, of course, have shifted ground on this. See Arneson (1989) and (2000b).

3. By way of illustration, Andrew Kuper argues that following Singer's imperative of massive redistribution from rich to poor is, in the case of the HIV/AIDS epidemic in South Africa, 'likely to seriously harm the poor' (Kuper, 2002, p. 110).

4. For an interesting inquiry into the nature of collective responsibility, with a particular emphasis on national responsibility, see Miller (2007), ch. 5.

5. Miller's own theory of global justice, of course, highlights the protection of basic human rights worldwide alongside fair terms of interaction between independent political communities. See Miller (1999b), (2000), (2007) and (2008).

7   Global Equality of Resources

1. This is not to say, of course, that Walzer offers no account of international morality. Yet the account he offers is a 'thin' morality centred around human rights as opposed to a 'thick' morality centred around the idea of global distributive justice. See Walzer (1994). Acknowledging the work of Beitz and other theorists of global distributive justice, Walzer states, 'I am inclined to think that, for now at least, ordinary moral principles regarding humane treatment and mutual aid do more work than any specific account of distributive justice' (Walzer, 1995, p. 293).

2. To clarify, the proposal is *not* that for any given plot of land P, the auctioneer puts under the hammer both liberal control rights L over P and religious control rights R over P. Rather, the auctioneer constructs two distinct lots constituted out of separate plots of land and control rights. This means that the person who successfully bids for lot one (P + L) owns all the permits associated with plot of land P, and the person who successfully bids for lot two (Q + R) owns all the permits associated with plot of land Q (which in this case is only R-type permits). Now Dworkin himself briefly considers the different proposal of Monopoly cards. We are asked to 'imagine that the auctioneer draws up a list, before the auction begins, of liberties he believes parties to the auction might find important, and then prints a limited number of cards (something like 'get out of jail' cards in Monopoly) each of which allows the bearer to exercise a particular liberty drawn from that list' (Dworkin, 1987a, p. 19). On this proposal, liberties are included within the auction but are sold separately from resources. He rejects this suggestion but not on the grounds that 'it would be nearly impossible to administer a post-action society in which people have different liberties'. Rather, the problem is that 'no one can intelligently, or even intelligibly, decide what to bid for

in an action, or what price to bid for it, unless he makes assumptions about how he will be able to use what he acquires' (p. 20). People would not be able to bid for resources until they had successfully bid for the relevant Monopoly cards. Yet they could not intelligently bid for certain Monopoly cards unless they could be sure of gaining the relevant resources. This is a catch-22. It seems to me, however, that the kind of catch-22 Dworkin describes would not afflict my proposal of having lots which comprise a set of control rights over particular resources or plots of land. Of course, if the auctioneer did put up for auction different control rights over the same particular resource or plot of land, then a similar problem would come to the fore. I cannot sensibly bid for one control right over a resource or plot of land without knowing how the other rights are going to be assigned and exercised. For example, I could not safely bid for the rental income from plot of land P without knowing how the person who purchases the use right (if not me) is going to exercise it. Maybe there will not be any rental income if he or she chooses to set P aside for environmental reasons. According to the version I propose, however, the auctioneer constructs lots which incorporate all the permits for each particular resource or plot of land (such as they are). This means that once a person successfully bids for the lot he does not have to worry about other persons owning some of the control rights associated with the resource or plot of land in question.

3. I thank Michael Otsuka for raising this concern.

4. For more on the question of what counts as personality rather than compensable circumstances, see Chapter 2.

5. Pogge, for example, frames this as a question about those persons who make more extensive use of the Earth's natural resources − wherever those resources happen to be located − than those persons who involuntarily make very little use. His solution is the Global Resources Dividend according to which 'states and their governments shall not have full libertarian property rights with respect to the natural resources in their territory, but can be required to share a small part of the value of any resources they decide to use or sell' (Pogge, 2002a, p. 196). For critical assessment of this proposal, see Crisp and Jamieson (2000), Haubrich (2004), Hayward (2005) and Heath (2007).

6. Miller makes a similar point using the case of the relative prosperity of Malaysia and Ghana. See Miller (2007), p. 241.

7. Of course, it is widely reported that in the aftermath of Hurricane Katrina the Bush administration refused offers of assistance from Cuba, Venezuela, Dominican Republic, Russia, Germany and many other countries.

8. For subsequent refinements of the view and replies to critics, see Singer (1993), (1999), (2002) and (2004). Interestingly Miller criticises Singer's duties partly on the grounds that they fail to take due account of the reasons why so many people around the world are poor. See Miller (2007), pp. 233–8.

9. Likewise, many Old Order Amish and Mennonites communities refuse to purchase home, health and life insurance on the grounds that it is their religious duty to provide for one another when misfortune strikes.

10. For a more complete account of negative duties not to support an unjust world order, see Pogge (2002a), pp. 66, 144 and (2005d), p. 33. An interesting

critique of, and alternative to, Pogge's account can be found in Gosselin (2006) and (2008).

8 Conclusion

1. Of course, like all statistics there is debate over the magnitude of that decline and how best to measure it. See Dollar (2007), p. 100, n. 3.

Bibliography

Abizadeh, Arash. (2007) 'Cooperation, Pervasive Impact, and Coercion: On the Scope (not Site) of Distributive Justice', *Philosophy and Public Affairs*, 35, 318–358.

Addison, Tony et al. (2005) 'Development Assistance and Development Finance: Evidence and Global Policy Agendas', *Journal of International Development*, 17, 819–836.

Amdur, Robert. (1977) 'Rawls' Theory of Justice: Domestic and International Perspectives', *World Politics*, 29, 438–461.

Anderson, Elizabeth. (1999) 'What is the Point of Equality?' *Ethics*, 106, 287–337.

Arneson, Richard. (1989) 'Equality and Equal Opportunity for Welfare', *Philosophical Studies*, 56, 77–93.

——— (1993) 'Equality', in R. Goodin and P. Pettit (eds.) *A Companion to Contemporary Political Philosophy* (Oxford: Blackwell).

——— (2000a) 'Welfare Should Be the Currency of Justice', *Canadian Journal of Philosophy*, 30, 497–524.

——— (2000b) 'Luck Egalitarianism and Prioritarianism', *Ethics*, 110, 339–349.

——— (2002) 'Review of Ronald Dworkin Sovereign Virtue', *Ethics*, 112, 367–371.

——— (2005) 'Do Patriotic Ties Limit Global Justice Duties?' *Journal of Ethics*, 9, 127–150.

Ashford, Elizabeth. (2007) 'The Duties Imposed by the Human Right to Basic Necessities', in T. Pogge (ed.) *Freedom from Poverty as a Human Right* (Oxford: UNESCO and Oxford University Press).

Auty, Richard. (1993) *Sustaining Development in Mineral Economies: The Resource Curse Thesis* (London: Routledge).

Bader, Veit. (1997) 'Fairly Open Borders', in V. Bader (ed.) *Citizenship and Exclusion* (Basingstoke: Palgrave).

Ban Ki-moon. (2008) Speech at the launch of the 2008 Consolidated Appeal, Geneva, 23 January, http://www.un.org/apps/news/infocus/sgspeeches/search—full.asp?statID=175.

Barnett, Michael and Weiss, Thomas G. (2008) *Humanitarianism in Question: Politics, Power, Ethics* (Ithaca: Cornell University Press).

Barry, Brian. (1973) *The Liberal Theory of Justice* (Oxford: Clarendon Press).

——— (1982) 'Humanity and Justice in Global Perspective', *NOMOS*, XXIV, 219–252.

——— (1995) *Justice as Impartiality* (Oxford: Oxford University Press).

——— (1998) 'International Society from a Cosmopolitan Perspective', in D. R. Mapel and T. Nardin (eds.) *International Society: Diverse Ethical Perspectives* (Princeton, NJ: Princeton University Press).

——— (2001) *Culture and Equality* (Cambridge: Polity).

——— (2005) *Why Social Justice Matters* (Cambridge: Polity Press).

Barry, Nicholas. (2006) 'Defending Luck Egalitarianism', *Journal of Applied Philosophy*, 23, 89–107.

Baubock, Rainer. (1996) 'Cultural Minority Rights for Immigrants', *International Migration Review*, 30, 203–250.

Beitz, Charles. (1975) 'Justice and International Relations', *Philosophy and Public Affairs*, 4, 360–389.

—— (1979) *Political Theory and International Relations* (Princeton, NJ: Princeton University Press).

—— (1983) 'Cosmopolitan Ideals and National Sentiment', *The Journal of Philosophy*, 80, 591–600.

—— (1999a) 'Social and Cosmopolitan Liberalism', *International Affairs*, 75, 515–529.

—— (1999b) 'International Liberalism and Distributive Justice', *World Politics*, 51, 269–296.

—— (2000) 'Rawls's Law of Peoples', *Ethics*, 110, 669–696.

—— (2001) 'Does Global Inequality Matter?' *Metaphilosophy*, 32, 95–112.

—— (2005) 'Cosmopolitanism and Global Justice', *Journal of Ethics*, 9, 11–27.

Benn, Stanley. (1967) 'Equality, Moral and Social', in P. Edwards (ed.) *Encyclopedia of Philosophy, Volume 3* (New York: Macmillan).

Berlin, Isaiah. (1969) *Four Essays on Liberty* (Oxford: Oxford University Press).

—— (1978) 'The Hedgehog and the Fox: An essay on Tolstoy's View of History', in H. Hardy (ed.) *Russian Thinkers* (London: Hogarth).

Bertram, Christopher. (2005) 'Global Justice, Moral Development and Democracy', in G. Brock and H. Brighouse (eds.) *The Political Philosophy of Cosmopolitanism* (Cambridge: Cambridge University Press).

—— (2006) 'Cosmopolitanism and Inequality', *Res Publica*, 12, 327–336.

Blake, Michael. (2001) 'Distributive Justice, State Coercion, and Autonomy', *Philosophy and Public Affairs*, 30, 257–296.

Bowles, Samuel. (2002) 'Globalization and Redistribution: Feasible Egalitarianism in a Competitive World', in R. Freeman (ed.) *Inequality around the World* (London: Palgrave Macmillan).

—— (2006) 'Egalitarian Redistribution in Globally Integrated Economies', in P. Bardhan, S. Bowles and M. Wallerstein (eds.) *Globalization and Egalitarian Redistribution* (Princeton, NJ: Princeton University Press).

Brooks, Thom. (2006) 'Is Global Poverty a Crime?' *Social Science Research Network*, http://ssrn.com/abstract=943762.

Brown, Alexander. (2005) 'Luck Egalitarianism and Democratic Equality', *Ethical Perspectives*, 12, 293–339.

—— (2007) 'An Egalitarian Plateau? Challenging the Importance of Ronald Dworkin's Abstract Egalitarian Rights', *Res Publica*, 13, 255–291.

—— (2008) 'Are There Any Global Egalitarian Rights?' *Human Rights Review*, 9, 435–464.

Brown, Chris. (1995) 'International Political Theory and the Idea of World Community', in K. Booth and S. Smith (eds.) *International Relations Theory Today* (Cambridge: Polity Press).

Brus, Marcel. (1995) *Third Party Dispute Settlement in an Interdependent World: Developing an International Framework* (Dordrecht: Martinus Nijhoff Publishers).

Buchanan, Allen. (1987) 'Justice and Charity', *Ethics*, 97, 558–575.

—— (1990) 'Justice as Reciprocity Versus Subject-Centered Justice', *Philosophy and Public Affairs*, 19, 227–252.

—— (1999) 'The Internal Legitimacy of Humanitarian Intervention', *Journal of Political Philosophy*, 7, 71–87.

————— (2000) 'Rawls's Law of Peoples: Rules for a Vanished Westphalian World', *Ethics*, 110, 669–721.

————— (2004) *Justice, Legitimacy, and Self-Determination: Moral Foundations for International Law* (Oxford: Oxford University Press).

Burnside, Craig, and Dollar, David. (2002) 'Aid, Policies, and Growth', *The American Economic Review*, 90, 847–868.

Busby, Joshua. (2007) 'Bono made Jesse Helms Cry: Jubilee 2000, Debt Relief and Moral Action in International Politics', *International Studies Quarterly*, 51, 247–275.

Caney, Simon. (1999) 'Nationality, Distributive Justice, and the Use of Force', *Journal of Applied Philosophy*, 16, 123–138.

————— (2001) 'Cosmopolitan Justice and Equalizing Opportunities', T. Pogge (ed.) *Global Justice* (Oxford: Blackwell).

————— (2003) 'Entitlements, Obligations, and Distributive Justice: The Global Level', in D. Bell and A. de-Shalit (eds.) *Forms of Justice: Critical Perspectives on David Miller's Political Philosophy* (Lanham, Maryland: Rowman and Littlefield).

————— (2005) *Justice Beyond Borders: A Global Political Theory* (Oxford: Oxford University Press).

————— (2006) 'Cosmopolitan Justice, Rights and Global Climate Change', *The Canadian Journal of Law and Jurisprudence*, 19, 255–278.

Carens, Joseph. (1992) 'Migration and Morality: A Liberal Egalitarian Perspective', in B. Barry and R. Goodin (eds.) *Free Movement: Ethical Issues in the Transnational Migration of People and Money* (Hemel Hempstead: Harvester Wheatcheaf).

————— (1995a) 'From Aliens to Citizens: The Case for Open Borders', in W. Kymlicka (ed.) *The Rights of Minority Cultures* (New York: Oxford University Press).

————— (1995b) 'Complex Justice, Cultural Difference, and Political Community', in D. Miller and M. Walzer (eds.) *Pluralism, Justice, and Equality* (Oxford: Oxford University Press).

CGAP. (2008) What Do We Know about the Impact of Microfinance? http://www.cgap.org/p/site/c/template.rc/1.26.1306, date accessed 2 August 2008.

Cohen, G. A. (1989) 'On the Currency of Egalitarian Justice', *Ethics*, 99, 906–944.

————— (1993) 'Equality of What? On welfare, Goods, and Capabilities', in M. Nussbaum and A. Sen (eds.) *The Quality of Life* (Oxford: Oxford University Press).

————— (1995) *Self-Ownership, Freedom and Equality* (Cambridge: Cambridge University Press).

————— (1997) 'Where the Action Is: On the Site of Distributive Justice', *Philosophy and Public Affairs*, 26, 3–30.

————— (1999) 'Expensive Tastes and Multiculturalism', in R. Bhargava, A. Kumar, R. Bagchi and R. Sudarshan (eds) *Multiculturalism, Liberalism and Democracy* (New Delhi: Oxford University Press).

————— (2000) *If You're an Egalitarian, How Come You're So Rich?* (Harvard, MA: Harvard University Press).

————— (2003) 'Facts and Principles', *Philosophy and Public Affairs*, 31, 211–245.

————— (2004) 'Expensive Tastes Rides Again', in J. Burley (ed.) *Dworkin and His Critics* (Malden, MA: Blackwell).

Cohen Christofidis, M. (2004) 'Talent, Slavery, and Envy', in J. Burley (ed.) *Dworkin and His Critics* (Malden, MA: Blackwell).

Cohen, Joshua, and Sabel, Charles. (2005) '*Global Democracy?*' *NYU Journal of International Law and Politics*, 37, 763–797.

―― (2006) 'Extra Rempublicam Nulla Justitia?' *Philosophy and Public Affairs*, 34, 147–175.

Collier, Paul. (2007) *The Bottom Billion* (Oxford: Oxford University Press).

Cramton, Peter, and Kerr, Suzi. (2002) 'Tradeable Carbon Permit Auctions: How and Why to Auction not Grandfather', *Energy Policy*, 30, 333–345.

Crisp, Roger, and Jamieson, Dale. (2000) 'Egalitarianism and a Global Resources Tax', in V. Davion and C. Wolf (eds.) *The Idea of a Political Liberalism* (Lanham: Rowman and Littlefield).

Dahl, Robert. (1999) 'Can International Organizations Be Democratic?' in I. Shapiro and C. Hacker-Cordon (ed.) *Democracy's Edges* (Cambridge: Cambridge University Press).

Daniels, Norman. (1990) 'Equality of What: Welfare, Resources, or Capabilities?' *Philosophy and Phenomenological Research*, 1, 273–296.

―― (2008) *Just Health: Meeting Health Needs Fairly* (Cambridge: Cambridge University Press).

Day, J. P. (1977) 'Threats, Offers, Law, Opinion, and Liberty', *American Philosophical Quarterly*, 14, 257–272.

Desch, Michael. (2003) 'It Is Kind to Be Cruel: The Humanity of American Realism', *Review of International Studies*, 29, 415–426.

Dollar, David. (2007) 'Globalization, Poverty and Inequality since 1980', in D. Held and A. Kaya (eds.) *Global Inequality* (Cambridge: Polity Press).

Dollar, David, and Levin, Victoria. (2006) 'The Increasing Selectivity of Foreign Aid, 1984–2003', *World Development*, 34, 2034–2046.

Donnelly, Jack. (2003) *Universal Human Rights: In Theory and Practice* (Ithaca, NY: Cornell University Press).

Dworkin, Ronald. (1973) 'The Original Position', *The Chicago Law Review*, 4, 500–533.

―― (1977) *Taking Rights Seriously* (London: Duckworth).

―― (1978) 'Liberalism', in S. Hampshire (ed.) *Public and Private Morality* (Cambridge: Cambridge University Press).

―― (1981a) 'What is Equality? Part 1: Equality of Welfare', *Philosophy and Public Affairs*, 10, 185–246.

―― (1981b) 'What is Equality? Part 2: Equality of Resources', *Philosophy and Public Affairs*, 10, 283–345.

―― (1983) 'Comment on Narveson: In Defense of Equality', *Social Philosophy and Policy*, 1, 24–40.

―― (1985) *A Matter of Principle* (Cambridge, MA: Harvard University Press).

―― (1986) *Law's Empire* (Cambridge, MA: Harvard University Press).

―― (1987a) 'What is Equality? Part 3: The Place of Liberty', *Iowa Law Review*, 73, 1–54.

―― (1987b) 'What is Equality? Part 4: Political Equality', *University of San Francisco Law Review*, 22, 1–30.

―― (1989) 'Liberal Community', *California Law Review*, 77, 479–504.

―― (1990) 'Foundations of Liberal Equality', in G. Peterson (ed.) *The Tanner Lectures on Human Values, Volume XI* (Salt Lake City: University of Utah Press).

―― (1993) *Life's Dominion: An Argument about Abortion and Euthanasia* (New York: Knopf).

—— (1994) 'Law, Philosophy and Interpretation', *Archiv für Rechts-und Sozialphilosophie*, 80, 463–75.

—— (1996) 'Objectivity and Truth: You'd Better Believe It', *Philosophy and Public Affairs*, 25, 87–139.

—— (2000) *Sovereign Virtue* (Cambridge, MA: Harvard University Press).

—— (2001) 'Do Values Conflict? A Hedgehog's Approach', *Arizona Law Review*, 43, 251–259.

—— (2002) 'Sovereign Virtue Revisited', *Ethics*, 113, 106–143.

—— (2003) 'Equality, Luck and Hierarchy', *Philosophy and Public Affairs*, 31, 190–198.

—— (2004a) 'Ronald Dworkin Replies', in Justine Burley (ed.) *Dworkin and His Critics* (Malden, MA: Blackwell).

—— (2004b) 'Hart's Postscript and the Character of Political Philosophy', *Oxford Journal of Legal Studies*, 24, 1–37.

—— (2004c) 'Rawls and the Law', *Fordham Law Review*, 72, 1387–1406.

—— (2006) *Is Democracy Possible Here?* (Princeton, NJ: Princeton University Press).

Easterly, William. (2003) 'Can Foreign Aid Buy Growth?' *Journal of Economic Perspectives*, 17, 23–48.

—— (2007) *White Man's Burden: Why the West's Efforts to Aid the Rest Have Done So Much Ill and So Little Good* (Oxford: Oxford University Press).

Egeland Jan. (2005) 'Niger Is Dying, and the World Is Merely Watching', *USA Today*, 7 August, http://www.usatoday.com/news/opinion/editorials/2005-08-07-niger-edit—x.htm.

European Commission Humanitarian Aid Office. (ECHO) (2005) *European Humanitarian Aid: Values and Principles*, http://www.reliefweb.int/library/documents/2005/echo-gen-13jun.pdf.

Fleurbaey, Marc. (2001) 'Egalitarian Opportunities', *Law and Philosophy*, 20, 499–530.

—— (2002) 'Equality of Resources Revisited', *Ethics*, 113, 82–105.

Franck, Thomas. (1995) *Fairness in International Law and Institutions* (Oxford: Oxford University Press).

Frankfurt, Harry. (1971) 'Freedom of the Will and the Concept of a Person', *Journal of Philosophy*, 68, 5–22.

—— (1988) 'Equality as a Moral Ideal', in his *The Importance of What We Care About* (Cambridge: Cambridge University Press).

Franklin, Thomas. (2008) 'Reaching the Millennium Development Goals: Equality and Justice as well as Results', *Development in Practice*, 18, 420–423.

Fransman, Jude et al. (2004) *Public Opinion Polling and the Millennium Development Goals, Working Paper No. 238* (Paris: OECD), http://www.oecd.org/dataoecd/52/43/33873214.pdf.

Freeman, Samuel. (2006) 'The Law of Peoples, Social Cooperation, Human Rights, and Distributive Justice', *Social Philosophy and Policy*, 23, 29–68.

—— (2007) *Rawls* (London: Routledge).

Fukuda-Parr, Sakiko. (2004) 'Millennium Development Goals: Why They Matter', *Global Governance*, 10, 395–402.

Gibbard, Allan. (1991) 'Constructing Justice', *Philosophy and Public Affairs*, 20, 264–297.

Gilabert, Pablo. (2005) 'The Duty to Eradicate Global Poverty: Positive or Negative?' *Ethical Theory and Moral Practice*, 7, 537–550.

Goodin, Robert. (1985) *Protecting the Vulnerable* (Chicago: University of Chicago Press).

—— (1988) 'What Is So Special about Our Fellow Countrymen?' *Ethics*, 98, 663–686.

—— (1995) *Utilitarianism as a Public Philosophy* (Cambridge: Cambridge University Press).

—— (2001) *Boundaries and Allegiances* (Oxford: Oxford University Press).

Goetz, Anne Marie, and Jenkins, Rob. (2002) *Hybrid Forms of Accountability and Human Development: Citizen Engagement of a New Agenda*, Background Paper for Human Development Report 2002 (New York: UNDP).

Gorr, Michael. (1989) *Coercion, Freedom and Exploitation* (New York: Peter Lang Publishing).

Gosselin, Abigail. (2006) 'Global Poverty and Responsibility: Identifying the Duty-Bearers of Human Rights', *Human Rights Review*, 8, 35–52.

—— (2008) *Global Poverty and Individual Responsibility* (Lanham, MD: Lexington Books).

Gosseries, Axel. (2008) 'How (Un)fair is Intellectual Property?' in A. Gosseries, A. Marciano and A. Strowel (eds) *Intellectual Property and Theories of Justice* (Basingstoke: Palgrave Macmillan).

Gould, Carol. (2004) *Globalizing Democracy and Human Rights* (Cambridge: Cambridge University Press).

—— (2007a) 'Transnational Solidarities', *Journal of Social Philosophy*, 38, 148–164.

—— (2007b) 'Coercion, Care, and Corporations: Omissions and Commissions in Thomas Pogge's Political Philosophy', *Journal of Global Ethics*, 3, 381–393.

Green, Leslie. (2004) 'Associative Obligations and the State', in J. Burley (ed.) *Dworkin and His Critics* (Malden, MA: Blackwell).

Griffin, James. (1986) *Well-Being* (Oxford: Oxford University Press).

Guest, Stephen. (1991) *Ronald Dworkin* (Stanford: Stanford University Press).

Haq, Inamul. (1979) 'From Charity to Obligation: A Third World Perspective on Concessional Resource Transfers', *Texas International Law Journal*, 14, 389–424.

Hattori, Tomohisa. (2003) 'The Moral Politics of Foreign Aid', *Review of International Studies*, 29, 229–247.

Haubrich, Dirk. (2004) 'Global Distributive Justice and the Taxation of Natural Resources: Who Should Pick Up the Tab?' *Contemporary Political Theory*, 3, 48–69.

Hayden, Patrick. (2002) *John Rawls: Towards a Just World Order* (Cardiff: University of Wales Press).

Hayter, Teresa. (1971) *AID as Imperialism* (Harmondsworth: Penguin).

Hayward, Tim. (2005) 'Thomas Pogge's Global Resources Dividend: A Critique and an Alternative' *Journal of Moral Philosophy*, 2, 317–332.

—— (2006) 'Global Justice and the Distribution of Natural Resources', *Political Studies*, 54, 349–369.

Heath, Joseph. (2004) 'Dworkin's Auction', *Politics, Philosophy and Economics*, 3, 313–335.

—— (2006) 'The Benefits of Cooperation', *Philosophy and Public Affairs*, 34, 313–451.

—— (2007) 'Rawls on Global Distributive Justice: A Defence', in D. Weinstock (ed.) *Canadian Journal of Philosophy Supplementary Volume* (Lethbridge: University of Calgary Press).

Heyd, David. (2007) 'Justice and Solidarity: The Contractarian Case against Global Justice', *Journal of Social Philosophy*, 38, 112–130.

International Federation of Red Cross and Red Crescent Societies (2004) Code of Conduct for the International Red Cross and Red Crescent Movement and NGOs in Disaster Relief, http://www.ifrc.org/publicat/conduct/code.asp.

Intergovernmental Panel on Climate Change (IPCC) (1995) *Second Assessment Report Climate Change 1995, Working Group III: Economic and Social Dimensions of Climate Change* (Cambridge: Cambridge University Press).

———— (2001) *Third Assessment Report Climate Change 2001, Working Group II: Impacts, Adaptation and Vulnerability* (Cambridge: Cambridge University Press).

James, Aaron. (2005) 'Constructing Justice for Existing Practice: Rawls and the Status Quo', *Philosophy and Public Affairs*, 33, 281–316.

Jones, Charles. (1999) *Global Justice: Defending Cosmopolitanism* (Oxford: Oxford University Press).

Jones, Peter. (1994) 'Bearing the Consequences of Belief', *Journal of Political Philosophy*, 2, 24–43.

Julius, A. J. (2006) 'Nagel's Atlas', *Philosophy and Public Affairs*, 34, 176–192.

Kamminga, Menno. (2006) 'Why Global Distributive Justice Cannot Work', *Acta Politica*, 41, 21–40.

Kant, Immanuel. (1785) Groundwork of the Metaphysics of Morals, in H. J. Paton (ed.) (1948) *The Moral Law* (London: Routledge).

———— (1793) *Religion within the Limits of Reason Alone*, in T. Greene and H. Hudson (trans.) (1934) (Chicago: Open Court).

———— (1795) Perpetual Peace, in H. Reiss (ed.) (1985) *Kant's Political Writings* (Cambridge: Cambridge University Press).

Kaufman, Alexander. (2004) 'Choice, Responsibility and Equality', *Political Studies*, 52, 819–836.

Kukathas, Chandran. (2005) 'The Case for Open Borders', in A. I. Cohen and C. H. Wellman (eds.) *Contemporary Debates in Applied Ethics* (Oxford: Blackwell).

Kuper, Andrew. (2002) 'More Than Charity: Cosmopolitan Alternatives to the "Singer Solution"' and 'Facts, Theories, and Hard Choices', *Ethics and International Affairs*, 16, 107–120, 125–126.

Kymlicka, Will. (2002) *Contemporary Political Philosophy, Second Edition* (Oxford: Oxford University Press).

Leys, Colin. (1996) *The Rise and Fall of Development Theory* (Bloomington: Indiana University Press).

Lippert-Rasmussen, Kasper. (2001) 'Egalitarianism, Option Luck, and Responsibility', *Ethics*, 111, 548–579.

Lumsdaine, David. (1993) *Moral Vision in International Politics: The Foreign Aid Regime (1949–1989)* (Princeton, NJ: Princeton University Press).

McDonnell, Ida et al. (2003) *Public Opinion and the Fight against Poverty* (Paris: OECD).

Macleod, Colin. (1998) *Liberalism, Justice, and Markets* (Oxford: Oxford University Press).

Margalit, Avishai, and Joseph Raz. (1990) 'National Self-Determination', *Journal of Philosophy*, 87, 439–461.

Markovits, Daniel. (2003) 'How Much Redistribution Should There Be?' *Yale Law Journal*, 112, 2291–2330.

Mason, Andrew. (2000) 'Equality, Individual Responsibility, and Gender Socialisation', *Proceedings of the Aristotelian Society*, 100, 227–246.

Meckled-Garcia, Saladin. (2008) 'On the Very Idea of Cosmopolitan Justice: Constructivism and International Agency', *Journal of Political Philosophy*, 16, 245–271.

Micro Insurance Agency. (2007) Weather-Indexed Crop Insurance, http://www.microinsuranceagency.com/crop—insurance.html, date accessed 20 May 2008.

Mieth, Corinna. (2008) 'World Poverty as a Problem of Justice? A Critical Comparison of Three Approaches', *Ethical Theory and Moral Practice*, 11, 15–36.

Miller, David. (1995) *On Nationality* (Oxford: Oxford University Press).

——— (1998) 'Limits of Cosmopolitan Justice', in D. Mapel and T. Nardin (eds.) *International Society: Diverse Ethical Perspectives* (Princeton, NJ: Princeton University Press).

——— (1999a) *Principles of Social Justice* (Cambridge, MA: Harvard University Press).

——— (1999b) 'Justice and Global Inequality', in A. Hurrell and N. Woods (eds.) *Inequality, Globalization and World Politics* (Oxford: Oxford University Press).

——— (2000) 'National Self-Determination and Global Justice', in his *Citizenship and National Identity* (Cambridge: Polity Press).

——— (2001) 'Distributing Responsibilities', *Journal of Political Philosophy*, 9, 453–471.

——— (2002a) 'Two Ways to Think about Justice', *Politics, Philosophy and Economics*, 1, 5–28.

——— (2002b) 'Cosmopolitanism: A Critique', *Critical Review of International Social and Political Philosophy*, 5, 80–85.

——— (2002c) 'Equal Opportunities and Cultural Commitments', in P. Kelly (ed.) *Multiculturalism Reconsidered* (Oxford: Polity).

——— (2005a) 'Against Global Egalitarianism', *Journal of Ethics*, 9, 55–79.

——— (2005b) 'Immigration: The Case for Limits', in A. Cohen and C. Wellman (eds.) *Contemporary Debates in Applied Ethics* (Oxford: Blackwell).

——— (2007) *National Responsibility and Global Justice* (Oxford: Oxford University Press).

——— (2008) 'National Responsibility and Global Justice' and 'A Response', *Critical Review of International Social and Political Philosophy*, 11, 383–399, 553–567.

Miller, Richard. (1998) 'Cosmopolitan Respect and Patriotic Concern', *Philosophy and Public Affairs*, 27, 202–224.

Moellendorf, Darrel. (2002) *Cosmopolitan Justice* (Boulder, Colorado: Westview Press).

Moore, Margaret. (2008) 'Global Justice, Climate Change and Miller's Theory of Responsibility', *Critical Review of International Social and Political Philosophy*, 11, 501–517.

Morgenthau, Hans. (1962) 'A Political Theory of Foreign Aid', *American Political Science Review*, 56, 301–309.

Morrissey, Oliver. (2001) 'Does Aid Increase Growth?' *Progress in Development Studies*, 1, 37–50.

Murphy, Liam. (1998) 'Institutions and the Demands of Justice', *Philosophy and Public Affairs*, 27, 251–291.

Nagel, Thomas. (1979) *Mortal Questions* (Cambridge: Cambridge University Press).

——— (1991) *Equality and Partiality* (Oxford: Oxford University Press).

——— (2005) 'The Problem of Global Justice', *Philosophy and Public Affairs*, 33, 113–147.

Narveson, Jan. (1983) 'On Dworkinian Equality' and 'Reply to Dworkin', *Social Philosophy and Policy*, 1, 1–23, 41–44.

——— (1998) 'Egalitarianism: Partial, Counterproductive, and Baseless', in A. Mason (ed.) *Ideals of Equality* (Oxford: Blackwell).

Noël, Alain, and Thérien, Jean-Philippe (1995) 'From Domestic to International Justice: The Welfare State and Foreign Aid', *International Organization*, 49, 523–553.

——— (2002) 'Public Opinion and Global Justice', *Comparative Studies*, 35, 631–656.

Nozick, Robert. (1974) *Anarchy, State, and Utopia* (Oxford: Blackwell).

Nussbaum, Martha. (1996) 'Cosmopolitanism and Patriotism', in J. Cohen (ed.) *For Love of Country: Debating the Limits of Patriotism* (Boston: Beacon Press).

OECD. (1996) *Shaping the 21st Century: The Contribution of Development Co-operation* (Paris: OECD), http://www.oecd.org/dataoecd/23/35/2508761.pdf.

——— (2008) Table 1: Net Official Development Assistance in 2007 and Chart 2: DAC Members Net ODA 1990–2007, 4 April, http://www.oecd.org/dataoecd/27/55/40381862.pdf.

O'Neill, Onora. (1986) *Faces of Hunger: An Essay on Poverty, Development and Justice* (London: George Allen and Unwin).

——— (1989) *Constructions of Reason: Explorations of Kant's Practical Philosophy* (Cambridge: Cambridge University Press).

——— (1998) 'Rights, Obligations and Needs', in G. Brock (ed.) *Necessary Goods: Our Responsibility to Meet Others' Needs* (Lanham, MD: Rowman & Littlefield).

——— (2000) *Bounds of Justice* (Cambridge: Cambridge University Press).

——— (2001) 'Agents of Justice', *Metaphilosophy*, 32, 180–195.

——— (2004) 'Global Justice: Whose Obligations?' in D. Chatterjee (ed.) *The Ethics of Assistance* (Cambridge: Cambridge University Press).

Opeskin, Brian. (1996) 'The Moral Foundations of Foreign Aid', *World Development*, 24, 21–44.

Oppenheim, Felix. (1970) 'Egalitarianism as a Descriptive Concept', *American Philosophical Quarterly*, 7, 143–152.

Orbinski, James. (1999) Nobel Lecture, Oslo, 10 December, http://nobelprize.org/nobel_prizes/peace/laureates/1999/msf-lecture.html.

Otsuka, Michael. (1998) 'Self-Ownership and Equality: A Lockean Reconciliation', *Philosophy and Public Affairs*, 27, 65–92.

——— (2002) 'Luck, Insurance, and Equality', *Ethics*, 113, 40–54.

——— (2003) *Libertarianism Without Inequality* (Oxford: Oxford University Press).

——— (2004) 'Liberty, Equality, Envy and Abstraction', in J. Burley (ed.) *Dworkin and His Critics* (Malden, MA: Blackwell).

Paine, Thomas. (1775) 'African Slavery in America', in M. Foot and I. Kramnick (eds.) *The Thomas Paine Reader* (1987) (Harmondsworth: Penguin).

Parekh, Bhikhu. (2000) *Rethinking Multiculturalism* (Basingstoke: Palgrave Macmillan).

Parfit, Derek. (1998) 'Equality and Priority', in A. Mason (ed.) *Ideals of Equality* (Oxford: Blackwell).

Pierik, Roland, and Robeyns, Ingrid. (2007) 'Resources versus Capabilities: Social Endowments in Egalitarian Theory', *Political Studies*, 55, 133–152.

Pogge, Thomas. (1989) *Realizing Rawls* (Ithaca: Cornell University Press).

——— (1992a) 'Cosmopolitanism and Sovereignty', *Ethics*, 103, 48–75.

——— (1992b) 'An Institutional Approach to Humanitarian Intervention', *Public Affairs Quarterly*, 6, 89–103.

——— (1992c) 'O'Neill on Rights and Duties', *Grazer Philosophische Studien*, 43, 233–247.

—— (1994) 'An Egalitarian Law of Peoples', *Philosophy and Public Affairs*, 23, 195–224.

—— (1999) 'A Global Resources Dividend', in D. Crocker and T. Linden (eds.) *Ethics of Consumption: The Good Life, Justice, and Global Stewardship* (Totowa, NJ: Rowman and Littlefield).

—— (2001) 'Priorities of Global Justice', *Metaphilosophy*, 32, 6–24.

—— (2002a) *World Poverty and Human Rights* (Cambridge: Polity Press).

—— (2002b) 'Cosmopolitanism: A Defence', *Critical Review of International Social and Political Philosophy*, 5, 86–91.

—— (2002c) 'Moral Universalism and Global Economic Justice', *Politics, Philosophy and Economics*, 1, 29–58.

—— (2004) 'The First United Nations Millennium Development Goal: A Cause for Celebration?' *Journal of Human Development*, 5, 377–397.

—— (2005a) 'World Poverty and Human Rights', *Ethics and International Affairs*, 19, 1–8.

—— (2005b) 'Severe Poverty as a Violation of Negative Duties', *Ethics and International Affairs*, 19, 55–82.

—— (2005c) 'Human Rights and Human Responsibilities', in A. Kuper (ed.) *Global Responsibilities: Who Must Deliver on Human Rights?* (London: Routledge).

—— (2005d) 'Real World Justice', *The Journal of Ethics*, 9, 29–53.

—— (2007) 'Why Inequality Matters', in D. Held and A. Kaya (eds.) *Global Inequality* (Cambridge: Polity Press).

Pogge, Thomas, and Reddy, Sanjay. (2002) 'How Not to Count the Poor' (New York: Mimeo, Barnard College).

Rakowski, Eric. (1991) *Equal Justice* (Oxford: Clarendon Press).

Ravallion, Martin. (2003) *How Not to Count the Poor? A Reply to Reddy and Pogge* (Washington DC: Mimeo/World Bank).

Rawls, John. (1971) *A Theory of Justice* (Oxford: Oxford University Press).

—— (1975) 'Fairness to Goodness', *Philosophical Review*, 84, 536–554.

—— (1980) 'Kantian Constructivism in Moral Theory', *Journal of Philosophy*, 77, 515–572.

—— (1982) 'Social Unity and Primary Goods', in A. Sen and B. Williams (eds.) *Utilitarianism and Beyond* (Cambridge: Cambridge University Press).

—— (1985) 'Justice as Fairness: Political not Metaphysical', *Philosophy and Public Affairs*, 14, 223–251.

—— (1996) *Political Liberalism* (New York: Columbia University Press).

—— (1999) *The Law of Peoples* (Cambridge, MA: Harvard University Press).

—— (2001) *Justice as Fairness: A Restatement* (Cambridge, MA: Harvard University Press).

Raz, Joseph. (1986) *The Morality of Freedom* (Oxford: Oxford University Press).

Rees, John. (1971) *Equality* (London: Pall Mall).

Riddell, Roger. (2007) *Does Foreign Aid Really Work?* (Oxford: Oxford University Press).

Ripstein, Arthur. (2007) 'Liberty and Equality', in A. Ripstein (ed.) *Ronald Dworkin* (Cambridge: Cambridge University Press).

Risse, Mathias. (2005) 'What We Owe to the Global Poor', *The Journal of Ethics*, 9, 81–117.

—— (2005b) 'How Does the Global Order Harm the Poor?' *Philosophy and Public Affairs*, 33, 349–378.

—— (2007) 'The Grounds of Justice', KSG Faculty Research Working Paper Series RWP07-048, October, http://ksgnotes1.harvard.edu/Research/wpaper.nsf/rwp/RWP07-048/$File/rwp—07—048—risse.pdf.

Robeyns, Ingrid. (2005) 'Assessing Global poverty and Inequality: Income, Resources and Capabilities', *Metaphilosophy*, 36, 30–49.

Roemer, John. (1993) 'A Pragmatic Theory of Responsibility for the Egalitarian Planner', *Philosophy and Public Affairs*, 22, 146–166.

—— (1998) *Equality of Opportunity* (Cambridge, MA: Harvard University Press).

Sachs, Jeffrey et al. (1995) 'Natural Resource Abundance and Economic Growth', NBER Working Paper 5398, http://www.nber.org/papers/w5398.

—— (2005). *The End of Poverty: Economic Possibilities for Our Time* (New York: Penguin).

Sandbu, Martin E. (2004) 'On Dworkin's Brute-Luck-Option-Luck Distinction and the Consistency of Brute-Luck Egalitarianism', *Politics, Philosophy and Economics*, 3, 283–312.

Sandel, Michael. (1982) *Liberalism and the Limits of Justice* (Cambridge: Cambridge University Press).

Sangiovanni, Andrea. (2007) 'Global Justice, Reciprocity, and the State', *Philosophy and Public Affairs*, 35, 3–39.

—— (2008) 'Justice and the Priority of Politics to Morality', *The Journal of Political Philosophy*, 16, 137–164.

Scanlon, Thomas. (1973) 'Rawls' Theory of Justice', *University of Pennsylvania Law Review*, 121, 1020–1069.

—— (1986) 'Equality of Resources and Equality of Welfare: A Forced Marriage?' *Ethics*, 97, 111–118.

—— (1998) *What We Owe to Each Other* (Cambridge, MA: Harvard University Press).

—— (2003) 'The Diversity of Objections to Inequality', in his *The Difficulty of Tolerance* (Cambridge: Cambridge University Press).

—— (2004) 'When Does Equality Matter?' http://politicaltheoryworkshop.googlepages.com/scanlonpaper.pdf, date accessed 12 October 2007.

Schachter, Oscar. (1976) 'The Evolving International Law of Development', *Columbia Journal of Transnational Law*, 15, 1–17.

Schaller, Walter. (1997) 'Expensive Preferences and the Priority of Right: A Critique of Welfare-Egalitarianism', *The Journal of Political Philosophy*, 5, 254–273.

Scheffler, Samuel. (1981) 'Natural Rights, Equality, and the Minimal State', in J. Paul (ed.) *Reading Nozick* (Oxford: Blackwell).

—— (2001) *Boundaries and Allegiences: Problems of Justice and Responsibility in Liberal Thought* (Oxford: Oxford University Press).

—— (2003) 'What is Egalitarianism?' *Philosophy and Public Affairs*, 31, 5–39.

—— (2005) 'Choice, Circumstance, and the Value of Equality', *Politics, Philosophy and Economics*, 4, 5–28.

Schemmel, Christian. (2008) 'On the Usefulness of Luck Egalitarian Arguments for Global Justice', *Global Justice: Theory Practice Rhetoric*, 1, 55–67.

Segall, Shlomi. (2007) 'In Solidarity with the Imprudent: A Defense of Luck Egalitarianism', *Social Theory and Practice*, 33, 177–198.

Sen, Amartya. (1973) *On Economic Inequality* (Oxford: Oxford University Press).

—— (1980) 'Equality of What?' in S. M. McMurrin (ed.) *The Tanner Lectures on Human Values, Volume I* (Salt Lake City: University of Utah Press).

——— (1982) *Choice, Welfare and Measurement* (Oxford: Blackwell).

——— (1985) *Commodities and Capabilities* (Amsterdam: North-Holland).

——— (1992) *Inequality Reexamined* (Oxford: Oxford University Press).

——— (1993) 'Capability and Well-Being', in M. Nussbaum and A. Sen (eds.) *The Quality of Life* (Oxford: Oxford University Press).

——— (1999) *Development as Freedom* (Oxford: Oxford University Press).

——— (2002) 'Justice across Borders', in P. deFreid and C. Cronin (eds.) *Global Justice and Traditional Politics* (Cambridge, MA: MIT Press).

Shue, Henry. (1980) *Basic Rights: Subsistence, Affluence, and U.S. Foreign Policy* (Princeton, NJ: Princeton University Press).

——— (1983) 'The Burdens of Justice', *Journal of Philosophy*, 80, 600–608.

——— (1999) 'Global Environment and International Inequality', *International Affairs*, 75, 531–545.

——— (2004) 'Limiting Sovereignty', in J. Welsh (ed.) *Humanitarian Intervention and International Relations* (Oxford: Oxford University Press).

Singer, Peter. (1972) 'Famine, Affluence, and Morality', *Philosophy and Public Affairs*, 1, 229–243.

——— (1993) *Practical Ethics, Second Edition* (Cambridge: Cambridge University Press).

——— (1999) 'The Singer Solution to World Poverty', *The New York Times Magazine*, September 5.

——— (2002) 'Poverty, Facts, and Political Philosophies: Response to "More Than Charity" ' and 'Achieving the Best Outcome: Final Rejoinder', *Ethics and International Affairs*, 16, 121–124, 127–128.

——— (2004) 'Outsiders: Our Obligations to Those Beyond Our Borders', in D. Chatterjee (ed.) *The Ethics of Assistance* (Cambridge: Cambridge University Press).

Sphere Project (2004) Humanitarian Charter and Minimum Standards in Disaster Response, http://www.sphereproject.org/, date accessed 3 May 2008.

Spiegelberg, Herbert. (1944) 'A Defence of Human Equality', *Philosophical Review*, 53, 101–124.

Steiner, Hillel. (1974–5) 'Individual Liberty', *Proceedings of the Aristotelian Society*, 75, 33–50.

——— (1994) *An Essay on Rights* (Oxford: Blackwell).

——— (1998) 'Choice and Circumstance', in A. Mason (ed.) *Ideals of Equality* (Oxford: Blackwell).

——— (1999) 'Just Taxation and International Redistribution', in I. Shapiro and L. Brilmayer (eds.) *Global Justice: NOMOS, Volume XLI* (New York: New York University Press).

Swift, Adam. (2001) *Political Philosophy* (Cambridge: Polity Press).

Tamir, Yael. (1991) 'The Right to National Self-Determination', *Social Research*, 58, 565–590.

——— (1993) *Liberal Nationalism* (Princeton, NJ: Princeton University Press).

Tan, Kok-Chor. (2004) *Justice without Borders* (Cambridge: Cambridge University Press).

——— (2008) 'Luck, Institutions, and Global Justice' presented at the ALSP Annual Conference, University of Nottingham, 27–29 March.

Tasioulas, John. (2002) 'International Law and the Limits of Fairness', *European Journal of International Law*, 13, 993–1023.

———— (2005) 'Global Justice Without End?' *Metaphilosophy*, 36, 3–29.

Taylor, Charles. (1989) *Sources of the Self: The Making of the Modern Identity* (Cambridge: Cambridge University Press).

———— (1992) 'The Politics of Recognition', in A. Gutmann (ed.) *Multiculturalism and the Politics of Recognition* (Princeton, NJ: Princeton University Press).

Taylor, Paul, and Curtis, Devon. (2004) 'The United Nations', in John Baylis and Steve Smith (eds.) *The Globalization of World Politics: An Introduction to International Relations, Third Edition* (Oxford: Oxford University Press).

Temkin, Larry. (1993) *Inequality* (Oxford: Oxford University Press).

Teson, Fernando. (1998) *A Philosophy of International Law* (Boulder, Colorado: Westview Press).

Thérien, Jean-Philippe. (2002) 'Debating foreign aid: right versus left', *Third World Quarterly*, 23, 449–466.

Tobin, James. (1982) 'A Proposal for International Monetary Reform', in his *Essays on Economics: Theory and Practice* (Cambridge, MA: MIT Press).

UN. (1960) *General Assembly Resolution 1522 (XV)*, 15 December, http://daccessdds.un.org/doc/RESOLUTION/GEN/NR0/152/96/IMG/NR015296.pdf?OpenElement.

———— (1968) Proceedings of the United Nations Conference on Trade and Development, Second Session, New Delhi, 1 February–29 March, 28 March.

———— (1991) General Assembly Resolution A/46/182, 19 December, http://www.reliefweb.int/OCHA—ol/about/resol/resol—e.html.

———— (2007) *The Millennium Development Goals Report 2007* (New York: UN), http://mdgs.un.org/unsd/mdg/Resources/Static/Products/Progress2007/UNSD—MDG—Report—2007e.pdf.

———— (2008) *MDG Gap Task Force Report 2008* (New York: UN), http://www.un.org/esa/policy/mdggap/mdg8report—engw.pdf.

UN CAP. (2008) Humanitarian Appeal 2008, http://ochadms.unog.ch/quickplace/cap/main.nsf/h—Index/CAP—2008—Humanitarian—Appeal/$FILE/CAP—2008—Humanitarian—Appeal—SCREEN.pdf?OpenElement.

UNDP. (1999) *Human Development Report* (Oxford: Oxford University Press).

US Census Bureau. (2007) 'Income, Poverty, and Health Insurance Coverage in the United States', August, http://www.census.gov/prod/2007pubs/p60-233.pdf.

Vandemoortele, Jan. (2005) 'Ambition Is Golden: Meeting The MDGs', *Development*, 48, 5–11.

van der Veen, Robert. (2002) 'Equality of Talent resources: Procedures or Outcomes?' *Ethics*, 113, 55–81.

———— (2008) 'Reasonable Partiality for Compatriots and the Global Responsibility Gap', *Critical Review of International Social and Political Philosophy*, 11, 413–432.

Vincent, Nicole. (2006) 'Equality, Responsibility and Talent Slavery', *Imprints*, 9, 118–139.

Voigt, Kristin. (2007) 'The Harshness Objection: Is Luck Egalitarianism Too Harsh on the Victims of Option Luck?' *Ethical Theory and Moral Practice*, 10, 389–407.

von Leyden, W. (1963) 'On Justifying Inequality', *Political Studies*, 11, 56–70.

Waltz, Kenneth. (1979) *Theory of International Politics* (Reading, MA: Addison-Wesley).

———— (2004) 'Neorealism: Confusion and Criticisms', *Journal of Politics and Society*, 15, 2–6.

Walzer, Michael. (1977) 'Interventions', in his *Just and Unjust Wars* (Harmondsworth, Penguin).

———— (1983) *Spheres of Justice* (Oxford: Blackwell).

———— (1994) *Thick and Thin: Moral Argument at Home and Abroad* (Notre Dame, Indiana: University of Notre Dame Press).

———— (1995) 'Response', in D. Miller and M. Walzer (eds.) *Pluralism, Justice, and Equality* (Oxford: Oxford University Press).

Wenar, Leif. (2003) 'What We Owe to Distant Others', *Politics, Philosophy and Economics*, 2, 283–304.

———— (2006) 'Accountability in International Development Aid', *Ethics and International Affairs*, 20, 1–23.

———— (2007a) 'Responsibility and Severe Poverty', in T. Pogge (ed.) *Freedom from Poverty as a Human Right* (Oxford: UNESCO/Oxford University Press).

———— (2007b) 'Property Rights and the Resource Curse', 5 April, http://siteresources.worldbank.org/INTDECINEQ/Resources/PropertyRights.pdf.

———— (2008) 'Human Rights and Equality in the Work of David Miller', *Critical Review of International Social and Political Philosophy*, 11, 401–411.

Williams, Andrew. (2002) 'Dworkin on Capability', *Ethics*, 113, 23–39.

———— (2004) 'Equality, Ambition and Insurance', *Aristotelian Society Supplementary Volume*, 78, 131–150.

Williams, Bernard. (1962) 'The Idea of Equality', in P. Laslett and W. G. Runisman (eds.) *Philosophy, Politics and Society, Second Series* (Oxford: Blackwell).

———— (2001) 'From Freedom to Liberty: The Construction of a Political Value', *Philosophy and Public Affairs*, 30, 3–26.

Wilson, John. (1966) *Equality* (London: Hutchinson).

World Bank. (1998) *Assessing Aid: What Works, What Doesn't and Why* (New York: Oxford University Press).

Zamora, Stephen. (1997) 'Economic Relations and Development', in C. Joyner (ed.) *The United Nations and International Law* (Cambridge: Cambridge University Press).

Index